MW01253379

Re-figuring the *Rāmāyaṇa* as Theology

The *Rāmāyaṇa* of Vālmīki is considered by many contemporary Hindus to be a foundational religious text. This understanding is in part the result of a transformation of the epic's receptive history, a hermeneutic project which challenged one characterization of the genre of the text, as a work of literary culture, and replaced it with another, as a work of remembered tradition.

This book examines *Rāmāyaṇa* commentaries, poetic retellings and praise-poems produced by intellectuals within the Śrīvaiṣṇava order of South India from 1250 to 1600 and shows how these intellectuals reconceptualized Rāma's story through the lens of their devotional metaphysics. Śrīvaiṣṇavas applied innovative interpretive techniques to the *Rāmāyaṇa*, including allegorical reading, *śleṣa* reading (reading a verse as a *double entendre*) and the application of vernacular performance techniques such as word play, improvization, repetition and novel forms of citation. The book is of interest not only to *Rāmāyaṇa* specialists but also to those engaged with Indian intellectual history, literary studies and the history of religions.

Ajay K. Rao is Associate Professor in the Department of Historical Studies (UTM) and the Department for the Study of Religion at the University of Toronto, Canada.

Routledge Hindu Studies Series
Series Editor: Gavin Flood, Oxford Centre for Hindu Studies

The *Routledge Hindu Studies Series*, in association with the Oxford Centre for Hindu Studies, intends the publication of constructive Hindu theological, philosophical and ethical projects aimed at bringing Hindu traditions into dialogue with contemporary trends in scholarship and contemporary society. The series invites original, high-quality, research-level work on the religion, culture and society of Hindus living in India and abroad. Proposals for annotated translations of important primary sources and studies in the history of the Hindu religious traditions will also be considered.

Epistemologies and the Limitations of Philosophical Inquiry
Doctrine in Mādhva Vedānta
Deepak Sarma

A Hindu Critique of Buddhist Epistemology
Kumārila on perception
The "Determination of Perception" chapter of Kumārila Bhaṭṭa's *Ślokarvārttika* translation and commentary
John Taber

Saṃkara's Advaita Vedānta
A way of teaching
Jacqueline Hirst

Attending Kṛṣṇa's Image
Caitanya Vaiṣṇava Mūrti-sevā as devotional truth
Kenneth Russell Valpey

Advaita Vedānta and Vaiṣṇavism
The philosophy of Madhusūdana Sarasvatī
Sanjukta Gupta

Classical Sāṃkhya and Yoga
An Indian metaphysics of experience
Mikel Burley

Self-surrender (Prapatti) to God in Śrīvaiṣṇavism
Tamil cats and Sanskrit monkeys
Srilata Raman

The Caitanya Vaiṣṇava Vedānta of Jīva Gosvāmī
When knowledge meets devotion
Ravi M. Gupta

Gender and Narrative in the Mahābhārata
Edited by Simon Brodbeck and Brian Black

Yoga in the Modern World
Contemporary perspectives
Edited By Mark Singleton and Jean Byrne

Consciousness in Indian Philosophy
The Advaita doctrine of 'awareness only'
Sthaneshwar Timalsina

Desire and Motivation in Indian Philosophy
Christopher G. Framarin

Women in the Hindu Tradition
Rules, roles and exceptions
Mandakranta Bose

Religion, Narrative and Public Imagination in South Asia
Past and place in the Sanskrit Mahābhārata
James Hegarty

Interpreting Devotion
The poetry and legacy of a female Bhakti saint of India
Karen Pechilis

Hindu Perspectives on Evolution
Darwin, dharma, and design
C. Mackenzie Brown

Pilgrimage in the Hindu Tradition
Salvific space
Knut A. Jacobsen

A Woman's Rāmāyaṇa
Candrāvatī's Bengali epic
Mandakranta Bose and Sarika Priyadarshini Bose

Classical Vaiśeṣika in Indian Philosophy
On knowing and what is to be known
Shashiprabha Kumar

Re-figuring the *Rāmāyaṇa* as Theology
A history of reception in premodern India
Ajay K. Rao

Re-figuring the *Rāmāyaṇa* as Theology

A history of reception in premodern India

Ajay K. Rao

Routledge
Taylor & Francis Group
LONDON AND NEW YORK

GUELPH HUMBER LIBRARY
205 Humber College Blvd
Toronto, ON M9W 5L7

First published 2015
by Routledge
2 Park Square, Milton Park, Abingdon, Oxon OX14 4RN

and by Routledge
711 Third Avenue, New York, NY 10017

Routledge is an imprint of the Taylor & Francis Group, an informa business

© 2015 Ajay K. Rao

The right of Ajay K. Rao to be identified as author of this work has been asserted by him in accordance with sections 77 and 78 of the Copyright, Designs and Patents Act 1988.

All rights reserved. No part of this book may be reprinted or reproduced or utilised in any form or by any electronic, mechanical, or other means, now known or hereafter invented, including photocopying and recording, or in any information storage or retrieval system, without permission in writing from the publishers.

Trademark notice: Product or corporate names may be trademarks or registered trademarks, and are used only for identification and explanation without intent to infringe.

British Library Cataloguing in Publication Data
A catalogue record for this book is available from the British Library

Library of Congress Cataloging in Publication Data
Rao, Ajay K.
Re-figuring the Ramayana as theology : a history of reception in premodern India / Ajay K. Rao.
pages cm. — (Routledge Hindu studies series)
Includes bibliographical references and index.
1. Valmiki. Ramayana. 2. Sri Vaishnava (Sect) 3. Hinduism—India, South—History. I. Title.
BL1139.26.R385 2013
294.5′922046—dc23
2012042917

ISBN: 978–0–415–68751–5 (hbk)
ISBN: 978–0–203–52149–6 (ebk)

Typeset in Times New Roman
by RefineCatch Limited, Bungay, Suffolk

Printed and bound in the United States of America by Edwards Brothers Malloy on sustainably sourced paper.

Contents

Illustrations

Figures

Tables

Acknowledgements

This book has been nourished over the years through the patient support and assistance of friends, teachers and family. First, thanks are especially due to Sheldon Pollock and Wendy Doniger, who first helped me envision this project as a dissertation. Not only did they see me through the dissertation and challenge me at every stage, they both served as role models in their mentorship and ethical scholarship. These pages bear the imprint of their guidance. Also at Chicago, Matthew Kapstein carefully read the dissertation and provided invaluable feedback. I thank Ronald Inden for his generosity, challenging discussions and hours spent watching black-and-white films of Pāñcarātra rituals.

In preparing this manuscript, I have benefited from responses to my ideas and comments on early drafts from many friends and colleagues, including Prasad Bidaye, Yigal Bronner, Whitney Cox, Lata Deokar, Mahesh Deokar, Arti Dhand, John Fritz, Jack Hawley, Emily Hudson, Robert Goldman, Sally Sutherland Goldman, Pasha Mohamad Khan, Lawrence McCrea, George Michell, Shyam Ranganathan, Rajam Raghunathan, Adheesh Sathaye, Prithvi Datta Chandra Shobhi and Valerie Stoker. I am especially grateful to Parimal Patil for conversations throughout the writing of the dissertation and to Guy Leavitt, who carefully read through a final draft of the book manuscript. I thank Candis Haak for assistance with photographs and the preparation of the map in Chapter 2. Patrick Cummins proofread the diacritics and translations. Vicki Low and Arun Brahmbhatt, my research assistants, provided crucial assistance copy editing. Maithili Thayanithy proofread the Tamil citations.

I have benefited from years of training with specialists in India who were incredibly open and willing to share their extensive knowledge. In Pune, I worked closely with M. G. Dhadphale. Vaman Shastri Bhagavat imparted his erudition in Sanskrit grammar to me during early morning readings in the last few years of his life. In Chennai, I consulted with A. Thiruvengadathan, M. Narasimhachary and K. Srinivasan on issues in the Sanskrit and Maṇipravāla sources. I worked for an extended period with N. T. Srinivasa Iyengar in Bangalore.

On a personal note, I wish to thank my parents and brother, Santosh, who were always a reservoir of support and encouragement. My dear son, Amar, was patient with me and supplied much joy and creative inspiration while I was writing. Lastly, I thank my wife, Rabea, whose loving spirit and intellectual and emotional support enabled me to complete this project. I dedicate this book to her.

1 Two conceptions of divinity

This book explores a transformation in the premodern receptive history of the Vālmīki *Rāmāyaṇa*. From 1250 to 1600, intellectuals from the Śrīvaiṣṇava community of South India developed innovative interpretive techniques enabling them to map theological concepts onto the epic narrative, in effect transforming the paradigmatic exemplar of literary culture (*ādikāvya*) into a soteriological work. The Śrīvaiṣṇava hermeneutic project marks a critical moment in the precolonial *prehistory* of the emergence of the Vālmīki *Rāmāyaṇa* as a foundational religious text for modern Hindus.

There have been two major strands in the textual scholarship on the *Rāmāyaṇa* in the past thirty-five years. The first consists of the multi-volume, full-length, annotated Princeton translations of the Vālmīki *Rāmāyaṇa* and accompanying critical essays, one of the most ambitious and synergistic collective translation projects ever undertaken by Indologists. The second involves collaborative and individual research on medieval and modern devotional, regional, folk and performative *Rāmāyaṇas*, with an emphasis on the multivocal nature of the Rāma story as a genre comprised of alternate tellings.[1] This study of Sanskrit commentaries and Sanskrit poetry based on the Vālmīki *Rāmāyaṇa* draws on both bodies of scholarship as it charts new territory, bringing into view the historical agency involved in contestation over the text between interpretive communities. The specific focus is on the way Śrīvaiṣṇavas challenged one characterization of the genre of the text, as a work of literary culture, or *kāvya*, and replaced it with another, as a work of remembered tradition, or *smṛti*. The historical agency involved in this project of textual hermeneutics may also help us to understand the motivations behind a parallel project also involving Śrīvaiṣṇavas, the construction of the first monumental royal Rāma temples in the Vijayanagara capital during the fifteenth and sixteenth centuries.

The Śrīvaiṣṇava *Rāmāyaṇa* tradition is historically significant for a number of reasons, though it has never previously been the object of an extended study.[2] Śrīvaiṣṇavas (from the ninth century) were the earliest to systematize a devotional reframing of the epic narrative and identify the figure of Rāma with icons in Vaiṣṇava temples; they were dominant in commentarial writing on the *Rāmāyaṇa*; and they were intimately involved in the promulgation of Rāma worship. Some background about the Śrīvaiṣṇava order: Śrīvaiṣṇavas are devoted to the paramount overlordship of the god Viṣṇu; they are active today throughout South India, especially Tamil Nadu, Karnataka and Andhra Pradesh, and are primarily constituted of Tamil-speaking groups. Śrīvaiṣṇavas were socially organized from the tenth century. The ideological orientation of Śrīvaiṣṇavas coalesces around the authority of both Tamil and Sanskrit sources: the devotional poetry of the Tamil Āḻvārs, the liturgical Pāñcarātra Āgamas and the philosophy of Viśiṣṭādvaita. Śrīvaiṣṇava metaphysics is encapsulated in the body-embodied relationship (*śarīrasarīrībhāva*): just as the body is related to the soul, so also the individual soul is related to the divine, with Viṣṇu present in all beings as the inner controller (*antaryāmin*). The Śrīvaiṣṇava concept most important for the interpretation of the *Rāmāyaṇa* is surrender, or *prapatti*, which, unlike *bhakti* (devotion to or participation in the divine), is available to everyone regardless of class or gender.

1.1 The divinity of Rāma

We can gain perspective on just what was at stake in the Śrīvaiṣṇavas' hermeneutic project by comparing two conceptions of divinity: that represented in the epic, with which Sanskrit Rāma *kāvyas* are overwhelmingly congruent, and that formulated in Śrīvaiṣṇava theology and projected onto the epic narrative by Śrīvaiṣṇava commentators.

Indologists since Jacobi in 1893 have held that much of the Bāla Kāṇḍa and the Uttara Kāṇḍa must be subsequent to the composition of books two through six, based on text-critical and stylistic criteria (e.g. in the Bāla Kāṇḍa, inconsistencies such as the incongruity between the *putrakāmeṣṭi* and *aśvamedha* rites performed by Daśaratha).[3] On the strength of this understanding of the poem's compositional history, a generation of modern *Rāmāyaṇa* scholars argued that the very representation of Rāma as divine in the epic reflects subsequent accretion. However, as Sheldon Pollock has convincingly argued, despite the unquestionable evidence of interpolations in the history of the textual transmission of the *Rāmāyaṇa*, many factors strongly militate against this view with regard to the 'authentic' books two through six, including the internal logic of the narrative, with Rāvaṇa's boon requiring him to be killed by a human/divine agent, and references to Rāma's identity with Viṣṇu at key junctures in the narrative belonging to the oldest strata of composition, as supported by the philological criteria of the critical edition.[4]

Pollock supports his conclusions with a general discussion of the morphological affinities the conception of divinity in the epic bears with other examples of the boon motif in Sanskrit literature, such as the stories of Sunda and Upasunda, Tāraka and the birth of Skanda, and the myth of Hiraṇyakaśipu, where a man-god is required to counteract the dangerous potency of an ascetic. One reason this conception of the divine has engendered such confusion is its contrast with Jewish and Christian or even later Hindu theism: the hero here is both *fully* human and also in some sense divine. Complicating matters is the fact that Rāma at times himself displays ignorance of his divine nature. This image of divinity mirrored another where the agent was both a man and a god: the ideal of divine kingship. The earliest expository discussion of this ideal occurs in the Rājadharma section of the *Mahābhārata*, and the association of Viṣṇu with kingship becomes a common theme in the Purāṇas. Following the Central Asian Śakas and Kuśāṇas, who on the precedent of the Indo-Greeks used the title 'king of kings' and 'son of God,' Gupta rulers implemented this ideal in the world, as evident in the reference to Samudragupta's participation in the being of Viṣṇu in the Allahabad Pillar Inscription of 379 CE. The conceptualization of royal power was as a series of concentric circles of overlordship emanating from the ruler and, ultimately, the divine itself; therefore any portent or disaster impacting the king, either identified with Viṣṇu or viewed as the paradigmatic devotee of Śiva, also affected the kingdom.[5] Rāma's identification with Viṣṇu is therefore closely related to the ideal nature of Rāma's rule, *rāmarājya*.

This conception of Rāma's divinity remains even in the sections of the epic where his identity with Viṣṇu differs from other gods and marks him as superior, as when the gods assemble and admonish Rāma after his rejection of Sītā; the clear force of the passage is that Rāma has forgotten his divinity and only thinks of himself as a man. The treatment of Rāma's identity with Viṣṇu is identical in Sanskrit Rāma *kāvyas*, for example in Kālidāsa's where the extended praise of Viṣṇu as universal deity before his descent as Rāma has no bearing on the narration of the epic plot itself. The contrast here with devotional *Rāmāyaṇas* such as Kampaṉ's *Irāmāvatāram* is striking: though in the *Irāmāvatāram* Rāma's treatment of Sītā is even more cruel, without the mitigating motivation of revealing her purity, there is no question of a transformation in Rāma's self-understanding, since he is clearly represented as god throughout – and this ontological consistency brings with it a difficult set of theological implications.[6]

Although Śrīvaiṣṇavas tapped into the basic representation of Rāma's divinity in the epic, their conception of divinity involved a distinctive theological metaphysics, which they brought to bear on the epic narrative through various sophisticated hermeneutic strategies. Elaborate Śrīvaiṣṇava views of the nature of divinity were formulated within philosophical Viśiṣṭādvaita. The fourteenth-century philosophers Sudarśana Sūri and Vedānta Deśika cast canonical sets of divine characteristics into the broader categories of transcendence (*paratva*), and accessibility (*saulabhya*), both of which are of significance for the hierarchical relationship between agents involved in surrender; for surrender to be efficacious, the one who gives refuge (*śaraṇya*) must be both capable and willing to provide refuge.

John Carman has shown that although Rāmānuja, the foundational figure in philosophical Viśiṣṭādvaita, himself never used the terms *paratva* and *saulabhya* in this technical manner, several aspects of his presentation prefigure the later theorization.[7] For example, the lists of Viṣṇu's auspicious qualities (*kalyāṇaguṇas*) that divide into two broad categories in Rāmānuja's introduction to the *Bhagavad Gītā Bhāṣya* serve as an epitome of the Śrīvaiṣṇava conception of the godhead. The six qualities (*ṣaḍguṇas*) conform neatly to the notion of the lord's transcendent nature or *paratva*: knowledge (*jñāna*), strength (*bala*), lordship (*aiśvarya*), energy (*vīrya*), power (*śakti*) and splendour (*tejas*). Later, another quite different set of qualities conforms to the notion of accessibility or *saulabhya*: compassion (*kāruṇya*), gracious condescension (*sauśīlya*), protective affection (*vātsalya*) and generosity (*audārya*); further along in the passage, Rāmānuja also lists the additional qualities of friendship (*sauhārda*) and love (*anurāga*).[8] While the Viśiṣṭādvaita philosophical conception of divinity rests on the metaphysics of Viṣṇu as the ensouler of the universe (contingently identified with the world on the analogy of coordinate predication statements), the basic concepts of *paratva* and *saulabhya* are more germane to the developing theory of surrender.

Also relevant to the Śrīvaiṣṇava understanding of the *Rāmāyaṇa* is their distinctive philosophy of divine descent, or *avatāra*. Post-Rāmānuja theologians grouped Viṣṇu's descents into a fourfold taxonomy: (1) *vibhava*, the lord's manifestation in incarnations; (2) *arcā*, the lord's presence in temple icons; (3) *vyūha*, the fourfold Pāñcarātra emanation; and (4) *antaryāmin*, the lord's presence as the inner controller within all beings. To demonstrate the relationship between these philosophical ideas and the Śrīvaiṣṇava approach to the *Rāmāyaṇa*, we can compare Rāmānuja's commentary on *Bhagavad Gītā* 4.8 and the long opening prose passage of the most important Sanskrit *Rāmāyaṇa* commentary, Govindarāja's *Bhūṣaṇa*. Rāmānuja discusses the purpose of Viṣṇu's incarnation:

> 1) [For the protection of the good]
> 'Sādhus,' the 'good,' are the best among Vaiṣṇavas practicing the described *dharma* who seek my protection. If they do not see me even for a moment they consider it to be an eternity, they find no solace in continuing to live and their limbs become weak – but the nature of my name and acts transcends language and cognition. I protect them by allowing them to see me and my acts and to speak with me.
> 2) [For the destruction of the wicked]
> 3) [For the establishment of *dharma*]
> For reinstating the Vedic *dharma*, which consists of venerating me, I make myself an object of veneration.
> 4) [I am born in every era].[9]

What is of particular interest in this key passage is that Rāmānuja casts all the *avatāras* of Viṣṇu as efforts to implement Vedic practice, identified with devotional worship and facilitated by the divine presence in the world.

Now notice the similar reasoning that Govindarāja gives for the birth of Rāma:

> The lord of Śrī, all his desires fulfilled, endowed with all auspicious qualities, the overlord, sat on his throne with his wives in the divine world of Vaikuṇṭha. Those who were eternally released (*nityamuktas*) always served his lotus feet, but he observed the ignorant beings who also deserved to serve his feet but did not attain him, stuck as they were to primeval matter at the time of dissolution like drops of gold stuck to beeswax. His mind filled with compassion, he gave them senses and bodies so that they could reach him. But as if diverted by the current of the river into the ocean with rafts meant

> for crossing the river, they became attached through their bodies to other objects. And even when he promulgated his own command in the form of the Veda so that they could discriminate between the real and the unreal, they did not respect it because of their incomprehension, false understanding and misinterpretation. Like a king desiring to approach and discipline his subjects transgressing his command, the lord decided to descend in the fourfold form of Rāma, etc., to teach living beings through his own conduct. In the meantime Brahmā and all the gods requested him to take birth. And so, in order to fulfill the desire of his devotee, Daśaratha, as well, he descended in four parts.[10]

The overlap between these two accounts is symptomatic of the normative dimension of the Śrīvaiṣṇava hermeneutic project and the degree to which systematic metaphysics and epistemology are brought to bear upon an understanding of the events depicted.

Govindarāja directly superimposes Śrīvaiṣṇava conceptions of divinity onto the narrative structure of the epic in his commentary on 1.5.1, where he explicates the eighteen traditional meanings of the *Rāmāyaṇa* passed down from Rāmānuja's maternal uncle, Śrī Śaila Pūrṇa. The first of the eighteen meanings employs the six contextual identifiers (*tātparyaliṅgas*) in Mīmāṃsā textual analysis to prove that the central purport of the *Rāmāyaṇa* is the supremacy of Viṣṇu. With the first of these identifiers, the commencement of the text (*upakrama*), Govindarāja identifies Rāma with Viṣṇu as *brahman*, the universal spirit, in congruence with the Upaniṣadic quote, 'Know that from which these beings are born, through which, being born, they live, and that into which they enter again. That is *brahman*' (*yato vā imāni bhūtāni jāyante yena jātāni jīvanti yat prayanty abhisaṃviśanti tad vijñānasva tad brahma*).[11] For the third identifier, repetition (*abhyāsa*), Govindarāja seeks to show how each book of the *Rāmāyaṇa* unfolds a separate aspect of Viṣṇu's supremacy:

> 1) In the Bāla Kāṇḍa, Viṣṇu creates the world; 2) in the Ayodhyā Kāṇḍa, Viṣṇu facilitates the sustenance of the world; 3) in the Āraṇya Kāṇḍa, Viṣṇu grants liberation (with Jaṭāyu); 4) in the Sundara Kāṇḍa, Viṣṇu possesses all virtues; 5) in the Kiṣkindhā Kāṇḍa, Viṣṇu destroys all; 6) in the Yuddha Kāṇḍa, Viṣṇu is the object of Vedāntic knowledge (as per the praise of Mandodarī); and in the Uttara Kāṇḍa, Viṣṇu's is the source of the creator himself.[12]

Govindarāja thereby effectively reduces the heterogeneity of the narrative to a set of propositions about Viṣṇu's divine nature, repeatedly shifting the interpretive frame back and forth between the story at hand and received conceptual schemata. In this section of the commentary, Govindarāja is able to accomplish the mapping of theological concepts at a macro level, but engaging the substance of the text in his commentary on specific verses often requires considerable interpretive effort.

1.2 Historical background

Śrīvaiṣṇavas did not access the Vālmīki *Rāmāyaṇa* unmediated by past interpretations but through the *Wirkungsgeschichte* of the epic in the Sanskrit literary–aesthetic tradition. Śrīvaiṣṇavas sought to engage with the generic categorization of the *Rāmāyaṇa* as *kāvya*, a work of literary culture, which originated from the identification of the epic as the first instance of poetry in its own frame narrative. Explicit mention of this status for the *Rāmāyaṇa* dates all the way back to Aśvaghoṣa in the second century and is repeated later by poets such as Kālidāsa (fourth or fifth century), Bhavabhūti (eighth century), as well as literary critics and aestheticians beginning with Ānandavardhana (ninth century), Rājaśekhara (tenth century) and Abhinavagupta (tenth century). Vālmīki's *Rāmāyaṇa* appears as the first poem in all genealogies prefacing Sanskrit *kāvyas* from the time of Bāṇa in the seventh century.[13] The strongest evidence we have for this receptive history is the plethora of Sanskrit *kāvya* versions of the epic, almost a class of literature unto itself, including some of the most famous works of Sanskrit poetry: Kālidāsa's *Raghuvaṃśa*, Bhāsa's *Pratimānāṭaka* and *Abhiṣekanāṭaka*, Bhavabhūti's *Mahāvīracarita* and *Uttararāmacarita*, Bhoja's *Campurāmāyaṇa*, etc. The influence of this particular history of evoking and recreating the Vālmiki *Rāmāyaṇa* should not, of course, lead us to overlook the existence of other important early *Rāmāyaṇa* narratives and alternative trajectories for the reception of Vālmīki's epic, including the Buddhist *Daśaratha Jātaka* and *Vessantara Jātaka*, the Jain *Paumacariya* and the *Rāmopākhyāna* of the *Mahābhārata.*[14] The emphasis in this book on the *Rāmāyaṇa* as *kāvya* is due to its centrality to the Śrīvaiṣṇava hermeneutic project.

Śrīvaiṣṇava approaches to the epic form part of a larger historical nexus between the Rāma story and the growth of devotional literary genres and traditions throughout the subcontinent, resulting in the composition of hundreds of written and performed *Rāmāyaṇa* poems in virtually every South Asian (and Southeast Asian) language. Broadly speaking, there appear to have been two partially intersecting trajectories of Rāma *bhakti* in the early second millennium, one northern and the other southern, each with separate histories of narrative adaptation, as well as differing theological and mythical sources. Important works from the north include the *Mokṣopāya* (tenth century) and its expansion into the *Yogavāsiṣṭha* (twelfth or thirteenth century), the *Bhuśuṇḍi Rāmāyaṇa* (fourteenth century), and *Adhyātmaramāyaṇa* (fifteenth century), Tulsīdās's *Rāmacaritamānas* (sixteenth century), the *Rāmatāpanīya Upaniṣad* and *Rāmarahasya Upaniṣad* (sixteenth or seventeenth century), and the full-length commentary on the *Rāmāyaṇa by* the grammarian Nāgeśa Bhaṭṭa, known as *Tilaka* (eighteenth century).[15] These share an idiosyncratic Advaita philosophy, the combination of Vaiṣṇava and Śaiva devotion, tantric elements and innovations in the basic plot such as the 'shadow' Sītā abducted by Rāvaṇa in place of the original Sītā. They also exhibit a wide set of Persian and vernacular influences and are closely connected with specific themes in the emerging genre of Hindavi Sufi romance, such as the significance of Lake Mānasa in the *Padmāvat* (sixteenth century) and the motif of the magic deer in the *Mirigāvatī* (sixteenth century).[16] The Rāmānandī order, a tradition centred on Rāma *bhakti*, likely dates to the fifteenth or sixteenth centuries.[17]

In the south, special mention must be made of Kampaṉ's monumental Tamil retelling, the *Irāmāvatāram* (twelfth century).[18] While the *Irāmāvatāram*, like the Sanskrit *kāvya* retellings, is an ornamental courtly poem and not the product of oral composition, it is squarely located in the larger milieu of Tamil *bhakti*, with Rāma appearing unequivocally as God rather than a composite man-god descent as in Vālmīki. It is curious that the *Irāmāvatāram* is almost completely without significance for Śrīvaiṣṇavas. Although an oral tradition identifies Kampaṉ as a Śrīvaiṣṇava and today one can find a special hall associated with Kampaṉ in the Śrīraṅgam complex (a Hoysaḷa construction of the thirteenth century), the *Irāmāvatāram* spawned no Śrīvaiṣṇava commentarial tradition; moreover, the *Irāmāvatāram* is rarely, if ever, cited in the *rahasya* literature despite its centrality to Tamil literary culture and its distinctive synthesis of Tamil *bhakti* with the Rāma story. It is possible that this absence was due to its perceived proximity to the emerging regional court of the Cōḻas, or to discrepancies between the idiosyncratic devotional anthropology of the *Irāmāvatāram* and aspects of Śrīvaiṣṇava theology invariably associated with their use of the epic paradigm.

Śrīvaiṣṇava engagement with the Rāma story occurred in three phases: (1) references in Tamil Āḻvār poetry (sixth to ninth centuries) interspersing specifically Tamil folk traditions and devotional veneration of Rāma with the basic outline of Vālmīki's telling; (2) the inscription of esoteric Maṇipravāla (mixed Tamil and Sanskrit) oral commentary on the Āḻvār poems and independent esoteric (*rahasya*) works (eleventh through fourteenth centuries); and (3) the composition of Sanskrit Rāma poems and full-length Sanskrit commentaries on the Vālmīki *Rāmāyaṇa* (thirteenth through sixteenth centuries). I focus especially on this last stage, where Śrīvaiṣṇavas directly engage with the literary–aesthetic receptive history of the *Rāmāyaṇa*, but the third stage is inextricably related to the second, because the Sanskrit works are invariably reformulations or translations of innovations in Maṇipravāla, as discussed in Chapter 2 of this book. Of the commentaries on the Āḻvār poetry (collectively called the Divyaprabandham), special status is attached to authoritative Maṇipravāla commentaries on the *Tiruvāymoḻi* of Nammāḻvār, considered by Śrīvaiṣṇavas to be revelation on a par with the Veda; these include the commentaries of Tirukkurukaippirāṉ Piḷḷāṉ (eleventh century), Nañcīyar (b. 1113), Vaṭakkutiruvītip Piḷḷai (b. 1217), Periyavāccāṉ Piḷḷai (b. 1228), and Vātikesari Aḻakiya Maṇavāḷa Cīyar (fourteenth century). The authors of the *rahasya* works, whose ideas formed the basis for the rival Vaṭakalai (northern) and Teṅkalai (southern) schools include Vedānta Deśika and Piḷḷai Lokācārya (b. 1205) (along with his influential commentator, Maṇavāḷamāmuni, b. 1370). Vedānta Deśika and his rough contemporary Periyavāccāṉ Piḷḷai wrote *rahasya* works devoted entirely to the *Rāmāyaṇa* (Vedānta Deśika's *Abhayapradānasāra* and Periyavāccāṉ Piḷḷai's *Abhayapradānasāra* and *Taniślokam*).

Vedānta Deśika was also the author of a series of Sanskrit poems on the Rāmāyaṇa. Deśika, who originated in Kāñcī in the period directly preceding the Vijayanagara Empire, was one of the seminal intellectual figures of the late-medieval Śrīvaiṣṇava community, and his sectarian positions formed the foundation for the Vaṭakalai school. His voluminous and diverse oeuvre includes philosophical works in Sanskrit, *rahasya* works in Maṇipravāla and poetry in Sanskrit and Tamil; altogether he is credited with over 130 works. Among these are a number of allegorical poems and praise-poems invoking the Rāma story including the *Haṃsasandeśa*, *Pādukāsahasra* and *Mahāvīravaibhava*. These works in many ways parallel the dynamics of Sanskrit commentaries, producing directly in poetic form the image of the *Rāmāyaṇa* envisioned by the commentators.

The majority of Śrīvaiṣṇava full-length, verse-by-verse Sanskrit commentaries on the Vālmīki *Rāmāyaṇa* were produced during the height of Śrīvaiṣṇava influence at the Vijayanagara Empire in the fifteenth and sixteenth centuries. Śrīvaiṣṇavas were the primary players in *Rāmāyaṇa* commentarial activity, which may to some degree be measured by the fact that four of the six commentaries used in the preparation of the Varodara critical edition are Śrīvaiṣṇava. The earliest extant Sanskrit commentary on the *Rāmāyaṇa* is the *Vivekatilaka* by Uḍāli Varadarāja.[19] This commentary is wholly concerned with text-critical issues (i.e. proper readings of variants, settling the literal meaning of difficult passages, etc.) and displays almost no trace of the religious affiliation of its author. In this sense it represents a line of interpretation distinct from the early Maṇipravāla *rahasya* works, and the differences between it and the commentaries that followed may indicate that more ambitious exegesis first required a more or less fixed recension, with editorial issues relegated to the background. V. Raghavan was able to trace references in the *Īṭu* commentary of Vaṭakkutiruvītip Piḷḷai to establish the terminus ad quem of the *Vivekatilaka* as 1250 CE.[20] The *Vivekatilaka* itself mentions that the author was a 'Cōḻa Paṇdita,' a member of a group of Brahmins who served under Cōḻa kings as military generals (with the title *Brahmamahārāja*). It also refers to earlier commentaries, although these have not survived.

Another extent commentary antedating Govindarāja is cryptically titled *Rāmānujīya*, a short work perhaps datable to the early fifteenth century expounding esoteric interpretations of select verses along the lines of the Maṇipravāla *rahasya* works. Virtually nothing is known about the actual author and the text's provenance. Shastri identifies this Rāmānuja as the Kantāṭai Rāmānuja Ayyaṅkār who was the *rājaguru* for the Vijayanagara king Sāluva Narasiṃha, but not much evidence for this claim is provided.[21] A more plausible explanation is that the Rāmānujīya is an eponymous work titled for the school of the Rāmānujīyas, i.e. the Śrīvaiṣṇavas. The only post-Govindarāja commentary rivalling Govindarāja's in terms of circulation is the *Tīrthīya* of Maheśvaratīrtha. Although not much is known about Maheśvaratīrtha except that he calls himself the son of Nārāyaṇatīrtha, Robert Goldman and Sally Sutherland Goldman have been able to track a number of places where Maheśvaratīrtha explicitly quotes the commentary of Kataka Mādhava Yogīndra, who perhaps lived in the seventeenth century, and they have thereby revised a previous consensus regarding the sequence of commentators and their relative dates.[22] Although there is some confusion regarding the relative dates of Maheśvaratīrtha and Govindarāja, it appears based on the analysis of Goldman and Sutherland Goldman that Govindarāja preceded Maheśvaratīrtha, since he lived before Kataka. Ātreya Ahobila's *Vālmīkihṛdaya* is an important post-Govindarāja commentary. Based on the fact that his teacher was Parāṅkuśa, the sixth pontiff of the Ahobila Maṭha, the text may be assigned to the first quarter of the seventeenth century. The composition of a great number of these commentaries within the Ahobila Maṭha indicates that this single institution, which flourished through Vijayanagara patronage, was the epicentre of Śrīvaiṣṇava commentarial activity on the *Rāmāyaṇa*.

I focus especially on Govindarāja's sixteenth-century *Bhūṣaṇa*, in part because this commentary represents a virtual compendium of previous Śrīvaiṣṇava interpretations, as the comments of earlier writers are incorporated verbatim directly into the body of the text. We can date Govindarāja's commentary on the basis of the identity of his teacher and his citations of other contemporary figures. Govindarāja credits the inspiration of Vedānta Śaṭakōpa Cīyar, the fifth head of the Ahobila Maṭha, who was counsellor to the chiefs of the Nāṇḍyāla family according to an inscription datable to 1548; this Śaṭakōpa Cīyar probably presided at Ahobila from 1548 to 1557.[23] Govindarāja also credits the encouragement of Bhāvanācārya, who lived during the reigns of the first Tuḷuva Vijayanagara kings in the early sixteenth century.[24] Finally, Govindarāja directly refutes the opinions of Appayya Dīkṣita, whose dates are 1520 to 1592. Combining these various references, 1550–1575 appears to be the probable range for the activity of Govindarāja. According to the colophons, Govindarāja belonged to the Kauśika *gotra* and was the son of Varadarāja; he also wrote a commentary on the *Taittirīya Upaniṣad*. In the invocatory verses of the *Bhūṣaṇa*, Govindarāja says that while visiting Tirupati he dreamt that crowds of devotees instructed him to compose his commentary. As with nearly all the commentators, it is unclear whether Govindarāja's sectarian affiliation was Vaṭakalai or Teṅkalai, if any, and this ambiguity may in part reflect the liminal status of the Ahobila Maṭha, which became an exclusively Vaṭakalai institution only with the seventh head, Ahobila Cīyar, according to Vīrarāghava's *Triṃśatpraśnottara*. Additional evidence for the Ahobila Maṭha's liminal status is the fact that it is the only Vaṭakalai institution that accepts the proto-Teṅkalai *Īṭu* commentary.

1.3 Outline of the book

In the second and third chapters of this book I explore several of these works in detail. My focus is especially on how, during the fourteenth through sixteenth centuries, Śrīvaiṣṇavas developed hybrid forms of Sanskrit poetic composition centred on the Rāma story and, in commentaries, applied innovative interpretive techniques to the *Rāmāyaṇa* as a text. Specific interpretive techniques included allegorical reading, *śleṣa* reading (reading a verse as a double entendre), and the application of vernacular performance techniques such as word play, improvisation, repetition and novel forms of citation.

Chapter 2 traces the translation of esoteric, performative exegesis from Maṇipravāla into scholastic Sanskrit. I discuss how Maṇipravāla represents the sedimentation of temple oratory and the 'voice' of cosmopolitan vernacular theology. I then examine the adaptation of Maṇipravāla methods into the Sanskrit poetry of Vedānta Deśika and the Sanskrit commentary of Govindarāja. Vedānta Deśika's *Haṃsasandeśa* is an atypical Sanskrit *kāvya* injecting Śrīvaiṣṇava theological elements into the literary series of Sanskrit Rāma *kāvyas*, as it subtly codes Rāma's message to Sītā via Hanumān as an allegory for the relationship between God and the individual soul. The second part of the chapter deals with Govindarāja's incorporation of Maṇipravāla verbatim into Sanskrit, often through transformations in idiom due to the grammatical and scholastic categories of Sanskrit commentary, resulting in the generation of new techniques involving a kind of hyperanalysis. The most extensive example of this practice is Govindarāja's treatment of the single most important event in the epic for Śrīvaiṣṇavas, the surrender of Rāvaṇa's brother, Vibhīṣaṇa, to Rāma. Here, without recourse to figuration, a relatively minor incident of political intrigue becomes the paradigmatic example for the theological concept of surrender.

Chapter 3 narrows the focus of analysis to a set of readings of a single verse: *mā niṣāda*, considered the first instance of poetic composition in Sanskrit. I begin the chapter with a review of the plethora of Sanskrit *kāvyas* patterned after the *Rāmāyaṇa* and the theorization of *kāvya* in Sanskrit aesthetics with the *Rāmāyaṇa* as exemplar. Given the centrality of *mā niṣāda* to both Sanskrit poetry and Sanskrit aesthetic theory, Govindarāja's reinterpretation of the verse represents perhaps his most direct challenge to the literary–aesthetic reception of the epic. Govindarāja reads the verse doubly, as a *śleṣa* (double entendre), provocatively transforming a mode of composition into a reading practice with the result that meaning itself becomes potentially destabilized. Through this reading, what appears in the original to be a curse is transformed into a Śrīvaiṣṇava benediction.

Chapter 4 charts connections between the composition of Rāma poems and *Rāmāyaṇa* commentaries and the rise of Rāma worship. Śrīvaiṣṇavas in mid-fifteenth- to sixteenth-century Vijayanagara were behind both of these parallel projects – textual hermeneutics and temple building – and in this chapter I draw on the preceding studies of texts to understand the actions of Śrīvaiṣṇavas on the ground in the imperial capital. I begin with the early history of the integration of the Rāma story into temples in the Tamil region and move to the construction of the first monumental Rāma temples at Vijayanagara. Evidence for the role played by Śrīvaiṣṇavas includes their influence at the Vijayanagara court during the Sāḷuva, Tuḷuva and Aravīḍu dynasties, culminating in their service as royal preceptors (*rājagurus*), as well as the Śrīvaiṣṇava affiliation of several of the key Rāma temples. The close partnership between kings and Śrīvaiṣṇavas at

Vijayanagara challenges the idea that the Rāma worship was a reaction to the expansion of Islamic rule in South Asia, in part because the dynamics of the Śrīvaiṣṇava theological treatment of the epic does not involve an appropriation of the epic's conceptual resources for othering, as is evident in the treatment of Rāvaṇa at junctures in the narrative of greatest significance to Śrīvaiṣṇavas. I conclude by situating the Rāma cult at Vijayanagara in the context of recent studies of the Islamicization of political culture at Vijayanagara.

2 Translating pearls into coral

Like a necklace made of pearls (*maṇi*) and coral (*pravāla*), 'Maṇipravāla' refers to the combination of Sanskrit with South Indian languages (Tamil, Malayalam, Kannada and Telugu). This chapter examines the historical pattern of adapting Maṇipravāla to Sanskrit in two sets of materials: the Sanskrit poetry of Vedānta Deśika and the Sanskrit commentary of Govindarāja. In Vedānta Deśika's poetry, the shadow of the vernacular is evident in the poem's allegorical form and crafting of regional space through the Śrīvaiṣṇava divine places. In Govindarāja's commentary, vernacular exegetical techniques were translated verbatim, resulting in the incorporation of performative improvisation into scholastic Sanskrit.

Translation from Maṇipravāla to Sanskrit captures the historical and logical trajectory of Śrīvaiṣṇava commentarial writing on the *Rāmāyaṇa*. All the earliest theological treatments of the *Rāmāyaṇa* occur in Maṇipravāla works: the Divyaprabandham commentaries and esoteric (*rahasya*) works of Piḷḷai Lokācārya, Periyavāccāṉ Piḷḷai, Vedānta Deśika and Maṇavāḷamāmuni. The composition of full-length Sanskrit commentaries incorporating these Maṇipravāla readings represents the final phase of Śrīvaiṣṇava hermeneutic activity directed towards the *Rāmāyaṇa*, with translation from Maṇipravāla marking a shift in hermeneutic orientation, a widening of audience from a restricted one to one that was in some sense universal. Nearly all of the Sanskrit commentaries date to the mid-fifteenth through sixteenth centuries, the period which witnessed the construction of major Śrīvaiṣṇava Rāma temples in Vijayanagara, as will be examined in the fourth chapter.

The lapidary metaphor that gives Maṇipravāla its identity may itself capture something of its capacity to mediate between linguistic, cultural and hermeneutic worlds. If Maṇipravāla represents the admixture of Tamil pearls and Sanskrit coral, it also moves directly between vernacular Tamil literary, devotional and folk traditions and cosmopolitan Sanskrit literary culture.[1] Through linguistic blending and translation, both Tamil and Sanskrit genres were subjected to a process of hybridity, whereby they became differentiated from conventional cultural forms, and this hybrid quality of Maṇipravāla facilitated an indirect transfer of distinctively Tamil practices (the pearls in the necklace remain pearls, and the coral remains coral) into Sanskrit. This chapter begins with a consideration of Maṇipravāla as the emblematic 'voice' of Śrīvaiṣṇava vernacular theology, and then moves to discussions of the redeployment of distinctively performative modes of Maṇipravāla exegesis into idioms more familiar to Sanskrit in the poetry of Vedānta Deśika and the commentary of Govindarāja.

2.1 Maṇipravāla and temple performance

Historically in early South Indian vernacular traditions, various patterns of combination received metalinguistic theorization as distinct language phenomena, though some forms of discourse bearing the marks of such linguistic hybridization were only retrospectively categorized as Maṇipravāla, as is the case with Śrīvaiṣṇava Maṇipravāla literature. Commentators on the Divyaprabandham and authors of Śrīvaiṣṇava *rahasya* works do not themselves use the term 'Maṇipravāla,' though their works have been subsequently characterized in such a way and constitute the most extensive examples of Tamil Maṇipravāla composition we possess. The authors are, however, explicit about another aspect of this literature – that it represents a record of temple oratory. Based on the close affinity many of these works bore with temple performance – i.e. the temple lecture (*upanyāsa* or *pravacana*) and the *araiyar* tradition of recitation, song and dramatic performance – we may go further and characterize the entire Śrīvaiṣṇava Maṇipravāla corpus as the sedimentation in writing of performative modes of oral discourse.

Within this corpus, as mentioned in the first chapter, special status was attached to the five authoritative commentaries on the *Tiruvāymoḻi* of Nammāḻvār written by Tirukkurukaippirāṉ Piḷḷāṉ (eleventh century), Nañcīyar (twelfth century), Vaṭakkutiruvītip Piḷḷai (thirteenth century), Periyavāccāṉ Piḷḷai (thirteenth century) and Vātikesari Aḻakiya Maṇavāḷa Cīyar (fourteenth century). Scattered references to oral antecedents occur in the commentaries themselves, but these are more frequent and explicit in later hagiographical literature, especially Piṉpaḻakīya Perumāḷ Cīyar's fourteenth-century *Guruparamparāprabhāva*.[2] Two anecdotes associated with the thirteenth-century teacher Nampiḷḷai are illustrative. One involves a local ruler witnessing a large number of people emerging from Nampiḷḷai's lectures, rivalling in size crowds at the worship chamber in Śrīraṅgam. The second is the most famous case of the circumscribed teacher–student transmission the *Īṭu* terms '*ōraṇvaḻi*,' involving an account of competing records of Nampiḷḷai's lectures produced by his two students, Periyavāccāṉ Piḷḷai and Vaṭakkutiruvītip Piḷḷai; unlike Periyavāccāṉ Piḷḷai, who received his teacher's permission to commit a commentary to writing, Vaṭakkutiruvītip Piḷḷai surreptitiously wrote his own by night. Temple lectures on the *Tiruvāymoḻi* provide a precedent for innovations in the Sanskrit texts examined in this chapter, including repetitive glossing of narremes, verses and lexical and morphological units, didactic genres, improvisational techniques, word play and novel forms of citation.

The hereditary *araiyar* tradition of *Tiruvāymoḻi* recitation, studied ethnographically by Vasudha Narayanan (1994b), appears to have been fairly widespread historically and practiced in a variety of temples, though today it is limited to Śrīraṅgam, Āḻvār Tirunagari and Śrīvilliputtūr. *Araiyar* recitation, which attains special prominence during the ten-day annual recitation festival in the month of Mārkaḻi, is distinguished by its ritual dimension: the standard performance is divided into two parts, with the performer facing the deity as audience in the first, or *mutal cēvai*, and facing away from the deity and towards devotees while reciting and expounding on the *Tiruvāymoḻi* in the second, or *iraṇṭāñ cēvai*.[3] Stories of musicians linked to the *araiyar* tradition in the *Kōyil Oḷuku*, the temple chronicle of the Śrīraṅgam temple, suggests that exegesis went hand in hand with song and dance, though in contemporary performances the musical element is limited to rhythmic beating accompanying recitation of verses and dramatic enactment. Narayanan highlights the homology between musical and exegetical improvisation in *araiyar* performance:

> There are repetitions of phrases, and a single line may be repeated and elaborated several times, in a manner akin to modern south Indian Carnatic musical performances. The *araiyar* conveys the depth of the *āḻvār*'s emotion or the philosophical import of the verse by going back to a phrase and expressing it in different ways, and it is here that we begin to understand what the community means when it calls the poem 'a text that is to be experienced,' *anubhava grantha*.[4]

In addition to these practices specific to Śrīvaiṣṇava temples, broader developments in the history of epic performance in the south likely impacted written commentary on the *Rāmāyaṇa*. The epics were inherently performative, in their compositional, no less than receptive, history, as foregrounded in the *Rāmāyaṇa*'s frame narrative, where the poem is described as being recited aloud and sung (*pāṭhye geye*) and set to music (*tantrīlayasamanvitam*).[5] In early history of the Tamil region, royal patronage of the public recitation of both the *Rāmāyaṇa* and the *Mahābhārata* is attested by inscriptions connected to periods of Paḷḷava, Coḻa and Pāṇṭiya rule.[6] However, in the second millennium Purāṇic exegetical and performative practices, closely associated with the emerging figure of the *vyākhyātṛ* or 'analyst' as reciter of Purāṇic stories in liturgical contexts, were increasingly brought to bear on the *Rāmāyaṇa*.[7] The modern tradition of *kathākālakṣepa* or *harikathā* in south India, combining elements of storytelling, lecture and music, is a much later extension of this integration of the epic into temple contexts, directly traceable to the influence of Marathi *kīrtankārs* in Tañjāvūr during Marāṭhā rule from the seventeenth century. There is anecdotal and documentary evidence for the existence of individual figures engaged in such performances of the *Rāmāyaṇa* in the centuries directly subsequent to the period in focus for this study, including Rāmabrahma, the father of the composer Tyāgarāja, who was an expert performer of Purāṇa *pravacana* and *upanyāsa* at the court of Tulajājī II (1763–1787) of Tañjāvūr, and Aruṇācala Kavirāyar (1712–1779), a performer of *prasaṅga* (discourse) who composed the musical drama *Rāma Nāṭaka*.[8] Despite the parallels between the integration of music and dance in *araiyar* recitation and in *kathākālakṣepa*, there are also important differences, including the greater emphasis on entertainment and humour and more fluid treatment of the epic story in the latter; recitation of the *Tiruvāymoḻi*, on the other hand, is of an invariably fixed text, envisioned as the Tamil equivalent to the Veda.

The affinity between the interpretation of texts in temple performance and in Maṇipravāla written commentary is evident, for example, in the contrasting evaluations of Bharata's relationship to Rāma in Piḷḷai Lokācārya's (b. 1205) *Śrīvacanabhūṣaṇa*, Vaṭakkutiruvītip Piḷḷai's (b. 1217) *Tiruvāymoḻi* commentary known as the *Īṭu*, and Vedānta Deśika's (b. 1228) *Abhayapradānasāra*, a *rahasya* work specifically devoted to the *Rāmāyaṇa*. In the first case Bharata's experience is disparaged in favour of conformity with divine will, in the second it is a model for measuring the Āḻvār's progressive spiritual development, and in the third it is contrasted to more active performances of surrender.

Piḷḷai Lokācārya and his commentator Maṇavāḷamāmuni contrast Rāma's refusal of Bharata's request to his intimacy with Guha, as they develop a classic Teṅkalai argument. Although accompanied by his ministers and army, Bharata fails to convince Rāma to return to Ayodhyā; on the other hand, Rāma himself approaches Guha and accepts him despite Guha's status as a tribal hunter (*niṣāda*). The message of the story, according to Maṇavāḷamāmuni, is that the lord's unmitigated independence (*niraṅkuśasvātantra*) entails that his will and his will alone determines liberation irrespective of a person's actions. Accordingly Bharata's apparently meritorious act of relinquishing the throne is transformed into a fault insofar as it conflicts with Rāma's own intention to defeat Rāvaṇa.[9]

Compare this disparaging of Bharata with the favourable treatment he receives in the third section of the general introduction (*mahāpraveśa*) of the *Īṭu*, where Vaṭakkutiruvītip Piḷḷai draws an extended comparison between Nammāḻvār and Bharata in terms of stages of servitude to the lord (*kaiṅkarya*), the state after liberation for Śrīvaiṣṇavas. Just as Bharata experiences intense grief upon returning from his maternal uncle's house and hearing Kaikeyī address him as king ('*rājan*'), similarly Nammāḻvār gives voice to the pain of separation from the lord in the *Tiruviruttam*. When Bharata travels to the Citrakūṭa forest with his ministers and army he bows his head to Rāma in an act of propitiation, a display of longing matched by the longing of Nammāḻvār's *Tiruvāciriyam*. Residing in Nandigrāma, Bharata's desire intensifies, as does Nammāḻvār's in the *Tiruvantāti*. Finally, after Rāma returns and is consecrated king, Bharata is reunited with him; so, too, Nammāḻvār finally realizes the lord with the *Tiruvāymoḻi*.[10]

Finally, Vedānta Deśika's comparison of the respective requests of Bharata and Lakṣmaṇa in the *Abhayapradānasāra* differs from both Piḷḷai Lokācārya's and Vaṭakkutiruvītip Piḷḷai's treatments of Bharata. Bharata's actions are not viewed as impertinence by Deśika, as they are by Piḷḷai Lokācārya, on the contrary they are valorized over Lakṣmaṇa's insistence, proving the superiority of passive dependence (*pāratantrya*) over active servitude (*kaiṅkarya*).[11] In his Sanskrit commentary, Govindarāja follows Vaṭakkutiruvītip Piḷḷai in the chapter dealing with Lakṣmaṇa's request (2.31) and follows Vedānta Deśika in the chapter dealing with Bharata's request (2.101, critical edition 2.95).

In these Maṇipravāla sources, the same event gives rise to multiple contrasting interpretations depending on the theological use the commentator wishes to make of it; it is uncontroversial to treat Bharata's request as an exemplar for *pāratantrya* or a foil for divine agency in soteriology. This flexibility in exegesis is evident in the fact that despite the significant divergences between Vedānta Deśika and Piḷḷai Lokācārya on doctrinal issues, they never argue about the proper adjudication of the purport of specific *Rāmāyaṇa* verses. Here we can imagine the similar practice of a lecturer in the temple, who has at her or his disposal a plethora of stories to apply to the doctrinal principle being imparted, the audience being addressed and the contextual situation. As we will see, traces of this pragmatic arena for interpretation linger, even in Sanskrit translations of the Maṇipravāla interpretations.

2.2 Maṇipravāla as a cosmopolitan vernacular

These adaptations of Maṇipravāla performative approaches into Sanskrit involved deliberative transformations of style and technique, as well as more direct linguistic translation. To better understand the dynamics of translation and the way Śrīvaiṣṇavas made these linguistic patterns their own, it will be helpful to briefly chart the history of Śrīvaiṣṇava Maṇipravāla and compare it with other forms of Maṇipravāla that were more explicitly theorized.

Although the earliest examples of Maṇipravāla-style discourse in Tamil appear in Paḷḷava inscriptions dating to the fifth century (called *meykkīrtti*), no reference to mixed language occurs in the early classification of linguistic borrowing in the classical Tamil treatise on grammar and poetics produced at approximately the same time, the *Tolkāppiyam*. Rather, the *Tolkāppiyam* divides words in Tamil into the following fourfold taxonomy: (1) Tamil words of everyday usage (*iyaṟ col*); (2) Tamil words found only in literary works (*tiri col*); (3) words borrowed from neighbouring regions (*ticaic col*); and (4) Sanskrit words (*vaṭa col*). This categorization precludes Maṇipravāla, since in the *Tolkāppiyam* Sanskrit vocabulary is normatively adapted to the phonemic features of Tamil (absence of aspiration, consonant clusters, etc.), while in contrast Maṇipravāla is characterized by the preservation of the phonemic qualities of Sanskrit words.

The first use of the term 'Maṇipravāla' in Sanskrit is by Abhinavagupta in his tenth-century *Bhārati* commentary on the *Nāṭya Śāstra*. Abhinavagupta's Kashmir milieu may seem distantly removed from southern language phenomena, but Abhinavagupta's integration of known forms of linguistic hybridity within the technical categories of Sanskrit grammar provides both a precise and relevant technical theorization. In identifying the preferable language for introductory stanzas in dramas (*dhruva* songs) as either 'half-Sanskrit' (*ardhasaṃskṛta*) or a Prakrit like Śaurasenī, Abhinavagupta defines Maṇipravāla as the mixture of Sanskrit nominal stems (*prātipadikas*) and regional language forms (*deśibhāṣya*). For Abhinavagupta, the term Maṇipravāla is restricted specifically to the south:

whereas half-Sanskrit in Abhinavagupta's native Kashmiri is called Śāṭakula, it is called Maṇipravāla when the combination is with southern languages.[12] This brief definition antedates the earliest Maṇipravāla literature composed by Śrīvaiṣṇavas, though the joining of Sanskrit verbal and nominal stems and compounds with Tamil endings is exactly what is found in Śrīvaiṣṇava Maṇipravāla. The immediate reference may be to Malayalam Maṇipravāla (which includes specific varieties used by temple drummers) or to Maṇipravāla courtly poetry.

The cultural dynamics of Maṇipravāla may be understood as a special case of what Pollock calls the cosmopolitan vernacular. According to Pollock, Maṇipravāla was emblematic of the way vernacular cultures from the end of the first millennium to 1500 domesticated the literary apparatus of Sanskrit, with local languages only gradually emerging with their own independent genres and theorization:

> Maṇipravāla embodied the very process of localization of the Sanskrit universal, in both political discourse and literature, that was occurring across southern Asia from this moment on, with the vernacular at first supplementing Sanskrit and later taking on an ever-increasing proportion as vernacularization gained power and confidence.[13]

This picture is complicated considerably in the Tamil region by the fact that Tamil, unlike other vernaculars, itself possessed a classical literature and sophisticated tradition of theoretical reflection beginning with the fourth-century *Tolkāppiyam*, rendering the adaptation of aesthetical and grammatical categories from Sanskrit unnecessary and redundant. Yet such an adaptation is precisely what took place with the eleventh-century *Vīracōḻīyam*, modelled closely on Daṇḍin's *Kāvyādarśa* in its adaptation of Sanskrit figures of sense (*arthālaṇkāras*) to Tamil literary examples.[14] It is significant that the *Vīracōḻīyam*, which contains the first definition of Maṇipravāla in Tamil, appears to refer to courtly poetry: unlike the mere adoption of Sanskrit phonemes called *viraviyal*, Maṇipravāla verse is defined not just as a mixture of Tamil and Sanskrit words but as verse in which the *etukai* second syllable rhyme of the lines of couplets is absent.[15] Yet we have no extant Tamil Maṇipravāla poetry from this period, in contrast to the Maṇipravāla literature that emerged from Kerala in the eighth or ninth century and was later elaborately theorized in the fourteenth-century (Sanskrit) *Līlātilaka*. In the Kerala region, Maṇipravāla composition was so widespread that it actually paved the way for the amalgamation of Sanskrit into the western dialects eventually termed Malayalam, as distinguished from the standardized Tamil of the east.[16] This large corpus of Malayalam Maṇipravāla may provide the best material for retrospectively reconstructing the Tamil Maṇipravāla poetry referred to in the *Vīracōḻiyam*.

The existence of this earlier corpus of courtly poetry means that the use of Maṇipravāla by Śrīvaiṣṇavas and Jainas was likely a derivative practice, the self-conscious appropriation of an existing cosmopolitan vernacular by religious communities. Śrīvaiṣṇava Maṇipravāla represents a highly specified usage proper to the Śrīvaiṣṇava temple that provided a distinctive 'voice' for Śrīvaiṣṇava vernacular theology.[17] The inscription of this voice, beginning with Tirukkurukaippirāṉ Piḷḷāṉ in the eleventh century, took shape through compositional styles involving differing ranges of the relative presence of Tamil or Sanskrit lexical items, as summarized by K. K. A. Venkatachari:

> Piḷḷāṉ, the first Śrīvaiṣṇava to use the Maṇipravāḷa prose used long compound sentences; when he uses Sanskrit words, he provides Tamil endings. Next, Nañjiyar avoided long compound sentences in favor of simple sentences; when he uses Sanskrit words, he provides Tamil endings. Vaṭakkutiruvītippiḷḷai and Periyavāccāṉpiḷḷai use more Tamil vocabulary (the ratio was about 2:1), while Piḷḷailokācārya used still more Tamil vocabulary (3:1) and introduced the *sūtra* style into Maṇipravāḷa prose. Vedāntadeśika reverted to a Sanskrit-dominated Tamil prose (3:2) . . .
>
> Aḻakiyamaṇavāḷaperumāḷnāyaṉār's Maṇipravāla is largely Tamil (4:1) and difficult prose, whereas Maṇavāḷamāmunikal who came after him used the simplest prose style of all the Ācāryas.

Linguistic hybridity was a novel factor apparent even in the orthography of Maṇipravāla:

> Maṇipravāla was generally written in Tamil script with grantha characters for those sounds not in Tamil, or else it was completely written in Telugu script with the addition of the Tamil characters for the two sounds peculiar to Tamil (underline l and underline r); when Tamil script was used, often the direct Sanskrit quotations were completely written in Grantha characters; or if a Sanskrit technical term or unfamiliar word was commonly used in Tamil, we find that the Sanskrit sounds may appear in Grantha characters, though often the word itself may have been in such common use that it was given a Tamil form.[18]

Assuming Maṇipravāla to be the reification of the self-image of Śrīvaiṣṇavism as the end of the two Vedas, Tamil and Sanskrit (*ubhayavedānta*, itself a fairly late appellation), obscures the sociocultural dynamics behind these developments. For instance, the very vernacularity of Maṇipravāla was at the same time cosmopolitan, not only because of the presence of Sanskrit but also through its use by native speakers of Kannada and Telugu from the fifteenth century. It may be productive to think of Śrīvaiṣṇava Maṇipravāla as a linguistic register, a language variety distinguished by situational context or purpose. Sociolinguistic studies of register, distinguished from dialect as referring to situational variety instead of varieties associated with speech groups, include several features associated with Maṇipravāla such as shared vocabulary, intonation, syntax and phonology, formulaic sequences and special terminology.[19] Although registers are normally associated with vocational domains or rhetorical modes of discourse, the formalized language of Maṇipravāla falls more easily within the category of register than speech genre or style. And the presence of idiomatic vocabulary recognizable only to Śrīvaiṣṇavas renders Maṇipravāla the ultimate 'insider' register, one that would be opaque to those not participating in the Śrīvaiṣṇava temple.

The formal process of translating from the circumscribed linguistic register of Maṇipravāla into Sanskrit generated new poetic and prose styles of regional Sanskrit composition. Translation from Maṇipravāla also mandated conspicuous accommodation to formal elements of Sanskrit: for the two examples examined in this chapter, to the messenger poem (*sandeśakāvya*), a distinctive subgenre of Sanskrit narrative poetry, in the case of Vedānta Deśika's *Haṃsasandeśa* and to a range of grammatical and scholastic categories, in the case of Govindarāja's *Rāmāyaṇa* commentary.

2.3 Comparing messengers

In the next part of this chapter, I examine in detail a key example of Sanskrit poetry inflected by vernacular forms, Vedānta Deśika's *Haṃsasandeśa*. I first situate this important poem within its Sanskrit genre of messenger poetry by comparing it with Kālidāsa's classic, the *Meghadūta*. I then explore elements that appear alien to the categories of Sanskrit *kāvya*: the poem's allegory and the crafting of regional space as divine space through the institutions of the Śrīvaiṣṇava community.

The *Haṃsasandeśa* of Vedānta Deśika recounts the imaginary vignette of a goose conveying a message to Sītā on behalf of Rāma. The familiar Sanskrit generic form of the messenger poem in turn evokes the plot of the *Rāmāyaṇa*, since the prototype of the genre, the *Meghadūta* of Kālidāsa, was itself patterned on Hanumān's message to Sītā in the Sundara Kāṇḍa. And yet, even as it betrays its close structural modelling on the *Meghadūta*, it is also a work of remarkable newness in its allegorical form, transforming a classical depiction of passion and longing into an esoteric meditation on devotional teaching. With the *Haṃsasandeśa's* allegory, Vedānta Deśika appears to have adapted a mode of Maṇipravāla exegetical practice as a model for Sanskrit poetic composition. At the same time, the *Haṃsasandeśa* is paradoxically rendered as a pastiche of the *Meghadūta* and the Sundara Kāṇḍa narrative of Hanumān's message, with the poem foregrounding its own intertextual connections with these antecedents at almost every stage.

Commentators on Kālidāsa's *Meghadūta* (more than sixty commentaries were produced after the tenth century) explicitly refer to the Sundara Kāṇḍa as a source, based on the many structural parallels: the separation of lovers, the non-human messenger, the message of reassurance and the aerial route. In the Sundara Kāṇḍa, Hanumān's meeting with Sītā concludes the part of the epic where the monkey's actions, rather than those of Rāma, take centre stage. Seated in a tall tree in the *aśoka* grove, Hanumān sings the praises of Rāma to gain Sītā's trust, speaks to her in sweet and clear Sanskrit and displays Rāma's signet ring. Sītā in turn tells him the story of the demonic crow (*kākāsura*) as an intimate anecdote to convey to Rāma.

Dakṣiṇāvartanātha, who most likely hailed from Tiruvalañculi, a small village near Kumbakoṇam in the Tamil region, makes the relationship between the *Rāmāyaṇa* and the *Meghadūta* the centrepiece of his *Pradīpa* commentary.[20] He explicates the obvious references to the epic – the setting in the Rāmagiri hermitage, the favourite Śaiva image of Rāvaṇa shaking Kailāsa (1.61), and the explicit comparison with Hanumān's message towards the end of the second half of the *Meghadūta* (2.40) – and also foregrounds deeper analogues. The *Meghadūta* resonates with imagery reminiscent of the *Rāmāyaṇa*, especially in the description of the *yakṣa*'s wife in the second half. Examples include her longing for his embraces, even in a dream:

niḥśvāsenādharakisalayakleśinā vikṣipantīṃ
śuddhasnānāt paruṣam alakaṃ nūnam āgaṇḍalambam/
matsaṃbhogaḥ katham upanamet svapnajo 'pīti nidrām
ākāṅkṣantīṃ nayanasalilotpīḍaruddhāvakāśam//

With sighs drying her shoot-like lips,
she must be blowing away the hair that falls over her face,
rough from washing in bare water.
She longs to sleep
so she can be united with me
if only in a dream.
And yet sleep evades her,
due to the constant flow of tears.[21]

svapne 'pi yady ahaṃ vīraṃ rāghavaṃ sahalakṣmaṇam/
paśyeyaṃ nāvasīdeyaṃ svapno 'pi mama matsarī//

If even in a dream
I were able to see heroic Rāma with Lakṣmaṇa,
I would not despair.
But even my dreams have become hostile.[22]

The braid of hair kept unkempt until it is tied by the *yakṣa* is an exact replica of a parallel image of Sītā:

ādye baddhā virahadivase yā śikhādāma hitvā
śāpasyānte vigalitaśucā tāṃ mayodveṣṭanīyām/
sparśakliṣṭām ayamitanakhenāsakṛtsārayantīṃ
gaṇḍābhogāt kaṭhinaviṣamām ekaveṇīṃ kareṇa//

When I left home on that day of parting,
I tied for her a single braid.
Released from sorrow at the end of this curse,
I will untie it.

She brushes it aside
with her hand, whose nails are uncut,
again and again.
It is hard, uneven, unpleasant to the touch.[23]

ekaveṇī dharāśayyā dhyānaṃ malinam ambaram/
asthāne 'py upavāsaś ca naitāny aupayikāni te//

Your single braid,
your sleeping on the ground, your brooding,
your dirty clothes,
your fasting at inappropriate times;
none of these things is appropriate for you.[24]

The auspicious quivering of the eye, described in the *Meghadūta* as likely to occur when the cloud arrives (*tvayy āsanne nayanam uparispandi śaṅke*), is just as it was with Sītā before Hanumān's arrival, as recounted by Trijaṭā (*dṛśyate ca sphurac cakṣuḥ padmapatram ivāyatam*).[25] And the *yakṣa's* clasping of snowy breezes in the hope that they have touched his wife is drawn from Rāma's statement to the same effect.

bhittvā sadyaḥ kisalayapuṭān devadārudrumāṇāṃ
ye tatkṣīrasrutisurabhayo dakṣiṇena pravṛttāḥ/
āliṅgyante guṇavati mayā te tuṣārādrivātāḥ
pūrvaṃ spṛṣṭaṃ yadi kila bhaved aṅgam ebhis taveti//

The snowy breezes suddenly unfold
the shoots of the pine trees
and blow to the south
spreading the fragrance of their sap.
I embrace them,
in the hope that earlier
they may have touched your limbs.[26]

vāhi vāta yataḥ kāntā tāṃ spṛṣṭvā mām api spṛśa/
tvayi me gātrasaṃsparśaś candre dṛṣṭisamāgamaḥ//

O breeze,
blow where my lover is,
touch her and then touch me.
Through you I touch her limbs.
Through the moon, I see her.[27]

The genre of messenger poems includes dozens of extant works in Sanskrit based on the *Meghadūta*, as well as works in Pali, various Prakrits and emerging vernacular literary cultures like Tamil, Telugu, Kannada, Malayalam, Sinhala and Tibetan. The Sanskrit poems follow a standard structure: (1) request to the messenger; (2) description of the route to be travelled; and (3) message. Many eulogize the love affairs and conquests of royal patrons, spatially mapping out the boundaries of the realm in the manner of a royal victory tour (*digvijaya*); for example, the collection of twenty-three sound-based paronomasia verses (*yamaka*) of Ghaṭakarpara (one of the nine jewels of Vikramāditya VI, 1076–1127 CE), the *Pavanadūta* of Dhoyī (patronized by the third Sena king, Lakṣmaṇasena, 1178–1206 CE), and the *Kokilasandeśa* of Uddaṇḍa (patronized by the Zamorin king Mānavikrāma, 1466–74 CE).[28] The specificity of the route as a conceptualization of politically meaningful space is evident in the last two of these poems: the wind in the *Pavanadūta* passes from the Malaya Mountains to the Pāṇṭiya country, the Tāmraparṇī River, Kāñcī, the Kāverī River, Godāvarī, Kaliṅga, the Narmadā river and finally the Sena capital, Vijayanagara, in effect tracing in reverse Lakṣmaṇasena's southern conquest; so too the bird in the *Kokilasandeśa* travels from Kāñcī to the Kampā River, the Co<u>l</u>a region, the Vāṅmayī River, Koṭṭayam, the Raṇakhala region and the capital at Jayantamaṅgala, significantly crossing through the north-eastern corner of the Hoysaḷa Empire. Different messengers are involved in different poems, resulting in a variety of titles: for example, the *Pavanadūta* ('the wind-messenger') of Dhoyī, the *Kokilasandeśa* ('message of the cuckoo bird') of Uddaṇḍa, the *Bhṛṅgasandeśa* ('message of the bee') of Vāsudeva, and the *Candradūta* ('message of the moon') of Jāmbukavi.

Messenger poems were especially popular in vernacular and regional Sanskrit traditions, where the aerial description of a concrete topos facilitated the poetic crafting of regional space in a manner analogous to the first vernacular versions of the epics. As we will see, Deśika's *Haṃsasandeśa* was paradigmatic in this regard. In addition to these regional reworkings, a number of Jaina intellectuals composed didactic messenger poems that provide a close parallel to the *Haṃsasandeśa*, including the *Pārśvābhyudaya* of Jinasena produced during the reign of Rāṣṭrakūṭa king Amoghavarṣa I (814–874), in which the route to Alakā is depicted as paved by Jaina temples, and the Jaina *Meghadūta* of Merutuṅga (born 1346, a generation after Vedānta Deśika), where the message is sent from the mendicant Neminātha to his bereaved, separated family. Finally, the Divyaprabandham itself contains a number of poems where birds serve as messengers, and it is the allegorization of poems of this variety in the Maṇipravāla commentaries on the *Tiruvāymo<u>l</u>i* that provides a direct antecedent to the allegory of the *Haṃsasandeśa*, which I will focus on in some detail.

The *Haṃsasandeśa* contains a high degree of what A. K. Ramanujan has called self-reflexive reflexivity, the meta level of intertextuality where a work makes explicit its linkages with other works.[29] The primary reflexive dimension – the fact that both Hanumān and the goose convey messages from Rāma to Sītā – is animated through ample hints to the reader, with the entire prospective action of the *Haṃsasandeśa* framed with the *Rāmāyaṇa* narrative in relief. As with the *Meghadūta*, this reflexivity breaks into the reader's awareness in the series of images in the second section, where descriptions of Sītā's forlorn state repeatedly evoke scenes from the epic. The description of divine women captured by Rāvaṇa waiting for Sītā to liberate them recalls two separate verses from the *Rāmāyaṇa*:

ugraiḥ śāpair upahatibhiyā rakṣasā dūramuktāḥ
dagdhuṃ yogyā hutavaham api tvatpriyāvarṇaśuddhāḥ/
utpaśyanto janakatanayātejasaiva svarakṣāṃ
rodhaṃ yasyām anuvidadhate lokapālāvarodhāḥ//

Rāvaṇa keeps the wives of the world-protectors
at a distance there
for fear of death from the terrible curse.
Though they are as pure as the white colour of your beloved
and could burn fire itself,
they wait for the protection
of the fiery power (*tejas*) of Sītā
and bear their imprisonment.[30]

asandeśāt tu rāmasya tapasaś cānupālanāt/
na tvāṃ kūrmi daśagrīva bhasma bhasmārha tejasā//

Because Rāma has not requested it,
and so that I may preserve my penance,
I do not reduce you to ashes, O ten-headed one,
though you deserve to be ashes.[31]

tapasā satyavākyena ananyatvāc ca bhartari/
api sā nirdahed agniṃ na tām agniḥ pradhakṣyati//

With her penance, true speech, and fidelity to her husband,
she herself could burn fire.
Fire cannot burn her.[32]

Both *Rāmāyaṇa* verses and the *Haṃsasandeśa* verse revolve around a symbolic nexus of images: fire, penance (*tapas*, also meaning heat) and *tejas*, which can mean lustre, brilliance or prowess, here associated with the fiery power of Sītā's chastity.

As Rāma describes Sītā and her locale to the goose, more direct resemblances follow in sequence. For instance, words uttered by the gods in the Bāla Kāṇḍa appear clearly to be the source for Vedānta Deśika's depiction of the *aśoka* grove:

īṣatkopāc cakitapavanām indusandigdhasūryāṃ
nityodārām ṛtubhir akhilair niṣkuṭe vṛkṣavāṭīm/
sītāśokajvalanasahajais tatra dīptām aśokair
āpadyethāḥ prathamalulitām āñjaneyapracārair//

You will reach an arbour
previously crushed by Hanumān's trampling,

where the wind is afraid of even slight anger on the part of Rāvaṇa,
where the sun appears like the moon,
where all the seasons are pleasant.
It is lit by *aśoka* blossoms,
and these are like the fire of Sītā's grief.[33]

nainam sūryaḥ pratapati pārśve vāti na mārutaḥ/
calormimālī taṃ dṛṣṭvā samudro 'pi na kampate//

The sun does not afflict him,
the wind does not blow at his side,
even the ocean with its tremulous waves
does not quiver upon seeing him.[34]

Other resemblances revolve around the description of Sītā's longing. The 'mixture of sorrow and pleasure' (*śokaprītivyatikaravatīṃ*) the goose will experience when seeing the beauty of Laṅkā's palaces and the terrible state of captured women therein (2.6) is similar to Sītā's words to Hanumān:

amṛtaṃ viṣasaṃsṛṣṭaṃ tvayā vānara bhāṣitam/
yac ca nānyamanā rāmo yac ca śokaparāyaṇaḥ//

What you have said, O monkey,
is like a mixture of poison and the nectar of immortality.
Rāma remains faithful to me,
but he is overcome with grief.[35]

Later, the following poignant verse develops Vālmīki's repeated accounts of Sītā's 'crying, heavy breathing' (*rodanād atiniḥśvasād*):

śūnyā dṛṣṭiḥ śvasitam adhikaṃ mīlitaṃ vaktrapadmaṃ
dhārākāraṃ nayanasalilaṃ sānubandho vilāpaḥ/
itthaṃ dainyaṃ kim api vidhinā durnivāreṇa nītā
sā me sītā tanutaratanus tapyate nūnam antaḥ//

Her eyes are empty,
she breathes heavily, her lotus-face shrivels,
the tears from her eyes flow
like a mountain waterfall,
she laments again and again
My Sītā is from some unavoidable fate
reduced to this pitiable state.
She is frail and despairs within.[36]

Even this passing reference to unavoidable fate ('*vidhinā durnivāreṇa*') seems to flow from words uttered by Sītā: 'Fate is unavoidable for living creatures' (*vidhir nūnam asaṃhāryaḥ prāṇinām*).[37] What results is a tapestry of correspondences enabling readers to focus attention back towards the familiar original, reprocessing the narrative and developing it in a new poetic idiom.

Vedānta Deśika's reflexive referencing of the generic norms of messenger poetry reprocessing the narrative of the Sundara Kāṇḍa is structured in an even more conspicuous manner. Some of the parallels are obvious: two sections of approximately fifty verses (in the *Meghadūta* called the *Pūrvamegha* and *Uttaramegha*, in the *Haṃsasandeśa* called the *Prathamāśvāsa* and *Dvitīyāśvāsa*), the *mandākrānta* metre, mirroring paths (Rāmagiri north to Kailāsa in the *Meghadūta*; Ṛṣyakūṭa south to Laṅkā in the *Haṃsasandeśa*), and matching seasons (the rainy season in the *Meghadūta*; the subsequent *śarad* season in the *Haṃsasandeśa*). But the modelling on the *Meghadūta* also occurs on a level of precise detail, as is evident in the first seven verses of both poems (see Table 2.1).

We can see that each verse in the *Haṃsasandeśa* corresponds closely to its counterpart in the *Meghadūta*. For example, the statement of the incongruity of an insentient cloud serving as a messenger in the fifth verse of the *Meghadūta* is transformed into a positive assertion of the merits of a goose over even Hanumān in the fifth verse of the *Haṃsasandeśa*; similarly, the seventh verse of the *Meghadūta* punning on the cloud's ability to protect from heat (*saṃtāpa*, also meaning suffering) is matched by a hyperbole (*atiśayokti*) in the seventh verse of the *Haṃsasandeśa* on the special status of geese as divine. Table 2.2 shows how this patterning, though not exact, continues for the entire poem.

Table 2.1 The first seven verses of the *Meghadūta* and the *Haṃsasandeśa*

MEGHADŪTA	*HAṂSASANDEŚA*
1. Setting: curse of the *yakṣa*, description of the lovers	1. Setting: Hanumān has returned from visiting Sītā; Rāma, separated from her, spends a sleepless night
2. Appearance of the cloud, state of the *yakṣa*	2. Appearance of a goose as Rāma is about to prepare the army
3. Reaction of the *yakṣa*, symbolism/association of the cloud	3. Resemblance to Sītā, Rāma's dumbfoundedness
4. Reasoning for sending the message; welcome from the *yakṣa*	4. Rāma's resolution to send the message; honouring of the goose
5. Anomaly of an insentient cloud being the messenger; confusion of one in the state of love	5. Reason for sending message with goose vs. cloud, mountain, etc.; more honour than Hanumān
6. Praise of the cloud as the servant of Indra; statement of helplessness on the part of the *yakṣa*	6. Praise of the goose, the transport of Brahmā; qualities of Sarasvatī
7. You protect all from heat and must protect me now, go to Alakā	7. Divinity of the goose, best of birds; appropriateness of condescending to send message

Table 2.2 Structural comparison of the *Meghadūta* and the *Haṃsasandeśa*

MEGHADŪTA	*HAṂSASANDEŚA*
1.1–11 Introduction	1.1–14 Introduction
1.12 Take leave of the Tuṅga Mountain	1.15 Taking leave of the lotus
1.13 Now listen to the path	
1.14–62 Path until Alakā	1.16–60 Path until Laṅkā
	(1.21–22 Description of Tirupati)
	(1.23–28 Description of Kāñcī)
(1.28–40 Long description of Ujjain, Avantī)	(1.38–46 Description of Śrīraṅgam)
2.1–14 Description of Alakā	2.1–9 Description of the *aśoka* grove, location of Sītā
2.15–21 Description of the *yakṣa*'s house	
2.22 Description of the *yakṣa*'s wife	2.10 Physical description of Sītā
2.23–32 Description of possible states of the wife	2.11–23 Description of states Sītā may be experiencing
2.33–37 Further descriptions, comments	2.24–27 Instructions to the goose
2.38 Preamble to the message	2.28–32 Preamble to message
2.39–52 Message	2.33–46 Message
2.53–54 Conclusion	2.47–50 Conclusion

The patterning works through a series of signals and allusions, only to be transformed through the *Haṃsasandeśa*'s implicit allegory.

As Bronner and Shulman have shown in their study of the *Haṃsasandeśa*, Vedānta Deśika's referencing of the *Meghadūta* involves explicit inversion and repudiation of the classic through structural reversals such as the redirection to a southern, rather than northern, path, and the contrast between the *śarad* season and the monsoon. Geese fly north to the Himalayas in the monsoon and fly south during *śarad*, a fact that provides Vedānta Deśika with an opportunity to craft a particularly pointed contrast: whereas in Kālidāsa's *Meghadūta* geese are companions of the cloud messenger, in the *Haṃsasandeśa* it is instead clouds who are companions of the goose:

> *kartuṃ yac ca prabhavati mahīm ucchilīndhrām avandhyāṃ*
> *tac chrutvā te śravaṇasubhagaṃ garjitaṃ mānasotkāḥ/*
> *ā kailāsād bisakisalayacchedapātheyavantaḥ*
> *saṃpatsyante nabhasi bhavato rājahaṃsāḥ sahāyāḥ //*
>
> Hearing that roar of yours,
> capable of filling the earth with mushrooms,
> pleasing to their ears,
> your companions, the royal geese,
> eager for Lake Mānasa and
> eating bits of lotus shoots on their travel,

will be at your side in the sky,
right up until Mount Kailāsa.[38]

sūkṣmākārair dinakaraiḥ kalpitāntaḥśalākāḥ
śāropāntāḥ śatamakhadhanuḥśeṣacitrāṃśukena/
ūḍhāḥ paścād upcitagatinā vāyunā rājahaṃsa
chatrāyeran nabhasi bhavataḥ śāradā vārivāhāḥ//

The autumn clouds will become an umbrella in the sky for you,
royal goose, with the sun's subtle rays as ribs.
Bits of rainbow appearing as the cloth
will make the umbrella multicoloured at the edges,
as it is carried by the fast-moving wind.[39]

Even as the phrase '*nabhasi bhavataḥ*' in the identical sequence in the fourth *pāda* draws the two verses together, they stand in opposition through the corresponding shapes and inverted size of (small) mushrooms and (giant) umbrella and the about-face in relative location – the cloud in the centre of the sky in the *Meghadūta* verse and the goose surrounded by clouds, who are merely there to serve, in the *Haṃsasandeśa* verse.[40]

2.4 The allegory of the *Haṃsasandeśa*

Beyond these tactics of subversion, it is through its allegorical form that the *Haṃsasandeśa* most clearly differentiates itself from the *Meghadūta*. The allegory takes the shape of a series of symbolic correspondences: Rāma stands for the lord, Hanumān for the *ācārya*, the ocean for the sea of transmigration (*bhavasāgara*), Laṅkā for the body, Rāvaṇa for the mind, his ten heads for the ten senses, the *aśoka* grove for the inner organ in which the lord resides and Sītā for the individual soul.[41]

The allegorical frame emerges through the poem spectrally and is especially unusual given the virtual absence of other examples of allegorical composition in Sanskrit literature. The very small class of what are known as *rūpaka* or *pratīka* dramas resembles allegory, with characters standing for abstract philosophical concepts (e.g. Kṛṣṇamiśra's twelfth-century Advaita *Prabodhacandrodaya*, to which Deśika's own *Saṅkalpasūryodaya* is the Viśiṣṭādvaita response). There are also a number of Jaina allegorical legends, including Siddharṣi's tenth-century *Upamitibhāvaprapañcakathā*. But aside from these few examples, allegory is not a compositional practice in Sanskrit literature, and it is also unknown to Sanskrit aesthetics. Its stream of two stable sets of meaning would seem similar to the simultaneous appearance (rather than superimposition as per the trope of metaphor, *rūpakālaṃkāra*) of non-contextual meaning in collapsed expression (*samāsokti*), and commentators of vernacular allegory sometimes employ this category in literary criticism. However, the temporal duration of allegory in narrative differs sharply from the momentary effect of *samāsokti*.

This absence contrasts with the presence, at least as a mode of interpretation (allegoresis), of allegory in Maṇipravāla, which Vedānta Deśika transformed into a form of Sanskrit poetic composition. Śrīvaiṣṇavas envisioned the *Tiruvāymoḻi* as a psychological drama encoding the emotional and spiritual development of the author, Nammāḻvār, with each decad (especially in *akapporuḷ* songs where Nammāḻvār takes on a female persona) associated with progress on the path and moments of union or separation. Norman Cutler has shown how Maṇipravāla allegoresis involves a creative extension of the poetics of Tamil Caṅkam poetry, with the imagined spiritual drama extending the convention of placing classical Tamil poems, including independent verses, within situational frames (historical for *puṟam* war poetry and universalized and interior for *akam* love poetry).[42] The allegoresis reaches a level of minutiae in Aḻakiyamaṇavāḷa Perumāḷ Nāyanār's *Ācārya Hṛdaya*, where even the heroine's ornaments bear a symbolic significance. Homologies between *Tiruvāymoḻi* allegoresis and Śaiva Siddhānta allegoresis of the *Tirukkōvaiyār*, passed down exclusively through oral history, strongly suggests that the *Tiruvāymoḻi* interpretations had their source in the didactic arena of temple performance. Most apposite to the *Haṃsasandeśa* is the allegoresis of *Tiruvāymoḻi* bird messenger songs, with the birds identified as *ācāryas* and their 'wings' as knowledge and right conduct, a direct parallel to the role of the goose in the set of relationships at the heart of the *Haṃsasandeśa*: Rāma/lord-goose/*ācārya*/-Sītā/soul. In each of the four decads (1.4, 6.1, 6.8 and 9.7) of the *Tiruvāymoḻi* containing references to bird messengers (storks, *koel* birds, *cakravāka* birds, herons, parrots and tiny *pūvai* birds, as well as geese as in the *Haṃsasandeśa*), different forms or aspects of the lord are invoked: (1) the Pāñcarātra emanations (*vyūha*); (2) the incarnations (*vibhava*); (3) the lord as transcendent and immanent (*paratva, antaryāmin*); and (4) the lord's presence in icons (*arcā*).

Vedānta Deśika is subtle in merging the allegoresis of the *Tiruvāymoḻi* with the generic norms of Sanskrit messenger poems, and the allegory of the *Haṃsasandeśa* remains highly enigmatic. Interpretive ambiguity is endemic to allegory, as the secondary sense necessarily emerges as supplement generated through reading, though authors often provide clues to reveal the allegorical framework of their works (e.g. explicit personification of characters, etc.). But the *Haṃsasandeśa* does not reveal its own allegory. It is likely that the allegory would be apparent to those familiar with the Maṇipravāla conventions regarding the allegorical significance of bird messengers as *ācāryas* in the *Tiruvāymoḻi*, but it is also likely that others not familiar with these conventions would not have read the poem in such a way, and therefore the *Haṃsasandeśa* could travel its own transregional route unencumbered by its esoteric vernacular theological associations. In this sense, the *Haṃsasandeśa* resembles works in the Western hermetic tradition where the precise figurative import remains shrouded in mystery.

The aesthetic fashioning of the erotic relationship between lovers in Sanskrit messenger poetry affords Vedānta Deśika with imaginative resources for the crafting of allegory that move beyond the schematic interpretation of the Maṇipravāla commentaries. This eroticism is evident in the many verses in the first half of the poem involving the trope of collapsed expression (*samāsokti*), where erotic symbolism is joined to natural imagery (1.11, 1.15, 1.20, 1.23, 1.24, and 1.52), as well as in the central *rasa*, passion-in-separation (*vipralambhaśṛṅgāra)* – the same *rasa* identified by Govindarāja in his commentary as the central *rasa* of the *Rāmāyaṇa* itself – adding a layer of intensity to the arduous nature of separation between devotee and lord as envisioned in the *Tiruvāymoḻi* commentaries. Vedānta Deśika's poem in many ways intensifies the emotional pathos of the separation of lovers, for instance in the culmination of the message delivered to Sītā that follows the lengthy description of her state:

dehasparśaṃ malayapavane dṛṣṭisaṃbhedam indau
dhāmaikatvaṃ jagati bhuvi cābhinnaparyaṅkayogam/
tārācitre viyati vitatiṃ śrīvitānasya paśyan
durībhūtāṃ sutanu vidhinā tvām ahaṃ nirviśāmi//

I touch your body in the Malaya wind,
in the moon our eyes meet,
we share the same home, the earth,
we share the same bed, the ground,
and the sky filled with stars is our roof.
Though, because of horrible fate, O beautiful one,
you are far away from me,
I enter into you.[43]

The separation is painfully real, not a mere prompt for allegorization.

The convergence of the erotic and the devotional is most idiosyncratic in a crucial verse at the middle of the second section:

cetovṛttiṃ śamayati bahiḥ sārvabhaume nirodhe
mayy ekasmin praṇayahitadhiyaṃ mānmathenāgamena/
abhyasyantīm anitarajuṣo bhāvanāyāḥ prakarṣāt
svāntenāntarvilayamṛdunā nirvikalpaṃ samādhim//

She restricts her mind from all other objects,
all states are held in check,
and as per the scripture of erotic love (*kāma*)
she affectionately places her mind in me alone.
Due to the excellence of her single-minded meditation
with her heart soft from inner melting,
she experiences concentration free from distinctions (*nirvikaplasamādhi*).[44]

Here Vedānta Deśika plays ironically on the erotic intensity of Sītā's longing and the philosophical implications of her carnal passion as a form of *bhakti*, as he pushes concepts in meditative yoga beyond their internal logic. The states mentioned in the first *pāda* of the verse refer to the first three of the five yogic stages associated with degrees of activity and inactivity; the latter two stages, one-pointedness (*ekāgratā*) and restriction (*niruddhatā*), are alluded to in the second and then in the third and fourth *pādas* respectively.

The last phrase of the verse, 'concentration free from distinctions' (*nirvikalpaṃ samādhim*) draws the yoga references toward a topic of significance for Viśiṣṭādvaita philosophy: attributive knowledge (*dharmabhūtajñāna*). As elaborated by Rāmānuja in *Śrībhāṣya* 1.1.1, Viśiṣṭādvaitins view knowledge as both qualified by the object perceived and self-luminating (*arthaprakāśika* and *svayaṃprakāśika*), with consciousness as a quality of the self (*ātman*) compared to a flame of a lamp or candle that illuminates objects with its light but is not dependent on objects for its luminous power. This view of consciousness is part of the Viśiṣṭādvaita critique of the Advaita perspective of consciousness not as a mere quality but the self itself. It is also related to Rāmānuja's theory of *bhakti* as outlined in his commentary on *Bhagavad Gītā* 9.34, where he characterizes *bhakti* as remembrance, a constant meditation on the lord similar to an unbroken stream of oil poured from one vessel to another, such that the normal distinction between knower and known is effaced.

And yet, as closely as these images would seem to adhere to standard Viśiṣṭādvaita concepts, one earlier phrase stands out as incongruous: Sītā is said to meditate on Rāma according to the 'scripture of erotic love' (*mānmathenāgamena*). The reader is left wondering whether the romantic context is in the service of the philosophical allegory or if the yogic meditation itself serves as a metaphor for Sītā's longing. In verses such as this, Vedānta Deśika playfully engages with categories of Viśiṣṭādvaita and brings into focus the novelty of crafting a devotional allegory in Sanskrit.

Uttamur Viraraghavacharya, in his twentieth-century commentary, provides an especially insightful perspective on the allegory of the *Haṃsasandeśa*, as he fleshes out esoteric meanings for every verse of the poem. Uttamur's provocative interpretations should of course not be conflated with the poem itself, but they do provide a useful insider's view on an earlier oral history regarding the allegory. What is especially notable about Uttamur's approach is that he lays out *two* separate allegorical levels based on the directionality of the message: (1) as sent from the individual soul (*jīva*) to the lord; (2) as sent from the lord to the individual soul. Hence the literal triad of Rāma–goose–Sītā gives rise to the allegorical triads of lord–*ācārya*–soul and soul–*ācārya*–lord, with the trajectory of the two allegorical readings following a distinct logic: the mirrored messages echo the reciprocity of the devotional relationship. It is clear that the allegory is entirely contextual, embedded in the immediate epic plot structure, and not ontological; Śrīvaiṣṇavas never view Hanumān as the *ācārya* or Sītā as the individual soul (or a fortiori Rāma as the soul) elsewhere.

Uttamur brings out esoteric meanings in an unusual manner, as he applies radical Maṇipravāla symbolic and figurative reading techniques to the *Haṃsasandeśa* itself, as for example in his commentary on the very first verse of the poem:

vaṃśe jātaḥ savitur anaghe mānayan mānuṣatvaṃ
devaḥ śrīmān janakatanayānveṣaṇe jāgarūkaḥ/

pratyāyāte pavanatanaye niścitārthaḥ sa kāmī
kalpākāraṃ katham api niśām āvibhātaṃ viṣehe//

The lord, husband of Śrī,
born in the faultless solar dynasty,
acted the part of a human.
Ever awake in his search for the daughter of Janaka,
full of passion, he made a resolution after Hanumān returned.
Somehow he endured a night
like an eon.[45]

Uttamur collapses the two allegorical levels in his reading of the verse. On the first allegorical reading (Rāma as soul, Sītā as lord), adjectival phrases describing Rāma also describe an aspirant seeking liberation: 'ever awake in his search for the daughter of Janaka' (*janakatanayānveṣaṇe jāgarūkaḥ*) means lost in the wheel of transmigration, i.e. engaged in seeking protection for one's parents and children, and so on (based on the meaning of the name, *Janaka*). On the second allegorical meaning, this same phrase means 'seeking souls who realize him as their progenitor (*janaka*) and hence are his offspring (*tanaya*).' Uttamur seems to be seeking to concretize the allegory through symbolic readings in Sanskrit. Elsewhere he often draws explicit connections between descriptions of the goose and the qualities of an *ācārya*, for example in the verse referred to above, 1.13, where clouds form an umbrella for the goose; according to Uttamur, on the allegorical level the wind that impels the clouds/umbrella stands for students of the *ācārya*.

Some details of these readings seem related to an earlier oral tradition. Take the following verse:

sthitvā tatra kṣaṇam ubhayataḥ śailaśṛṅgāvatīrṇaiḥ
srotobhedair adhigataguṇaṃ cāruviṣphāraghoṣaiḥ/
lakṣyīkurvan daśamukhapurīṃ saumya patraprakṛṣṭo
velācāpaṃ śara iva sakhe vegatas tvaṃ vyatīyāḥ//

Wait a moment there.
Make Laṅkā, the city of the ten-headed one, your target.
Like an arrow with wonderful feathers
quickly cross over the beach, O gentle friend.
It takes on the qualities of a bow
from the beautiful twang of the streams
flowing from the mountains on both sides.[46]

The verse maps a series of metaphors: just as the goose as a whole is compared to the arrow, so its wings also resemble the feathers of the arrow, the shore of the ocean is like a long bow, the two mountain peaks are the two front portions of the bow, and the rivers flowing down from them are the bow-strings; just as these rivers produce a resonant sound, the bow-strings are also sonorous. Uttamur develops his reading through a comparison with a verse from the *Muṇḍaka Upaniṣad*:

praṇavo dhanuḥ śaro hy ātmā brahma tallakṣyam ucyate/
apramattena veddhavyam śaravat tanmayo bhavet//

The bow is the *om*, the arrow is the soul.
One should be diligent in knowing the universal soul (*brahman*)
which is said to be its target
and be like the arrow, fixed on it.[47]

Here the symbolically rich set of images of bow, arrow and target are appropriated to the context of soteriological knowledge. The esoteric level of meaning is developed from the basic metaphor of the verse, as in the umbrella verse. The close correspondence suggests an earlier history of esoteric citation and exegesis developed around the *Haṃsasandeśa*, or even that Vedānta Deśika used the *Muṇḍaka Upaniṣad* verse as a model for his own verse.

The relationship between the *Haṃsasandeśa*'s allegory and exegetical practices specific to the temple may become clearer if we compare the poem with another authored by Deśika, the *Pādukāsahasra*, which merits attention in its own right as a significant engagement with the generic features of Sanskrit Rāma *kāvya*. Studies of oral epics in South Asia have highlighted the common performance of segments of longer narratives, in part due to practical limitations of what can be covered in a particular setting or set of songs, which gain in significance as independent stories as they continue to be performed.[48] Just as the *Haṃsasandeśa* revolves around the single episode of the message to Sītā, so the *Pādukāsahasra* elaborates the episode of Rāma's bestowal of his sandals on Bharata over a stretch of nearly one hundred verses.

The *Pādukāsahasra* is a long devotional praise poem (*stotrakāvya*) dedicated to the sandals of Raṅganātha, the icon at Śrīraṅgam. The relevance of the *Pādukāsahasra* to our study involves the verses associating these sandals of Raṅganātha with those of Rāma. Praise for Rāma is rendered hyperbolic through the veneration of this simple possession, intimacy with which engenders a greater distance from Rāma himself. Typical are verses 4.8 and 4.10:

pādāvani prabhavato jagatāṃ trayāṇāṃ
rāmād api tvam adhikā niyataṃ prabhāvāt/
no cet kathaṃ nu bharatasya tam eva lipsoḥ
pratyāyanaṃ paripaṇaṃ bhavatī bhavitrī//

O sandal, your majesty surely outweighs that of even Rāma,
the source of the three worlds.
For if not, how would Bharata accept you as collateral
when he really wanted Rāma to return?[49]

pādāvani prabhutarān aparādhavargān
soḍhuṃ kṣamā tvam asi murtimatī kṣameva/

yat tvāṃ vihāya nihatāḥ paripanthinas te
devena dāśarathinā daśakaṇṭamukhyāḥ//

O sandal, you are forgiveness embodied,
capable of tolerating the most extreme crimes.
For only after Rāma left you behind
did he defeat Rāvaṇa and other enemies.[50]

The parental compassion of the sandal contrasts directly with the image of Rāma as conqueror in a far more dramatic manner than the standard contrast between Viṣṇu and the goddess. This salvific role of the sandal becomes the central theme of the retelling of the Rāma–Bharata encounter in the *Pādukāsahasra*. Among the innovative aspects of the *Pādukāsahasra* is Deśika's fashioning of the embodiment of the sandal through the frequent use of the figure of poetic supposition (*utprekṣā*), as he creates, in the process, a new form of personification as unknown to Sanskrit poetics as the allegory of the *Haṃsasandeśa*. It seems likely that, as with the allegory of the *Haṃsasandeśa*, the personification of the sandal in the *Pādukāsahasra* was a stylization of the devotional elaboration of a single epic episode in oral exegesis, with the deep theological meditation drawing the episode out of its immediate context. Adapting the didactic and figurative application of individual stories to Sanskrit *kāvya* resulted in nothing less than the generation of new methods of Sanskrit poetic composition.

2.5 Mapping divine space

Beyond its allegorical form, the *Haṃsasandeśa* also displayed its relation to vernacularity in Sanskrit through the specific route travelled by the goose. Arguing that 'this genre, more than any other, heralds the crystallization of an independent regional Sanskrit tradition,' Bronner and Shulman emphasize the intensification of space and time in regional Sanskrit poetry such as the *Haṃsasandeśa* (with the intertextual connections between messenger poems bringing together multiple topoi and temporalities into the consciousness of readers) and the interconnectedness of vast domains of vernacular and Sanskrit poetic and scientific discourses.[51] Regional Sanskrit often evinced metrical and linguistic features originating in vernacular poetry; for example the short non-quantitative metres, songs and end-rhyme of Jayadeva's *Gītagovinda* (twelfth-century Bangla region), the head rhyme in Śākalya Malla's *Udārarāghava* (fourteenth-century Tamil region), and the semantic overriding of metrical caesura in Śrīdhara Veṅkaṭeśa's *Śāhendra Vilāsa* (seventeenth-century Andhra region). Bronner and Shulman take the *Haṃsasandeśa* to be a paradigmatic example of the following features of second-millennium Sanskrit poetry:

1 localization within a specific region;
2 the aesthetic conceptualization of regional space, regional identities and regional polities;
3 a local rather than transregional audience;

4 the incorporation of vernacular syntax and morphology; and
5 the integration of Sanskrit scholastic and literary genres with emerging vernacular traditions.

What results, according to Bronner and Shulman, is great 'depth' on the levels of both space and time.[52]

As with the many other Sanskrit messenger poems produced from the thirteenth century, the description of the route in the *Haṃsasandeśa* is not incidental but crafted in a purposeful manner. In what follows, I will try to show that as the *Haṃsasandeśa* maps regional space it projects the *Rāmāyaṇa*'s mythic action directly onto the institutions of the medieval Śrīvaiṣṇava community through the category of divine places (*divyadeśa*). When travelling towards Sītā, the goose is exhorted to pass through no fewer than seven of the divine places, including the central triad of Tirupati, Kāñcī and Śrīraṅgam (Figure 2.1).

Śrīvaiṣṇavas demarcated the boundaries of their social community in ways that both overlapped with and moved beyond other vectors (agrarian, linguistic, etc.) of the construction of space in late medieval south India. Spaces of region and locality were produced in part through shifting patterns of agricultural exchange mediated between geography or distribution on the one hand, and sociocultural imagination on the other. David Ludden has studied the diachronic series of agrarian zones and territories of ethnic identity in the Tamil country, which are all subsets of the four macro-regions described in the Caṅkam corpus: Toṇṭaimaṇṭalam (land of the Paḷḷavas), Cōḻamaṇṭalam, Pāṇṭiyamaṇṭalam, and Cēramaṇṭalam.[53] These macro-regions are an important frame against which Vedānta Deśika charts the space of the Śrīvaiṣṇava community. Conceptions of space were closely correlated, with Śaiva and Vaiṣṇava temple centres forming a critical component of the political consolidation of regional space from the time of the Coḻas.[54] The local spaces of Tamil language use and of Tamil literary culture oriented to the emerging regional courts (the two were not coextensive) were also highly significant to Śrīvaiṣṇavas in their claim of revelatory status for the Tamil *Tiruvāymoḻi*. But as the material geography of a religious community, the spatial imaginary of the *Haṃsasandeśa* was both narrower and broader than that of region. Such a distinction need not entail characterizing the divine places as reified sacred space in the mode of Eliade, whose account of an 'inherent capacity' realized through theophany, hierophany or signs obscures the collective agency involved in the way societies construct spatial meaning even in the case of sites believed to be autochthonous, as borne out in south India by the composition of *māhātmyas* or *sthalapurāṇas* associated with particular temples describing the mythic history and the adventures of the worshipped deity.[55]

The divine places were normatively catalogued as a list of the 108 pilgrimage centres described in the poetry of the Āḻvārs.[56] Lists of the *divyadeśas* include a classification according to the *maṇṭalams* with the addition of a northern region (Vaṭamaṇṭalam). Śrīvaiṣṇavas understand these to be sites in which Viṣṇu is not just represented iconographically but where he himself descends in an iconic form (*arcāvatāra*); the emphasis, therefore, is on the direct presence of the lord on earth.

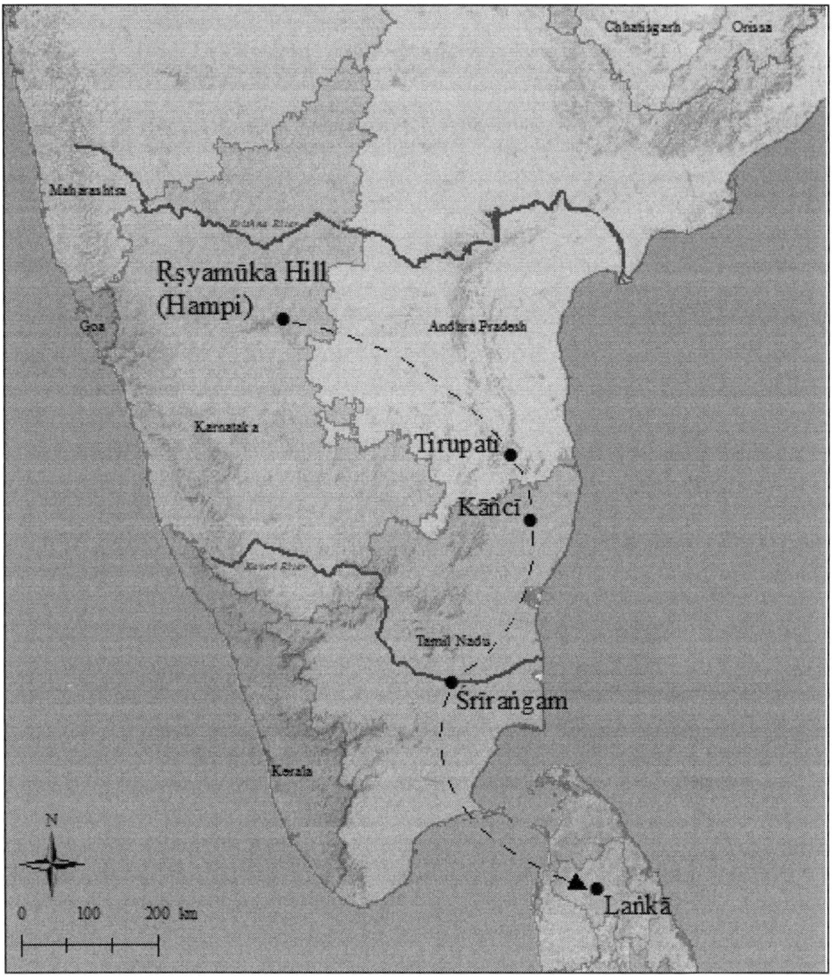

Figure 2.1 The route of the goose.

Various Sanskrit and Tamil terms, dating to the time of Rāmānuja's immediate disciples, are used synonymously to refer to these sites: *ukantaruḷiṉanilaṅkaḷ* (places that are beloved and blessed), *ukanta-ūrellām* (all beloved places), *vilakṣaṇasthānāni* (unique places), *ukantaruḷiṉadeśaṅkaḷ* (places graciously loved) and, simply, *aṣṭottaraśatasthānāni* (108 places). The standard list accepted today was compiled by Aḻakiyamaṇavāḷa Tācar. The four most significant sites are those believed to have been frequented by Rāmānuja: Śrīraṅgam, Tirupati, Kāñcī and Melukoṭe. While ninety-six of the 108 sites are in South India (primarily in the Tamil country), two are not of the earth: the milk ocean upon which Viṣṇu sleeps and his heavenly realm of Vaikuṇṭha. What we have, then, is a demarcation of space predicated on the relationship between human and divine worlds, a spatial mapping of the local as coterminous with the divine.

In redirecting the route from north (Rāmagiri to Alakā in the Himalayas in the *Meghadūta*) to south (the Deccan to Laṅkā in the *Haṃsasandeśa*), the poem makes an implicit valorization of southern locales. But Vedānta Deśika is also explicit about what he believes to be the most significant features of the southern landscape – the presence of divine places (*sthānair divyair*), among other features:

sthānair divyair upacitaguṇāṃ candanāraṇyaramyāṃ
muktāsūtiṃ malayamarutāṃ mātaram dakṣināśām/
asmatprītyai janakatanayāijīvitārthaṃ ca gacchan
ekam rakṣaḥpadam iti sakhe dośaleṣam sahethāḥ//

Go to the southern regions,
adorned with divine places.
It is lovely with its sandal forests,
mother of the Malaya winds and full of pearls.
Go in order to revive Sītā and for my sake.
But endure this minor fault: it is filled with demons.[57]

This conception of southern space is reinforced by Rāma's exhortation to choose one of two potential trajectories to the south:

mārgau ṣamyaṅ mama hanumatā varṇitau dvau tayos te
sahyāsanno 'py anatisubhagaḥ paścimo nityavarṣaḥ/
prācīneṣu pratijanapadaṃ saṃhatāv adbhutānāṃ
magnā dṛṣṭiḥ katham api sakhe matkṛte te nivāryā//

Hanumān described to me two paths:
a (shorter) western path close to the Sahya Hills near Koḍagu,
always rainy and unpleasant,
and an eastern path filled with wondrous sites and kingdoms.
Take the latter path,
but avert your eyes from these distractions,
for my sake.[58]

The pragmatic instruction to avoid the western path on account of rains facilitates a contortion of the route from the western edge of the Deccan to the southeastern edge of the Bay of Bengal – the exact area in which Tamil is spoken. Yet, for Vedānta Deśika, the Tamil region is important insofar as it is specially favoured by the lord, with the path clearly marked by the primary centres of Śrīvaiṣṇava intellectual and cultural activity, Kāñcī, Tirupati and Śrīraṅgam, towards which attention is ironically directed by the admonition to avoid the wondrous sites present 'in every kingdom' (*pratijanapadaṃ*).

The first point at which regions are named in the poem is 1.20, when reference is made to Kannada- and Telugu-speaking women in the rural border area. As elsewhere, Vedānta Deśika retrospectively projects contemporary spatial realities into the hoary past, such that the speaking communities of Kannada, Telugu and Tamil are conceived of as reified transhistorically. Interestingly, Deśika mentions no specific sites for the entire Kannada region, including the important Śrīvaiṣṇava centre at Melukoṭe; it is a particularly Tamil regional space that Vedānta Deśika chooses to foreground. However, it is not only the Kannada region, but also vast swaths of Cōḻa and Pāṇṭiya land that are cast in the background in favour of a restricted set of temples.

The route proper begins at Tirupati. The Tirumalai Hill was widely considered to be the outer boundary for the Tamil region, as attested first in the *Tolkāppiyam*. As S. Krishnaswami Aiyangar points out:

> These hills form a feature of the frontier half a degree to the north of Madras, extending the whole length from the Mysore plateau and stretching eastwards to almost near the coast at Ponneri, and thus constitute a prominent feature of the northern extremity of the Tamil land.[59]

Aside from the geographic prominence of the hills, even in the earliest references there is an awareness of a shift in language use in this area, from Tamil to the '*vaṭuku*' language, a somewhat amorphous category used in reference to Telugu.

Tirupati is the most important divine place in the northern region, or Vaṭamaṇṭalam. Vedānta Deśika's description of the site covers four verses, 1.21–1.24, and includes descriptions of the hill, the main icon in the Tirupati temple and the Kanakamukharā River where Śrīvaiṣṇavas believe Śiva worshipped Viṣṇu. The first verse is typical of how Vedānta Deśika introduces these pilgrimage sites, with poetic imagery weaving mythic associations with the physical landscape:

> *viṣṇor vāsād avanivahanād baddharatnaiḥ śirobhiḥ*
> *śeṣaḥ sākṣād ayam iti janaiḥ samyag unnīyamānaḥ/*
> *abhrair yukto 'laghubhir acirānmuktanirmokakalpaiḥ*
> *agre bhāvī tadanu nayane rañjayan añjanādriḥ//*
>
> Just ahead the Añjanādri Mountain (Tirupati)
> will please your eyes.
> People rightly consider it to be serpent *Śeṣa* himself.
> It is where Viṣṇu resides,
> it bears the earth,
> it has jewels inlaid in its peaks/hoods,
> and it is joined with large clouds
> appearing like skin just cast off.[60]

The verse plays upon the idea that the places of Viṣṇu's residence are his dependents (*śeṣas*), even as Tirupati itself appears like the divine serpent (also called Śeṣa) on which the lord rests. As with the other divine places, the overall description of the site is immediately followed by an image of the icon located therein:

> *tatrārūḍhair mahati manujaiḥ svarghibhiś cāvatīrṇaiḥ*
> *sattvonmeṣād vyapagatamithastāratamyādibhedaiḥ/*
> *sādhāraṇyāt phalapariṇateḥ saṃghaśo badhyamānāṃ*
> *śaktyā kāmaṃ madhuvijayinas tvaṃ ca kuryāḥ saparyām//*

> You can worship the destroyer of Madhu there,
> just as the crowds do,
> both gods descended on earth
> and mortals climbing up.
> Their mutual inequality is erased
> by the common preponderance of purity (*sattva*).[61]

The effacing of mutual differences references a specific point in Śrīvaiṣṇava soteriology regarding the absence of hierarchy (*tāratamya*) between beings in liberation regardless of differences in caste or gender subject to *karma*.

The description of Kāñcī is more detailed than that of Tirupati, covering eleven verses (1.25–1.35), with special emphasis on Vedānta Deśika's own birthplace near Kāñcī (at Viḷakkoḷi Kōyil). Here is yet another parallel to the *Meghadūta* – Kālidāsa also devotes eleven verses to describing his hometown, Avantī. Vedānta Deśika covers three of the divine places located in Kāñcī: Tirukkacci (Kāñcī proper), Tiruttaṅkā and Tiruvega (the Veghavatī River), with the most space devoted to the Hastiśaila or Varadarāja shrine at Kāñcī, historically one of the most important Vaiṣṇava centres in the south and the subject of another major work of Sanskrit poetry by Vedānta Deśika, the *Varadarājapañcāśat*. Vedānta Deśika first introduces Kāñcī with a verse embellished by an elaborate double-entendre (*śleṣa*) playing on the name 'Kāñcī' as a word for a particular kind of ornament:

> *nānāratnair upacitaguṇāṃ nityasaṅgītanādāṃ*
> *bhūmer drakṣyasy ucitavibhavaṃ bhūṣaṇam tatra kāñcīm/*
> *yasyāṃ nityaṃ nihitanayano hastiśailādhivāsī*
> *dvandvātītaḥ sa khalu puruṣo dṛśyate satyakāmaḥ//*

> The lord of Hastiśaila,
> who is beyond all opposites and is fulfilled in his desires,
> has his eyes forever transfixed
> on that waist-ornament of the earth inlaid with many jewels,
> tinkling with beautiful musical sounds,
> Kāñcī.[62]

Though the suggestion of an amorous relationship between Viṣṇu and the earth is a form of apparent contradiction (*virodhābhāsa*, since the lord 'is beyond all opposites,' *dvandvātīta*, and not subject to desire), the image of the belt with bells and jewels dangling around the hips is a suggestive way of emphasizing the nexus between divine and mundane believed to be at work in the divine places.

Verse 1.25 describes the legendary account of Hastigiri. According to the story, Viṣṇu, who is 'the bridge for all worlds' (*sakalajagatām ekasetuḥ*, i.e. for crossing the ocean of transmigration) once took the form of a bridge to assuage the anger of goddess Sarasvatī towards her husband, Brahmā, who had partnered with another woman, Satyavratā, while performing a sacrifice there. The verses immediately following draw a direct connection between the myth and the icon, with Rāma enjoining the goose in 1.27 'to bow down with head bent in devotion' (*bhaktinamreṇa mūrdhnā*). The most vivid description occurs in 1.33:

lakṣmīvidyullalitavapuṣaṃ tatra kāruṇyapūrṇaṃ
mā bhaiṣīs tvaṃ marakataśilāmecakaṃ vīkṣya megham/
śuddhair nityaṃ paricitapadas tvādṛśair devahaṃsair
haṃsībhūtaḥ sa khalu bhavatām anvavāyāgrajanmā//

Do not be frightened
seeing that compassionate emerald-coloured black cloud,
streaked with the lightning of Lakṣmī.
Divine geese like yourself worship at his feet.
It is told that becoming a goose himself,
he was your ancestor.[63]

Vedānta Deśika's description dovetails closely with the *Hastigirimāhātmya*, the *sthalapurāṇa* of the Varadarāja temple in Kāñcī forming part of the *Brahmāṇḍa Purāṇa*. The deep significance of the Varadāraja temple for Deśika is evident in his authorship of an experimental Maṇipravāla dance-drama with this same title, *Hastigirimāhātmya* (or *Meyviratamāṉmiyam*), in addition to the *Varadarājapañcāśat* and these verses in the *Haṃsasandeśa*.

No sites in the Coḻa region before Śrīraṅgam merit attention from Vedānta Deśika, and Rāma urges the goose in 1.36 to 'cross over the intervening areas' (*janapadam atho madhyamaṃ laṅghayitvā*). After a poetic description of the Kāverī River, Deśika skips over major Cōḻa urban centres including Tañjāvūr and Kumbakoṇam. It appears that these silences are emblematic of the perceived difference between the permanence of the divine places (transcending details of the temples and icons that appear therein) and the modernity of socially produced urban space, a convenient artifice for reducing both the epic space of the *Rāmāyaṇa* and that of the Tamil region to an institutionalized Śrīvaiṣṇava geography.

The verses describing Śrīraṅgam (1.38–1.46) are of special interest because the mythic origin of the Raṅganātha icon at Śrīraṅgam is for Śrīvaiṣṇavas the strongest and oldest material link with the epic narrative. From the early Āḻvār poetry, the Raṅganātha icon was identified with the family heirloom (*kuladhana*)

Rāma gave to Vibhīṣaṇa as recompense for his assistance in ousting Rāvaṇa, as described in the last *sarga* of the Yuddha Kāṇḍa (specifically, 6.131.88, where Rāma presents gifts to Hanumān, Sugrīva, Lakṣmaṇa and Vibhīṣaṇa upon ascending the throne at Ayodhyā). Deśika covers two divine places – Tiruveḷḷaṟai and Śrīraṅgam – and also provides an extended description of the Kāverī River as it passes through the area. He devotes three full verses (1.38–1.41) to the relatively minor Tiruveḷḷaṟai shrine, including a comparison of the Śvetādri Hill and the serpent Śeṣa risen from the nether regions (1.38) that directly parallels the description of Śeṣa at Tirupati, as well as an intricate double entendre (*śleṣa*) conflating the lustre of the divine gaze with a lamp in the temple (1.39). Tiruveḷḷaṟai, like Tirupati and later Tirumāliruñcōlai (1.49, on Vṛṣabha), is situated on a mountain, and it may be that Deśika's emphasis on the site is related to the logistical requirement of having the goose touch down periodically to recover. The environs depicted in 1.38 (the western part of the Cōḻa country called Varṣa), 1.40–1.41 (the forest and areca grove nearby) and 1.42–1.43 (the Kāverī river containing crocodiles and pearls) are closely echoed by descriptions in the *Śrīraṅgamāhātmya*.

More than anywhere else in the poem, it is in the section on Śrīraṅgam that Vedānta Deśika addresses the possibility of anachronism involved in the conflation of contemporary pilgrimage sites with the ancient action of the *Rāmāyaṇa*. Beyond Tiruveḷḷaṟai, the only material object described is the ancient Puṣkariṇī tank associated with the removal of the disease of the moon. And Vedānta Deśika is careful to have Rāma describe the Śrīraṅgam icon prospectively:

tīre tasyā viracitapadaṃ sādhubhiḥ sevyamānaṃ
sraddhāyogād vinamitatanuḥ śeṣapīṭhaṃ bhajethāḥ/
yasmin asmatkuladhanatayā saumya sāketabhājaḥ
sthānaṃ bhāvyaṃ munibhir uditaṃ śrīmato raṅgadhāmnaḥ//

On that bank there is a spot frequented by good people.
Worship the *Śeṣapīṭha*,
your body bowed down with respect.
The sages tell us that our family heirloom in Ayodhyā
will one day be the icon of Śrī Raṅganātha there.[64]

sattve divye svayam udayatas tasya dhāmnaḥ prasaṅgān
mañjūṣāyāṃ marakatam iva bhrājamānaṃ tadantaḥ/
ceto dhāvaty upahitabhujaṃ śeṣabhoge śayānaṃ
dīrghāpāṅgaṃ jaladhitanayājīvitaṃ devam ādyam//

My mind races
to the ancient god with long eyes, the life-breath of Lakṣmī.
He will lie on the bed of Śeṣa's hoods
resting on the pillow of his arm, shining within that self-existent site,
like an emerald in a jewel-box.[65]

This is a vivid description of how the famous reclining Viṣṇu icon in Śrīraṅgam *will* appear after installation. As Bronner and Shulman have argued, the description of the icon is an excellent example of the dizzying temporal depth of regional Sanskrit – involving future action in the prospective flight of the goose; the past action of the *Rāmāyaṇa* narrative; the present landscape of the south; and the plethora of futures, pasts and presents of other intertextually related messenger poems beginning with the *Meghadūta*.[66] Here we get a glimpse of an implicit argument against anachronism that rests on the peculiar construction of space in the *Haṃsasandeśa*: unlike the rest of the south, the divine places are deemed to be eternal sites of the lord's presence on earth.

2.6 Intertextuality and reflections

The dynamics through which the *Haṃsasandeśa* develops its allegory and distinctive charting of space through intense, non-derivative intertextual connections with the *Meghadūta* and Sundara Kāṇḍa warrants additional consideration. There is no existing major study of intertextuality in South Asian literary cultures, and the most insightful analysis on the topic remains Ramanujan's eloquent discussion of 'reflections' and translation in South Asian retellings and embedded narratives. While reflexivity for Ramanujan includes many forms of intertextuality – 'awareness of self and other, mirroring, distorted mirroring, parody, family resemblances and rebels, dialectic, antistructure, utopias and dystopias, the many ironies connected with these responses, and so on,' the expansive category of translation also overlaps with intertextuality.[67] Ramanujan speaks of the vertical relationship between works through a series of semiotic typological triads schematizing positive influence or negative subversion, meta-levels of textuality and local variation. The three types of reflection are:

> (1) *responsive*, when text A responds to text B in ways that define both A and B; (2) *reflexive*, where text A reflects on text B, relates itself directly or inversely; (3) *self-reflexive*, where a text reflects on itself or its kind.[68]

The three types of translation are arranged according to the Piercian triad: (1) iconic, (2) indexical and (3) symbolic. In the reflection triad, whereas responsive texts redefine both texts A and B, reflexive texts react inversely to text A; similarly, in the translation triad, whereas iconic texts geometrically resemble their predecessors and indexical texts are focused on concrete historical contexts, symbolic texts produce a counter-text.

Ramanujan's analysis and many cited examples highlight the way narrative in South Asia is saturated with histories of retellings distilling earlier voices, such that familiar stories such as the *Rāmāyaṇa* are performed and re-performed hundreds of times with subtle variations that do not exhaust the capacity to generate new meaning. Storytelling in this sense parallels Sanskrit commentarial writing, where innovation is often paradigmatically rendered through engagement with sources from the past rather than the creation of a new 'original.' Ramanujan develops the useful idea of 'clusters' in story traditions, whereby an individual poem is distinct from the broader Rāma *kathā* or story as 'not merely a set of texts, but a genre with a variety of instances.'[69] There is an open-endedness to this generic category:

> One may go further and say that the cultural arena in which *Rāmāyaṇas* are endemic has a pool of signifiers (like a gene pool), signifiers that include plots, characters, names, geography, incidents, and relationships; oral, written, and performance traditions, phrases, proverbs, and even sneers carry allusions to the Rāma story.

Each new text, 'dips into' the genre 'and brings out a unique crystallization.'[70]

Ramanujan's discussion brings out aspects of intertextuality specific to premodern South Asia corresponding to recent studies of genre in literary studies. A text is not a closed system – a hermetic whole – because of its intersection with other texts on the levels of both composition and reception: just as the author is also a reader of other texts, the reader brings to the text associations from other texts she or he has read. However, intertextuality does not only entail centrifugal forces of meaning undermining unity in a text, but also elements bringing texts together. For example, Genette's notion of the architext includes categories such as thematics, modes of enunciation, etc. that lie behind any text.[71] Jauss's reader-oriented approach emphasizes relationships between works through 'overt and covert signals, familiar characteristics, implicit allusions,' which are occasionally overturned – in effect transforming the genre itself.[72] Ramanujan's discussion points to genre as a more fluid category in South Asia and an emphasis on modes of imitation or transposition. The intertextual cluster of Rāma *kathā* includes nodes or smaller clusters such as the genre of messenger poems itself, and the *Haṃsasandeśa* reorients *sandeśakāvya* back towards its source in the *Rāmāyaṇa* while at the same time radically expanding the network of intertextual connections to include Maṇipravāla allegoresis. In its unique allegorical form, the *Haṃsasandeśa* is an example of positive influence, whereby text B iconically invokes text A yet radically alters our awareness of A (the antecedent), indexically connecting it to a specific historical context and interpreting it symbolically.

One sign of the lasting imprint the *Haṃsasandeśa* made on the later history of *sandeśakāvya* is the existence of several works also called '*Haṃsasandeśa*' produced in places as far away as Kerala and the Bangla region.[73] The dissemination and replication of the *Haṃsasandeśa* throughout the breadth of the subcontinent demonstrates how regional Sanskrit *kāvya* could become transregional, especially in the case of a poem like the *Haṃsasandeśa* which adumbrates its esoteric aspects resistant to universalization. Among these *Haṃsasandeśas*, perhaps of most interest is that of Vāmana Bhaṭṭa Baṇa, who wrote in the Andhra region just thirty years after Vedānta Deśika.

In his recent study of this work, Bronner has shown that already for Vāmana Bhaṭṭa Baṇa, Deśika's poem had become an exemplar of *sandeśakāvya* on par with the *Meghadūta*, as is evident from his absorption and appropriation of elements of Deśika's poem while reorienting the template of the messenger poem away from its *Rāmāyaṇa* prehistory and back to the classic model of Kālidāsa. Even as he adopts the goose as a messenger, Vāmana Bhaṭṭa Baṇa reverts to Kālidāsa's *yakṣa* (rather than Rāma) as the sender of the message; he incorporates both southern and northern routes (inclusive of the entire subcontinent) but follows Kālidāsa's south to north orientation, ending in Alakā in the Himālayas. He also incorporates and reverses Vedānta Deśika's crafting of space, with the sites now being almost exclusively Śaiva and not Vaiṣṇava.[74] This work and others like it demonstrate the degree to which Vedānta Deśika's poem found a comfortable place within the genre of messenger poems. In this regard it is of interest that there is no allegorical dimension to the *Haṃsasandeśa* of Vāmana Bhaṭṭa Baṇa, raising two possibilities: either Vāmana Bhaṭṭa Baṇa did not perceive the allegory in Deśika's poem, or he chose not to adapt it. If the former, it appears that Vedānta Deśika's *Haṃsasandeśa* could be read in at least two registers – one exclusive to the shared understanding of the Śrīvaiṣṇava community and another regional in orientation but also capable of travelling far beyond the Tamil region.

2.7 Stories of surrender

In the remainder of this chapter, I shift towards a discussion of the translation from Maṇipravāla in Govindarāja's sixteenth-century Sanskrit *Rāmāyaṇa* commentary. This juxtaposition of Sanskrit poetry and commentary may be helpful in exploring the confluence of creative and hermeneutic elements in various discursive modes. As might be expected, the influence of Maṇipravāla exegetical methods is deeper and more direct in Govindarāja's commentary. The performative origins of Govindarāja's theological reading are especially apparent in the list of eighteen traditional meanings of the *Rāmāyaṇa* passed down from Śrī Śaila Pūrṇa and in the commentary on episodes treated as paradigms of surrender.

A helpful analytic resource for understanding the appearance of specific linguistic markers of performance in Govindarāja's Maṇipravāla sources and in Govindarāja's commentary itself is Richard Bauman's comparative folklore theory of performance. Bauman refers to the 'keying' of performance as 'a transformation of the basic referential . . . uses of language,' a metacommunicative indication to the receiver of a message to interpret it in a special way.[75] The idea of keying relates to Bateson's and Goffman's theories of interpretive frames for messages. Since performance is an event and not a text, there are aspects of keying that are often elided in written transcription, including paralinguistic features such as rate, length, duration of pausing, qualities of voice (tenor, intonation, etc.), as well as the referential features Emanuel Schegloff calls conversational 'detritus': personal pronouns, discourse markers and indexical linguistic forms such as deictics.[76] Nevertheless, there do seem to be markers of the keying of performance that are evident in Maṇipravāla and even Sanskrit written texts. Philip Lutgendorf has highlighted the embedding of performative keying and framing in the dialogical storytelling context in Purāṇic, epic and vernacular literary traditions. In the

Rāmacaritamānas of Tulsīdās, the metaphor of the lake in the title relates to the characterization of the seven books as 'stairways' or 'descents' (*sopan*) that are multiple ingresses to the poem's meaning, indicating 'that there can never be a single definitive interpretation of the text.'[77] Popular recitation of the *Rāmacaritamānas* is also organized into a series of dialogues (*saṃvād*), further embedding the reception of the poem in a performative context.

Bauman's list of keys includes special codes, figurative language, parallelism, special paralinguistic features, special formulae, appeals to tradition and disclaimers of performance. Of these, the first two are clearly involved in Maṇipravāla sources: Maṇipravāla as a linguistic medium is just such a performative code, delimited to those within the Śrīvaiṣṇava community, and distinctive forms of figuration were associated with Maṇipravāla performative exegesis. Several other keys are also involved in Maṇipravāla works, most notably parallelism, characterized by Bauman, following Jakobson, as 'the repetition, with systematic variation, of phonic, grammatical, semantic, or prosodic structures, the combination of invariant and variant elements in the construction of an utterance.'[78] Bauman presents his list as a preliminary one, since keying occurs differently in each different culture. A form of keying resembling, but not delimited to, parallelism is the culturally specific style of improvisation termed by South Indian musicians and dancers *manodharma*, which, as Narayanan points out with respect to Tirukkōnēri Dāsyai's commentary on the *Tiruvāymoḻi*, finds its way into Maṇipravāla exegesis:

> The techniques of using a word or phrase and interpreting it dozens of ways is an integral part of singing and dancing in the Indian tradition. A singer may repeat a phrase from the Tiruvāymoḻi several times, exploring the nuances of a raga. A dancer may interpret a phrase in many ways, each time bringing new associations to the original meaning. Dāsyai seems to have applied a performing art technique to a verbal commentary.[79]

In the temple lecture, improvisation is oriented around a fixed doctrinal frame. Sometimes as a result of direct or indirect translation from Maṇipravāla and sometimes through his own creative application, Govindarāja's commentary contains many examples of such proliferation of meanings.

Another culturally specific key of performance in temple lecture is the use of non-formal didactic genres such as allegory, personification, parable and aphorism, which as we saw Vedānta Deśika developed into forms of poetic composition. Studies have shown that certain metaphors or genres are used more commonly in non-narrative discourse (such as the temple lecture) and conversation, including didactic forms such as aphorisms or parables, which, even if preformulated, are used by performers with great flexibility depending on social context.[80]

Govindarāja's incorporation of Maṇipravāla performative exegesis involves significant reinscription into the norms of Sanskrit scholastic commentary, as well as the integration of readings of isolated episodes into verse-by-verse commentary on these episodes in their original narrative context. Govindarāja accomplishes this task in an insidious fashion, as his comments on the vast majority of verses involve straightforward grammatical analysis or text-critical analysis aimed at ironing out apparent inconsistencies or ensuring that the text plausibly represents actually occurring events, as Goldman has shown.[81] The grammatical dimension in particular, however, offers Govindarāja possibilities for a kind of hyperanalysis or overinterpretation only hinted at in Maṇipravāla works.

In his comment on 1.5.1, under the rubric of the eighteen meanings of Śrī Śaila Pūrṇa, Govindarāja provides a schematic overview of his translation from Maṇipravāla – all the interpretations are adapted directly from the works of three roughly contemporary fourteenth-century authors, Vaṭakkutiruvītip Piḷḷai's *Īṭu*, Periyavāccāṉ Piḷḷai's *Taniślokam* and *Abhayapradānasāra*, and Vedānta Deśika's *Abhayapradānasāra*. These eighteen meanings constitute a précis, with economy of presentation, of stories of surrender analysed in the *rahasya* works. The four Maṇipravāla works differ greatly in structure and style. Periyavāccāṉ Piḷḷai's *Taniślokam* is a free-flowing stream of consciousness meditation on individual verses. Although the verses are organized according to their order of appearance in the epic, Periyavāccāṉ Piḷḷai employs improvisational techniques and provocatively picks them apart syllable by syllable without regard to narrative sequence, through associations with a wide array of sources and colloquial expressions. For example, he frames the first verse examined, 1.19.14 (1.18.14), (Viśvāmitra requesting Daśaratha for Rāma's assistance) with corresponding elements in the *Puruṣa Sūkta*; later, he offers dozens of mutually contrasting interpretations of 5.21.2–3 (5.19.3) (Sītā placing a blade of grass between herself and Rāvaṇa).[82] The *Abhayapradānasāras* of both Periyavāccāṉ Piḷḷai and Vedānta Deśika, on the other hand, revolve around the specific event of Rāma's granting protection to Vibhīṣaṇa, though these works also retain identifiable features of the Maṇipravāla style of interpreting verses out of context. Finally, the *Īṭu* is not a work focused on the *Rāmāyaṇa* but one of the classic commentaries on the *Tiruvāymoḻi*.

In what follows I go over the eighteen meanings and the specific *Rāmāyaṇa* episodes used as illustrations. The first meaning, discussed in the first chapter, is the supremacy of Viṣṇu, identified by Govindarāja as the predominant theme of the *Rāmāyaṇa* on the basis of the six Mīmāṃsā contextual identifiers (*tātparyaliṅgas*).[83] As per the indicator of repetition (*abhyāsa*), Govindarāja provides a *kāṇḍa* by *kāṇḍa* analysis of the many passages in the *Rāmāyaṇa* that he believes demonstrate Rāma's identity with a specifically Śrīvaiṣṇava conception of the godhead: as receptacle of all auspicious qualities, supreme, eternal, unknowable, primeval cause, refuge of all and, most significantly, meaning of the word Nārāyaṇa. Govindarāja uses verses cited by Periyavāccāṉ Piḷḷai and other Maṇipravāla verses as support and develops his analysis in rebuttal of the counterposition of Appayya Dīkṣita that the *Rāmāyaṇa* actually suggests the supremacy of Śiva.[84] It is of interest that this bird's-eye view of the narrative emplotment of the epic stands in contrast with those offered in the context of the *mā niṣāda* verse (discussed in detail in the next chapter), where the devotional refiguring of the emplotment is contingent upon the precedent of *rasa* theory in the aesthetic tradition.

The second meaning is the central Śrīvaiṣṇava soteriological concept of surrender (*prapatti*), which becomes so closely identified with the theological reading of the *Rāmāyaṇa* that Govindarāja and others refer to the epic itself as the 'systematic discourse on surrender' (*prapattiśāstra*). The acts of surrender cited from the *Rāmāyaṇa* are used as exemplars for almost all of the eighteen meanings: the gods to Rāma, Triśaṅku and Śunaḥśepa to Viśvāmitra, Lakṣmaṇa to Rāma, Bharata to Rāma, the sages of Daṇḍakāraṇya to Rāma, the demonic crow (*kākāsura*) to Rāma, Sugrīva to Rāma, Vibhīṣaṇa to Rāma, Rāma to the ocean and Trijaṭā to Sītā. Each exemplifies a different aspect of surrender.[85] Whereas some of the stories are major turning points in the narrative, others are minor incidents in which the phrasing or structuring of the depiction is especially apposite to the dynamics of surrender. Lakṣmaṇa's request to accompany Rāma to the forest demonstrates that one should perform surrender in the presence of a mediator (*puruṣakāra*) such as Sītā. According to Govindarāja (following Vedānta Deśika), the fact that Rāma did not return with Bharata does not imply that he failed to honour Bharata's request, it instead reflects the relative priority of acts of surrender, since the gods had earlier asked Viṣṇu that Rāvaṇa be defeated, and the sandals therefore become emblems not only of Rāma's reign but also of his eventual fulfillment of Bharata's surrender upon returning to Ayodhyā. This revisionary chronicling of events transforms the narrative logic, with acts of surrender replacing the dramatic flow of the surface emplotment.

The tangential stories receiving substantial attention from Govindarāja likely reflect their independent treatment in temple lectures and performances, with specific incidents serving as definitional resources for the conceptualization of surrender. For example, the transference of Trijaṭā's surrender to the female demons (and Vibhīṣaṇa's to his four companions) conduces to the popular notion that Rāmānuja's performance of surrender is transferred to all Śrīvaiṣṇavas. Similarly, the perceived failure of Rāma's entreaty to the ocean on the grounds of a lack of the requisite power disparity between suppliant and protector corresponds to the discussion of restrictions on the object of surrender (*viṣayaniyama*) in Piḷḷai Lokācārya's *Śrīvacanabhūṣaṇa*, cited in this context by Govindarāja:

> *prapattikku deśaniyamamum kālaniyamamum prakāraniyamamum atikāriniyamamum palaniyamamum illai. viṣayaniyamamey uḷḷatu.*
>
> Even though there is no restriction regarding the place, time, means, qualified aspirant and purpose of surrender, still there is a restriction with respect to the object of surrender.[86]

It is possible to perform surrender to other beings, but the paradigmatic protector is Viṣṇu, and the criteria for identifying an appropriate object of surrender – one who is both capable (*samartha*) and compassionate (*kāruṇika*) – correspond to the two key qualities of Viṣṇu according to Viśiṣṭādvaita: transcendence (*paratva*) and accessibility (*saulabhya*). The theological and exegetical perspectives are so apposite that it seems certain that early Śrīvaiṣṇava theologians had these *Rāmāyaṇa* incidents in mind while formulating the doctrine of surrender.[87]

The third meaning, servitude (*kaiṅkarya*), is the state of active service to Viṣṇu occurring after surrender, defined as a 'pleasure-generating activity' (*prītijanakavyāpāraviśeṣa*); the term is a secondary derivation from *kiṅkara*, servant, which is in turn etymologically derived from the phrase a servant may utter, 'What may I do?' (*kiṃ karomi*). The concept is grounded in Viśiṣṭādvaita metaphysics, where the relationship between human and divine operates on the grammatical analogy of the relationship between property and owner (*sva-svāmi bhāva*). Govindarāja begins his discussion of servitude by stating, 'The *Rāmāyaṇa* demonstrates that the goal of this practice [*prapatti*] is servitude accompanying the attainment of the lord' (*asya copāyasya prāpyaṃ bhagavatprāptipūrvakaṃ tatkaiṅkaryam eveti rāmāyaṇena pratipādyate*). The terminology used for surrender is significant: while in the *rahasya* works the word *prapatti* is generally used, here Govindarāja makes similar use of the near synonym *śaraṇāgati* (literally, 'seeking protection'), which unlike *prapatti* occurs frequently in the passages analysed. Govindarāja ties these passages to the conceptual structure of *prapatti* by arguing, crucially, that the immediate results sought in each of these incidents are ancillary (*ānuṣaṅgika*) to the ultimate goal of servitude, and in this sense all the various performances of surrender can be seen as being oriented towards soteriological ends. For example, the gods' explicit request to Rāma to defeat Rāvaṇa:

> It is said that when the gods surrendered to Viṣṇu in the beginning of the poem, their primary goal was to serve Rāma. For it is recounted that each of them was born in a womb of an *apsarā* just so that they could attend on him.[88]

Govindarāja offers similar explanations for each story, which together demonstrate not only that surrender is the primary subject (*pradhānaviṣaya*) of the *Rāmāyaṇa*, but also that the *Rāmāyaṇa* as a totality constitutes an extended act of surrender (*śrīrāmāyaṇam dīrghaśaraṇāgatiḥ*). All other meanings are subordinate to this unifying thematic focus.

Meanings four through eleven elaborate additional technical dimensions of the concept of surrender: (4) the mediator (*puruṣakāra*); (5, 6 and 7) the threefold taxonomy of qualified aspirants (*adhikārasvarūpa*); (8) the five secret forms of knowledge (*arthapañcakajñāna*); (9) the state of helplessness (*ākiñcanya*, *ananyagatitva*); (10) the *ācārya*; and (11) final release from transmigration (meanings twelve to eighteen cover subsidiary topics). The section on qualified aspirants (meanings five through seven) demonstrates the substantial distance between the didactic imperative to generate exemplary models and the interpretation of the plot according to narrative context. Govindarāja draws this entire section directly from comments in the *Īṭu*, the commentary where the allegorical drama of the progression of Nammāḻvār's states is most clearly developed.[89] Govindarāja, following Vaṭakkutiruvītip Piḷḷai, identifies each member of Viṣṇu's fourfold *avatāra* with different aspects of surrender: Rāma (the lord), Lakṣmaṇa (the embodiment of servitude), Bharata (the embodiment of dependence), and Śatrughna (the embodiment of dependence on the lord's devotees, *bhāgavatapāratantrya*).[90] What is interesting in this taxonomy is that there is a progressive hierarchy of the modes of practice outlined here in the *rahasya* works, with dependence valorized over servitude and dependence on the lord's devotees valorized in turn over mere dependence (because it more closely approaches the ideal of absolute subservience). But extolling Śatrughna over Bharata directly contradicts the hierarchies represented in the epic narrative itself, because the former accompanies the latter as subordinate at every stage. Govindarāja occasionally attempts to traverse the distance between theological use and grammatical, text-critical and historical analyses, but more often than not the two levels of reading are not collapsed together, though they are also rarely separated off in the commentary.

2.8 Exegesis in context

Applying this theological analysis of the series of stories of surrender while commenting on the relevant passages in their contexts requires considerable hermeneutic effort on the part of Govindarāja, and although in some places he is able to reproduce the repetition, word play and improvisational techniques from Maṇipravāla nearly verbatim, in others he modifies these significantly and harmonizes them into the standard protocols of Sanskrit commentary. Translation from the *rahasya* works usually only occurs where such a treatment seems apposite, such as Lakṣmaṇa's servitude, Sītā's forbearance, Jaṭāyu's liberation and Vibhīṣaṇa's surrender.

An example of Govindarāja's exegesis in context is his interpretation of Lakṣmaṇa's request for servitude (*nityakaiṅkarya*) in 2.31. For Govindarāja, Lakṣmaṇa's persistent entreaties to Rāma to allow him to accompany Rāma to the forest chart the stages of servitude, beginning with the performance of surrender and proceeding to the formal request for servitude. In 2.31.2, Lakṣmaṇa first responds to the news that Rāma has been exiled:

> *sa bhrātuś caraṇau gāḍhaṃ nipīḍya raghunandanaḥ/*
> *sītām uvācātiyaśā rāghavaṃ ca mahāvratam//*
>
> That famed descendant of Raghu firmly grasped his brother's feet
> and addressed Sītā and Rāghava of the great vow.
>
> 'He' was one who had no other means to attain his objective of following Rāma. The word, 'brother,' because it implies a permanent connection, indicates Rāma's being a protector (*śaraṇyatvam*), and 'grasping his feet' refers to the act of surrender. 'Firmly,' i.e. tightly, indicates great trust. 'Raghunandanaḥ' is Lakṣmaṇa. 'Famed one' means that he has avoided evil and intends good. First he addresses Sītā, taking her to be the mediator, and then, with her assistance, he addresses the one distinguished by the 'great vow,' an allusion to Rāma's later statement, 'I would not in any way abandon [such a person]; this is my vow' (6.18.3, critical edition 6.12.20). Mentioning the name 'Rāghava' also suggests that protecting those who have surrendered is the well-known family

> *dharma*, as is evident in the later discussion between Rāma and Vibhīṣaṇa. 'Said' means that since surrender allows one to attain all goals, he communicated his own desired goal. 'Grasped' is a reference to the description of surrender in the first part of the *dvaya mantra* [*śrīmannārāyaṇacaraṇau śaraṇam prapadye*]. 'He said to Rāghava' is a reference to the request for the result of surrender in the second part of the *dvaya mantra* [*śrīmate nārāyaṇāya namaḥ*]. 'He said to Sītā' refers to the goddess as mediator as expressed in both parts [i.e. *śrīman, śrīmate*].[91]

Govindarāja links the fact that Lakṣmaṇa addresses both Rāma and Sītā with the necessary presence of a mediator in surrender, and he identifies the grasping of Rāma's feet as an act of surrender. Other elements of the verse correspond to the six components (*aṅgas*) of surrender, derived from Pāñcarātra sources: (1) intention for good (*ānukūlyasaṅkalpa*); (2) avoidance of evil (*prātikūlyavarjana*); (3) great trust (*mahāviśvāsa*); (4) the request for protection (*goptṛtvavaraṇa*); (5) entrusting one's self (*ātmanikṣepa*, also considered the principal, *aṅgin*, of the other components); and 6) helplessness (*kārpaṇya*). These six components represent analytically the progressive performance of surrender and constitute a point of controversy between Vaṭakalais and Teṅkalais regarding whether surrender is a unified or composite act. Govindarāja sees grasping 'firmly' (*gāḍha*) as a sign of great trust (*mahāviśvāsa*) and Lakṣmaṇa's being 'famous' (*atiyaśā*) as an indication of his intention to do good (*ānukūlyasaṅkalpa*) and avoid evil (*prātikūlyavarjana*). Specific elements of the verse also correspond to the *dvaya* mantra, one of the three key Śrīvaiṣṇava mantras.

Govindarāja pursues the analogy in more detail in a few key verses. Lakṣmaṇa asks:

> *yadi gantuṃ kṛtā buddhir vanaṃ mṛgagajāyutam/*
> *aham tvānugamiṣyāmi vanam agre dhanurdharaḥ//*
>
> If your mind is set on going to the forest
> full of deer and elephants,
> then I will accompany you to the forest
> walking in front of you and bearing a bow.[92]
>
> *mayā sameto 'raṇyāni bahūni vicariṣyasi/*
> *pakṣibhir mṛgayūthaiś ca saṃghuṣṭhāni samantataḥ//*
>
> With me by your side you will wander many forests,
> with birds and herds of animals resounding on all around.[93]

These verses include the formal request for servitude: 'With the words "many, etc.," he makes his request for servitude suitable for all places, times and situations' (*bahūnītyanena sarvadeśakālasarvāvasthocitasarvavidhakaiṅkaryaprārth anaṃ kṛtam*).

Govindarāja views verse five as a statement of the absence of an ulterior motive (*ananyaprayojanatva*), another key aspect of servitude.

na devalokākramaṇaṃ nāmaratvam aham vṛṇe/
aiśvaryaṃ vāpi lokānāṃ kāmaye na tvayā vinā//

Without you I would not desire conquest over the gods,
immortality or even lordship over the worlds.[94]

Govindarāja's commentary here plays on the words of the *Rāmāyaṇa* while transposing set conceptual patterns onto the narrative, as is clear in his effort to recast Lakṣmaṇa's series of denials of other-worldly enjoyments in verse five as denials of alternative conceptions of liberation:

> 'Conquest over the gods,' as per the quote, 'The city of the gods is unassailable,' means I would not want to attain the highest state without you. The sense is, I would not desire even liberation, if it were not accompanied by servitude to you. 'Immortality' refers to the conception of liberation known as isolation (*kaivalya*), as per the phrase, 'liberation from old age and death' (*Bhagavad Gītā* 7.29). 'Lordship over the worlds,' i.e. being ruler over the three worlds, is tantamount to being *brahman*; the idea is: if I don't desire even liberation why would I want isolation (*kaivalya*), etc.? Or else the sequence is one of descending desirability: I don't desire even lordship over the worlds; thereby the fault of illogical classificatory hierarchy is avoided. Rendering the verse as 'I would not want to reach the world of the gods, become a god or become Indra' is off the mark.[95]

The fact that Lakṣmaṇa does not desire conquest over the gods indicates that he rejects liberation without servitude; his refusal of immortality refers to the state of isolation (*kaivalya*) advocated by Advaitins and in Sāṃkhya; and similarly his disavowal of lordship over the worlds is identified by Govindarāja as the Advaita ideal of becoming *brahman*. The analysis of specific words and phrases and the contrast with Advaita here resemble the precision of scholastic commentaries on the *Brahma Sūtras* or *Bhagavad Gītā*. At the same time, Govindarāja's sequential elaboration of the phrases in this verse is strongly reminiscent of the South Indian improvisational repetition of phrases.

This practice of unfolding multiple concatenated readings while exploiting Sanskrit grammatical analysis to dilate minutiae in the text is especially conspicuous in Govindarāja's commentary on 2.31.22:

kuruṣva mām anucaraṃ vaidharmyaṃ neha vidyate/
kṛtārtho 'ham bhaviṣyāmi tava cārthaḥ prakalpate//

Make me your servant, there is no impropriety in it.
I will accomplish my goal,
and your needs will also be taken care of.

> 'Me,' i.e. your subordinate (*śeṣa*). 'Make me your servant,' i.e. one fit for the servitude (*kainkarya*) that is associated with being a subordinate (*śeṣa*). The use of the middle voice (*ātmanepada*) indicates that this would be in your own

interest. 'There is no impropriety in it' means if you make me your servant, there will be no transgression of our respective duties as master and servant, for your duty as master is fulfilled by being served, and my duty as servant is fulfilled by my being your natural subordinate. Or else 'there is no impropriety' means that it will not result in something undesired, as you had suggested in your logically faulty argument to dissuade me. If you ask, what do I stand to gain from making you my servant, my response is, 'your needs will be taken care of,' i.e. you will be able to eat meals of fruit, roots, etc. without making any effort. And 'I will accomplish my goal' means I will attain my goal of servitude to you. Or one could take 'me' as referring to my essential nature as a subsidiary/the serpent Śeṣa, 'make me your servant' as referring to conformity with my nature as subsidiary/the serpent Śeṣa, and 'there is no impropriety in it' as consistency with my state of being a subsidiary. Servitude is then the result attained by knowing that this is my inherent nature. 'I will accomplish my goal' addresses the question, what would I lose were I not to perform servitude (*kaiṅkarya*)? If I did nothing, I wouldn't retain the status of being a subordinate (*śeṣatva*). The goal to be accomplished by servitude is indicated in the phrase 'and your,' with 'and' specifying that only your goal, and not mine, will be accomplished. The idea is that only servitude that benefits another is an ethical objective. Here is the secret meaning: the decision to be a subordinate is the means, and the result is other-directed servitude without self-interest. Some also analyse the verse in an altogether different way. 'There is no impropriety' because an elder brother is the same as one's father, and 'I will accomplish my goal,' since it will be of mutual benefit to us.[96]

Here, the loading of esoteric meanings is especially intense, through an extended series of multiple readings. The mere reference to Lakṣmaṇa being a follower or servant (*anucara*) provides Govindarāja with an opening to identify the verse as a definitional statement on *kaiṅkarya*, and Govindarāja supplies the qualifier 'who am a subordinate' (*śeṣabhūtam*; in technical discussions, *śeṣa* is closely tied to *kaiṅkarya*) in his gloss of the word 'me.' Govindarāja pushes Sanskrit grammatical and scholastic analysis to squeeze meaning out of every possible element of the verse. Stretching the standard usage of the morphology of the verb itself, he reads the middle voice of 'make' (*kuruśva*) as an indication that Lakṣmaṇa's act of surrender will also be beneficial to the lord himself ('for *you*'). He also applies terminology from Sanskrit epistemology, for Rāma's previous statement is a logical syllogism (*hetu*) suffering from the technical defect of *anyathāsiddhi*. In his comment on this verse and others where he draws on Maṇipravāla sources, Govindarāja's phrasing includes a high number of indexicals, which as discussed above occur commonly in performative discourse but are often elided in writing; here they build on the pronouns used in the verse itself ('me' and 'you').

The several options offered for interpreting the verse allow it to be used as a prop for a deeper reflection on surrender that squeezes meaning in the style of Śrīvaiṣṇava performative discourse. For example, Govindarāja reads Lakṣmaṇa's argument regarding the absence of impropriety (*vaidharmyaṃ neha vidyate*) two completely different ways, either as an indication that the relationship of servant to lord, the essence of *kaiṅkarya*, will not be violated or that the untoward events earlier warned of by Rāma will not occur. The locative 'in this/him' (*asmin*) may refer to the act of following Rāma (no impropriety regarding the relationship of subordinate–superordinate) or to Lakṣmaṇa himself (no impropriety in his state of being a subordinate). When the locative refers to Lakṣmaṇa himself, the verse is transformed through a word play on Lakṣmaṇa's traditional association with the serpent vehicle of Viṣṇu, *Śeṣa*, whose name is the same as the word translated here as subordinate (*śeṣa*) (recall that this word play also occurs in Vedānta Deśika's *Haṃsasandeśa*). So Govindarāja renders the request as a call to restore the intrinsic nature of Lakṣmaṇa as subordinate/serpent (*śeṣa/ Śeṣa*), and the absence of impropriety is only the lack of any contradiction with Lakṣmaṇa's/ Śeṣa's eternal state of being a subordinate. 'Your needs' may refer to Rāma's status as superordinate, to his more mundane needs of subsistence in the forest, or to the fact that servitude must be other-directed and not self-directed. The phrase 'I will accomplish my goal' refers to the possible objection 'If you don't perform servitude, what do you lose?' According to Govindarāja, what Lakṣmaṇa stands to relinquish is his very essence.

As is typical for Govindarāja, each reading fits neatly within the parameters of the doctrinal understanding of servitude, and their very profusion adds to the relishing of the verse. He develops their basic outline from the *Īṭu* and the *Taṉiślokam* (Periyavāccāṉ Piḷḷai comments on two of the verses discussed here, 2.31.2. and 2.31.25).[97] Of the comparisons with *Rāmāyaṇa* characters in the *Īṭu*, noted above, the comparison with Lakṣmaṇa and his request for servitude is the most frequent and most significant; a single verse, 2.31.25 (*bhavāṃs tu saha vaidehyā girisānuṣu raṃsyate/ ahaṃ sarvaṃ kariṣyāmi jāgrataḥ svapataś ca te*), is cited by Vaṭakkutiruvītip Piḷḷai fourteen times.[98]

Another example of the translation of performative exegesis is Govindarāja's comment on the verse known to Śrīvaiṣṇavas either as Sītā's 'last' verse (*carama-śloka*, on the model of the 'last' verse of the *Bhagavad Gītā*, another of the three Śrīvaiṣṇava *rahasya* mantras) or Sītā's protection-granting verse (*abhayapradāna-śloka*, parallel to Rāma's own protective statement to Vibhīṣaṇa described below):

> *pāpānāṃ vā śubhānāṃ vā vadhārhāṇāṃ plavaṅgama/*
> *kāryaṃ karuṇam āryeṇa na kaścin nāparādhyati//*
>
> Whether dealing with the sinful or the virtuous,
> or even those deserving to be killed, oh monkey,
> a noble person should be compassionate.
> No one is free from faults.[99]

The verse is embedded in a long passage near the end of the Yuddha Kāṇḍa, where Sītā advocates forgiveness and seeks to prevent Hanumān from attacking the female demons who had threatened her during her imprisonment in the *aśoka* grove. Sītā's protection-granting verse is memorized and recited by Śrīvaiṣṇavas and is thought to be the classic example of the goddess's role as mediator. The context of the verse resembles the context of Rāma's own granting of protection to Vibhīṣaṇa: those whose fate is in question are in both cases demons, enemies whose character appears dubious to those advocating punishment, and in each case the statement is framed by a legendary account, for Rāma with the vignette of the dove, and for Sītā with the words of the bear. The Maṇipravāḷa sources are again the *Īṭu* and the *Taniślokam*.

Govindarāja's first significant move is to supply the story of the bear referred to by Sītā in 6.116.43 (6.101.34):

> Long ago a hunter chased by a tiger climbed a tree. The tiger, now at the trunk of the tree, said to a bear at the top of the tree, 'He is a natural enemy to us, the animals of the forest. Push him down from the tree.' The bear responded by saying that he would never push someone who had come to his own home, as this would be ignoble, and he fell asleep. Then the tiger turned to the hunter and said, 'Look, I'll protect you, just make that sleeping bear fall,' and encouraged by the tiger the hunter did just that. But because he was very experienced, the bear caught onto another branch and did not fall. At this point, the tiger said to the bear many times, 'Push the hunter, after all he just double-crossed you.' But the bear refused. 'Even though he has greatly wronged me,' he said, 'I will not hand him over to you,' and the bear protected the hunter. So goes the ancient story.[100]

This account of the interaction between the tiger, the hunter and the bear is Govindarāja's own; the *Rāmāyaṇa* itself only refers to the words uttered by a bear without providing any details, and Periyavāccāṉ Piḷḷai does not mention it. Not only does Govindarāja supply the story, but the length of the commentary at this juncture expands in a way that assigns inordinate weight to what is a mere passing reference in the original, in comparison to the one- or two-line gloss allotted the remaining verses in the chapter. The story resembles the predominant mode of parables, insofar as Govindarāja has Sītā as a character draw a comparison with an external situation.[101] As discussed above, parable as a didactic genre (like aphorism) is commonly employed in performative conversation rather than storytelling, and in this and other ways Govindarāja would seem to be adapting the style of the temple lecture without the benefit of a Maṇipravāla antecedent.[102]

Similarly, Govindarāja devotes great care to his reading of the last part of the verse, the phrase 'no one is free from faults,' *na kaścin nāparādhyati* (which might better translate as, 'nobody's perfect'), a phrase that becomes for Śrīvaiṣṇavas a kind of aphorism cited out of context in conversation or in lecture. The entire reading is predicated on an a priori assumption of Sītā's identification with the goddess Śrī, which is an ontological rather than situational equivalence as in the allegoresis of Hanumān's message. Govindarāja directly translates in abridged form sections of the *Īṭu* and the *Taniślokam* to construct an imaginary, ironic dialogue between Sītā and an interlocutor (presumably Hanumān), thereby inserting a dialogical mode into the commentary along the lines of his commentary on 2.31.22:[103]

> The phrase 'the sinful or the virtuous' implies that although you think they are sinful, from my perspective they are virtuous. That's what Rāma meant when he said, 'even if the person is at fault' (6.18.3, 6.12.3). Only someone who is dirty needs a bath. Only those who are sinful need me, what do the virtuous need me for? Their good deeds already protect them. So I seek out sin. But if you adopt such an approach, won't you be violating the *dharmaśāstra* principle that those who deserve to be punished should be punished, and not the innocent? Well, if this is your objection, aren't you yourself violating the special principle that even those who have faults should be protected? Monkey, you desire something that you should not desire. 'A noble person,' i.e. a magnanimous person, would be compassionate. Forget about whether they are sinful or not, look at how much they need our compassion right now. Or, on the other hand, 'whether virtuous' could be taken as an analogy. Just as we would be compassionate towards a virtuous person who is about to be killed, so too we ought to be compassionate towards a sinful person. 'No one is free from faults' is a response to the possible objection that not punishing those who have committed crimes amounts to an over-extension of this principle. The idea is that everyone commits offenses.[104]

The peculiar effect of the translation from Maṇipravāla is an informal conversational style, replete with indexicals, that also mimics the conventions of a formal Sanskrit scholastic debate. In Govindarāja's word-by-word gloss, each new phrase becomes a further development in an argument by Sītā whose ultimate objective is to convince Hanumān to forgive the female demons. Govindarāja begins by reinscribing the aporia in the verse (whether sinful or virtuous) into pseudo-scholastic alternative positions, with Sītā in effect declaring 'either wicked, which is *your* meaning, or virtuous, which is *my* meaning.'

But this stance is immediately undermined when Govindarāja's Sītā alludes to the Śrīvaiṣṇava (Teṅkalai) notion of the lord's hyperbolic preference for human sins, like dirt that requires bathing. The rhetorical shift here reverts to the idea that those in question are, in fact, sinful (even though Sītā's first statement asserted their virtue). The second statement renders the first into an ironic remark, whose ultimate meaning would be as follows: I, Sītā, consider them to be virtuous because their sin is, for me, a virtue. Govindarāja continues the conversational tête-à-tête between Sītā and Hanumān while dispensing with an objection voiced from the perspective of *dharmaśāstra*. It would seem that Sītā's extreme position vitiates the basic rule of *dhārmic* justice, whereby only those deserving punishment are punished and not the innocent (*daṇḍyo daṇḍanīyaḥ nādaṇḍyaḥ*), but Sītā directly rebuts this position by arguing that the more contextual (theological) principle of surrender trumps all other ethical norms. And yet with the next phrase, 'even one deserving to be killed,' the entire flow is again turned around, with Govindarāja now having Sītā use 'virtuous' merely as an analogy: sinful people, like virtuous people, should be treated with compassion if there is a threat of their being killed. In response to a final objection regarding the possibility of an unwarranted overextension (*atiprasaṅga*) of the principle of compassion, Sītā simply responds with the laconic last phrase, 'nobody's perfect' (*na kaścin nāparādhyati*). What is evident from this example is that the extreme detail of Govindarāja's reading (and that of his Maṇipravāla sources) allows him to transform an ancillary passage into a major theological statement while seeming to build on the literal meaning without resorting to figuration.

Govindarāja's theological reading is sometimes more overt than in the context of the Lakṣmaṇa and Sīta episodes, such as his treatment of the liberation of Jaṭāyu. The description of Jaṭāyu's death occurs towards the end of the Āraṇya Kāṇḍa (3.67–3.68, critical edition 3.63–3.64) after Rāma and Lakṣmaṇa have discovered Sītā's absence. The precedent for the treatment of these chapters appears to be neither the *Īṭu* nor the *Taniślokam* but the life of the important Śrīvaiṣṇava figure Parāśara Bhaṭṭar in the *Guruparamparāprabhāva*. Both Govindarāja and Maheśvaratīrtha focus attention on a few specific verses. In 3.67.9, Govindarāja explains the use of the adjective 'illustrious' (*mahābhāgam*) as a reference to the glory of Jaṭāyu having abandoned his body, indeed his very life, for the lord.[105] In 3.67.22, Maheśvaratīrtha views the description of Rāma's face being covered with tears (*bāṣpapūrṇamukhaḥ*) as the lord's distress on seeing a calamity befall his devotee.[106]

These brief remarks prepare the reader for the more detailed interpretation of Rāma's bestowal of liberation in 3.68.29–30 (3.64.29–30):

yā gatir yajñaśīlānām āhitāgneś ca yā gatiḥ/
aparāvartināṃ yā ca yā ca bhūmipradāyinām//
mayā tvaṃ samanujñāto gaccha lokān anuttamān/
gṛdhrarāja mahāsattva saṃskṛtaś ca mayā vraja//

O king of vultures,
I give you permission to go by the paths of
those devoted to sacrifice,
those who keep the fires,
those who do not return,
those who give up the earth.
Go to the highest worlds, O noble soul,
go consecrated by me.[107]

In the clearest echo yet of the improvisational repetition from Maṇipravāla, Govindarāja offers four separate readings for the verse, each of which places special weight on the contrast between the ultimate liberation of Jaṭāyu and ordinary life after death.[108] First, Govindarāja views each of the paths as a world corresponding to the earthly life-stations (*āśramas*, in the sequence of the verse): householders, forest-dwellers, renunciates and perpetual students. Or, on the second reading, the paths may refer respectively to sacrifice (*yajña*), charity (*dāna*), penance (*tapas*) and renunciation (*sanyāsa*); in either case, Jaṭāyu will proceed not only to these worlds, but beyond them to the heavenly world of Viṣṇu. On the third reading, Rāma's consecration and permission are grouped together, with emphasis placed on the last phrase now reinscribed as 'come to me' (*mayā vraja* becomes *māṃ vraja*). On the last reading, the permission after consecration is linked to specific mantras that qualify one for each respective world. The multiple interpretations (often introduced by the phrase 'or else,' *yad vā*) demonstrate a playful engagement with the verse, but each option, supported by extensive Vedic quotations, develops a progressively stronger Vaiṣṇava understanding of liberation, from the identification of the worlds of Viṣṇu to the construal of a devotional relationship and specification of esoteric mantras.[109]

2.9 Vibhīṣaṇa's surrender

The most extensive application of Maṇipravāla exegetical methods occurs in Govindarāja's expansive commentary on 6.17–18 (6.11–12), describing the surrender of Rāvaṇa's brother, Vibhīṣaṇa, to Rāma. The epic representation of this most famous act of surrender is in the idiom of calumny, political intrigue and strategic policy. Whereas the structuring of the episode provides a showcase for Rāma's ideal embodiment of benevolent royal virtues, for Śrīvaiṣṇavas it takes on far greater significance as the prototype for theological conceptions of surrender. The entire dialogue rings with the immediate political context: spying, usurping kingship, treason and asylum – but the language used to describe the dynamics between Vibhīṣaṇa and Rāma, including related words for protection (*śaraṇa*), seeking protection (*śaraṇāgati*) and protector (*śaraṇya*), provide ample openings for Śrīvaiṣṇava commentators to interpret through the prism of theological surrender. No other event, including the banishment of Rāma, the abduction of Sītā or the killing of Rāvaṇa, merits such rigorous attention from Śrīvaiṣṇava commentators. The direct Maṇipravāla sources are the two *rahasya Abhayapradānasāras* of Vedānta Deśika and Periyavāccān Piḷḷai, both of which are devoted entirely to Vibhīṣaṇa's surrender and culminate in Rāma's protection-granting verse (*abhayapradānaśloka*). In my discussion of Govindarāja's commentary on Vibhīṣaṇa's surrender, I focus especially on the way Govindarāja incorporates idiomatic, colloquial Maṇipravāla expressions while at the same time making extensive use of Sanskrit scholastic framing devices.

At the end of chapter 6.16 (6.10), Vibhīṣaṇa abandons Rāvaṇa after repeatedly advising him to let Sītā return to Rāma, and in the beginning of chapter 6.17 (6.11), he appears in the sky opposite where the monkeys and Rāma have gathered to prepare for war. He announces himself as the estranged brother of the wicked Rāvaṇa who would like to be brought immediately before Rāma, the protector of all (*sarvalokaśaraṇyāya*). A lengthy discussion between the monkeys ensues, with each stating reasons why Vibhīṣaṇa should not be trusted: some believe him to be a spy, while others disdain him simply because he is a demon (and that too, a demon who has just abandoned his own brother); some want to send a counter-spy to have Vibhīṣaṇa pass a test of faithfulness, or just to kill him (with a sharp stick, '*daṇḍena tīvreṇa*'). Finally, Hanumān expresses a dissenting opinion. Strategically, he sees faults in each of the previous views, since Vibhīṣaṇa could not be tested without being entrusted with an important task, and this would lead to either his ascertaining the monkeys' intentions and deceiving them or, if he is actually sincere, in their losing his friendship; furthermore, Vibhīṣaṇa's appearance and demeanour engender trust, and so Hanumān advocates accepting him.

Hanumān's words provide an opening for Rāma, whose response represents one of his more gracious acts in the epic. The framing of Rāma's words with the cynical perspectives of the monkeys couched in the technical language of political strategy (*nītiśāstra*), augments the representation of Rāma's benevolent rule as an embodiment of ideal kingship in a way that resembles Rāma's beneficent encounters with Ahalyā and Jaṭāyu. As with those encounters, the language and analogies conduce to Śrīvaiṣṇava conceptions of divinity and soteriological concepts. After listening to what Hanumān has to say, Rāma says that he too has an opinion about Vibhīṣaṇa: one should never abandon someone who approaches in friendship, even if they have faults. On the level of pure realpolitik, Rāma points out that rivalries are quite common in royal families and it should not surprise the monkeys if Vibhīṣaṇa wants to overthrow Rāvaṇa. But Rāma adds, matching the monkeys' bellicose rhetoric, that for him, Vibhīṣaṇa's intentions are immaterial since he himself can kill anyone with just his little finger. Finally, Rāma presents a series of clinching arguments: (1) the story of the dove; (2) the words of Kaṇḍu, son of Kaṇva; and (3) the protection-granting verse. He asks Sugrīva to bring forward whoever it may be that is asking for protection, whether Vibhīṣaṇa or Rāvaṇa himself, and Sugrīva at last accepts.

Just as with the episode of Lakṣmaṇa's request for *kaiṅkarya*, Govindarāja frames the narrative through the conceptual schema of the six components of surrender:

> The eight preceding chapters have shown intention for good (*ānukūlyasya saṅkalpaḥ*) and avoidance of evil (*prātikūlyasya varjanam*) on the part of Vibhīṣaṇa, the one wishing to surrender, in accordance with the verse, 'Surrender is sixfold: intention for good, avoidance of evil, trust that the protector will protect, a request to be protected, self-surrender and the condition of helplessness.' Vibhīṣaṇa's repeated advice to Rāvaṇa showed his great trust (*mahāviśvāsa*), and now the poet describes his actual surrender and demonstration of helplessness.[110]

According to Govindarāja, Vibhīṣaṇa's possession of the first two ethical components, intention for good and avoidance of evil, is already evident through his continued counsel to Rāvaṇa, and similarly his great trust is on display when Vibhīṣaṇa leaves Rāvaṇa in full faith that Rāma will accept him. Vibhīṣaṇa's statement to the monkeys demonstrates his helplessness, and his request for surrender and performance of surrender take place through his encounter with the monkeys and Rāma.

Govindarāja develops his application of the six components from Vedānta Deśika's *Abhayapradānasāra*, although Deśika provides more details in his *rahasya* discussion.[111] Vedānta Deśika identifies the request for surrender in verse fourteen, when Vibhīṣaṇa himself says, 'I have surrendered to Rāma' (*rāghavaṃ śaraṇaṃ gataḥ*), and in the next verse when he asks the monkeys, 'Immediately introduce me to the great Rāma, the protector of all, as Vibhīṣaṇa who is close at hand.'[112] Deśika specifically identifies the request as an exemplification of the complete submission of the burden of protection (*rakṣābharasamarpaṇa*) manifest in the Śrīvaiṣṇava double mantra (*dvaya*). Maheśvaratīrtha, on the other hand, presents a slightly different analysis from that of Deśika and Govindarāja, with both the avoidance of evil and request for surrender occurring in verse fourteen. The differences in the use of the six components again indicates the desideratum of creative application of schema to the narrative, without the necessity of a final, authoritative rendering. The text itself (and by extension the events to which it refers) itself becomes a schema that may be arranged and rearranged according to the logic of surrender.

The now familiar pattern of improvisation through optional readings is apparent in Govindarāja's incorporation of Maṇipravāla readings for a key verse in Rāma's counterargument:

> *mitrabhāvena saṃprāptaṃ na tyajeyaṃ kathaṃcana/*
> *doṣo yady api tasya syāt satām etad agarhitam//*
>
> I cannot in any way abandon
> someone whom I meet in friendship,
> even if the person is at fault.
> And good people would not censure this.[113]

Consider the many possible meanings offered for the single compound *mitrabhāvena*:

> 'In friendship' can mean just acting as if one is a friend, even if there is no real friendship. Friendship amounts to surrender. For Vibhīṣaṇa already said, 'I surrender to Rāma,' and he will later say, 'I surrender to the protector.' Sītā earlier began a speech saying, 'He is famed to be someone who knows *dharma* and is gracious to those who have surrendered' and concluded 'Therefore you should seek friendship with him, if you desire to live.' Or else the word 'friend' is from Rāma's perspective, since it is appropriate to consider someone who has surrendered as worthy. Or 'in friendship' could refer to friendly actions, i.e. pretending to be a friend and requesting surrender without it really being in one's heart, since it has been said, 'Such a statement becomes a request for protection even if it is made unintentionally.' Although he should have said, 'in surrender,' the lord says 'in friendship' because he considers a person taking just the first initial steps towards surrender to be like one dependant on him. When the goddess said 'therefore you should seek friendship with him, if you desire to live,' she meant surrender. Or 'in friendship' means as a friend, as per the quote '*suhṛdaṃ sarvabhūtānāṃ*' (BG 5.29), the lord is inherently amiable towards all beings.

> Or 'in friendship' refers to the intention to do good, etc. [the first of the six components of surrender]. Or, the word friend (*mitram*) means without limits, based on its etymology; one should engage in helpful acts thinking that these are being offered to the lord. Or 'friendship' is a place of trust, the idea being that he is trustworthy.[114]

The 'or else' (*yad vā*) constructions occur here in an almost rhythmic pattern. While the main point is a simple one – 'in friendship' is essentially synonymous with surrender – the many ways this point can be made drives it home and brings out subtle nuances.

The phrase 'even if the person is at fault' (*doṣo yady api tasya syāt*) closely resembles 'whether sinful' (*pāpānām vā*) in Sītā's protection-granting verse, and here as in the other verse the emphasis is on the lord's enjoyment of human faults. What is of interest in Govindarāja's gloss of the phrase is the way he makes use of Sanskrit grammatical categories to extend the practice of Maṇipravāla improvisational repetition. Govindarāja exploits the vast semantic range of the optative tense (*vidhi liṅ*) for the verbs to be (root *as*) and abandon to (root *tyaj*) in this phrase and the one preceding it: 'I cannot in any way abandon' (*na tyajeyaṃ kathaṃcana*). In addition to the way I have rendered it in my translation, Govindarāja glosses the optative for to be (*as*) as an imperative (*vidhi*): he should be full of faults. And later this same optative becomes even more pointed as an entreaty (*prārthanāyāṃ liṅ*): may he have faults.[115] He makes a similar move with respect to the optative for to abandon (*tyaj*). First, again, the optative is glossed as an imperative (*vidhi*): I *may not* abandon him. Next, this same optative expresses possibility (*sambhāvanāyāṃ liṅ*) generating a rhetorical statement: how could I possibly abandon him?[116]

Govindarāja's exploiting of the precise grammatical analysis of epic commentary occurs in the chapters on Vibhīṣaṇa's surrender with such frequency that the practice may be said to constitute its own reading technique. The impression that this interpretation is a literal one is important because Śrīvaiṣṇavas were concerned to demonstrate that Vibhīṣaṇa's surrender was actually an act of surrender in the theological sense. This concern is apparent in both Vedānta Deśika's and Govindarāja's arguments against the possibility that Vibhīṣaṇa's surrender is a mere stratagem for usurping kingship (a refrain voiced not only by the monkeys, but also by Rāma himself in 6.18.9 when he raises the more subtle, *sūkṣmataram*, point about familial rivalries). The clinching evidence for Deśika, and for Govindarāja, is: (1) when Vibhīṣaṇa receives a boon from Brahmā, as recounted in Uttara Kāṇḍa 7.10.31–34 (7.10.27–29), he asks only to always have his mind intent on *dharma* (identified by Deśika and Govindarāja as the *dharma* of surrender); and (2) it appears from Uttara Kāṇḍa 7.108.27–29 (7.98.21–23) that Rāma in effect *orders* Vibhīṣaṇa to accept kingship when he grants him the Ikṣvāku family heirloom (the Śrīraṅgam icon). While these arguments refurbish Vibhīṣaṇa's propensity for surrender, a more direct argument is based on the simple psychological application of a distinction imported from grammatical theory between what is internal (*antaraṅga*) and external (*bahiraṅga*).[117] Vibhīṣaṇa's own words carry more weight in ascertaining his intentions than those of others.

Govindarāja's close grammatical analysis also affords him theological opportunities in his gloss of the seemingly insignificant qualifier 'with Lakṣmaṇa,' *salakṣmaṇaḥ* in 6.17.1 (6.11.1), a mere reference to the co-presence of Rāma and Lakṣmaṇa that warrants no special analysis elsewhere. In order to be a case of surrender, the scene requires the presence of a mediator, which Govindarāja identifies as Lakṣmaṇa and the monkeys, according to the principle that a distinguished devotee (*bhāgavata*) may qualify as the mediator even though this role is paradigmatically fulfilled by the goddess or an *ācārya*. Govindarāja explains that the reluctance of Lakṣmaṇa and the monkeys to accept Vibhīṣaṇa is due to their overwhelming emotion and concern for Rāma's safety, and this does not disqualify them from serving as mediators. The phrase 'with Lakṣmaṇa' (*salakṣmaṇaḥ*) is critical to this identification. Govindarāja explains that while this reference to Lakṣmaṇa may be a mere identifier (*vyāvartaka*) of Rāma, it also indicates the presence of a mediator (*puruṣakārasānnidhyam*), i.e. Lakṣmaṇa.[118]

Unlike grammatical analysis, other keys of Maṇipravāla performative discourse appear conspicuous in their distinction from the standard modes of Sanskrit, such as the use of colloquial, idiomatic expressions. Several occur in the comments on 6.17.1 (6.11.1) and 6.17.2 (6.11.2). The dexterity of Vibhīṣaṇa approaching Rāma within a moment (*muhūrtena*) is first compared to someone walking over hot coals (*aṅgāranikaraparikṣipte vartmani padanyāsavat*) and, later, more poignantly, to a freed calf who rushes forward refusing to see anything except his mother's udder (*vigalitabandharajjor vatsasya māturadhaḥ sparśam antareṇa madhyadeśādarśaṇavat*), a metaphor drawn from the *Taniślokam* and based on *Tiruvāymoḻi* 1.30. In the next verse, we are told that Vibhīṣaṇa comes as if from a forest fire into a cool lake (*davāgner nirgatya śītalahrade patitum ivāgacchantam*). Some of these idiomatic expressions may be traced back to the two Maṇipravāla *Abhayapradānasāras*, but others are found only in Govindarāja, suggesting that Govindarāja and other Sanskrit commentators themselves incorporated vernacular and folk elements.

These translations are all the more conspicuous in the commentary on Vibhīṣaṇa's surrender because the section is also replete with formal classificatory frames proper to scholastic Sanskrit. Govindarāja organizes Rāma's arguments on accepting Vibhīṣaṇa according to the fivefold source of *dharma* laid out in the *Yājñavalkyasmṛti*:

> *śrutiḥ smṛtiḥ sadācāraḥ svasya ca priyam ātmanaḥ/*
> *samyak saṅkalpajaḥ kāmo dharmamūlam idaṃ smṛtam//*
>
> The source of *dharma* is declared to be fivefold: 1) revelation (*śrutiḥ*); 2) remembered tradition (*smṛtiḥ*); 3) right conduct (*sadācāra*); 4) one's own benefit (*svasya ca priyam ātmanaḥ*) and 5) desire born of purposeful intention (*saṅkalpajaḥ kāmo*).[119]

According to classic *dharmaśāstra* theory, the evaluation of normative conduct is through the precedent of Vedic tradition and the conduct of practitioners of this tradition. Govindarāja foregrounds this schema in relation to the decisive moment in the acceptance of Vibhīṣaṇa, Rāma's protection-granting verse, where he lays out the five sources in Rāma's argument. Although Vedānta Deśika also makes reference to the *Yājñavalkyasmṛti* verse, Govindarāja goes much further and uses it to analyse Rāma's entire speech in this chapter:

> *sakṛd eva prapannāya tavāsmīti ca yācate/*
> *abhayaṃ sarvabhūtebhyo dadāmy etad vrataṃ mama//*
>
> I give protection
> to anyone who surrenders to me even once
> saying, 'I am yours.'
> This is my vow.
>
> As per the fivefold schema laid out in the *Yājñavalkyasmṛti*, four of the valid means for establishing *dharma* have been established with regard to the position that someone who has surrendered should be protected. 'Therefore they do not reject someone who has surrendered, even if the person deserved to be killed' (*Taittirīya Saṃhitā* 6.5.6.3) is the *śruti* source. The *smṛti* source is the verses of Kaṇḍu. Right conduct is shown in the story of the pigeon. Rāma demonstrates the benefit to himself by asserting his own view and casting off those of his interlocutors. Now with this verse the fifth valid means is described.[120]

This key verse, perhaps the most famous in the entire *Rāmāyaṇa* for Śrīvaiṣṇavas, provides the culminating point for the two Maṇipravāla works and their titles ('granting protection,' *abhayapradāna*).

Govindarāja cites a highly apposite verse from the *Taittirīya Saṃhitā* as the *śruti* source, which is presumably seen as the inspiration for 6.18.3 (6.12.3), discussed above. The next logical step is corroboration through remembered tradition (*smṛti*), identified as the verses of Kaṇḍu referred to by Rāma in 6.18.26 (6.12.13) and quoted in 6.18.27–28 (6.12.14–15):

> *badhāñjalipuṭaṃ dīnaṃ yācantaṃ śaraṇāgatam/*
> *na hanyād ānṛśaṃsyārtham api śatruṃ parantapa//*
>
> Scorcher of foes, out of compassion
> one should not harm a helpless suppliant
> who seeks protection (*śaraṇāgatam*)
> with hands folded.
>
> *ārto vā yadi vā dṛptaḥ pareṣāṃ śaraṇāgataḥ/*
> *ariḥ prāṇān parityajya rakṣitavyaḥ kṛtātmanā//*
>
> If one is self-possessed
> one should protect an enemy seeking protection from others,

even at the cost of one's own life,
whether the enemy be proud or in distress.[121]

The source for these verses (the *Kaṇḍugāthā*) is unknown, but Govindarāja seems to locate them in a *dharmaśāstra* work.

The precedent of established practice (*śiṣṭācāra*) is rendered through the story of the pigeon:

śrūyate hi kapotena śatruḥ śaraṇam āgataḥ/
arcitaś ca yathānyāyaṃ svaiś ca māṃsair nimantritaḥ//

It is told that a pigeon
honoured the enemy who had come to him.
He offered his own flesh when asked,
doing what was right.

If this pigeon, who is not even qualified for *dharma*, acted in such a way, why shouldn't we? The hunter was a natural enemy of the pigeon who had actually taken away his wife. Vibhīṣaṇa bears no such relation to us. So then why should we be so harsh and not offer him protection? Needing protection, the hunter by chance came to the foot of the tree where the pigeon resided. He folded his hands and addressed the forest deity (and not the pigeon): 'I surrender to the deity who lives here.' 'Honoured' refers to the pigeon honouring him by throwing his own body into the fire to satisfy his hunger, even though it would have made sense to try to kill him since he was his enemy, a hunter, who had taken away his wife. On the other hand, we honour Vibhīṣaṇa by saying things like, 'Let's kill him along with his ministers with a sharp stick.' 'Doing what was right' means he treated him with respect and without inner disgust until his hunger subsided, as if he were a good friend. Or it refers to his not tricking the hunter with sweet words, etc. 'He offered his own flesh': he didn't just host the hunter and offer him food brought from somewhere, some belongings or some part of his body; he offered his whole body. The ignorant take the body to be the self but the wise acknowledge it as the basic instrument for ethical conduct, and so he fell into the fire thinking, like Śarabhaṅga, 'this is a great penance.'[122]

The story of the pigeon in many ways resembles that of the bear alluded to in the context of Sītā's own protection-granting verse, with Govindarāja again supplying the details. In this case the source is clearer, as the story is described in the Mahābhārata.[123] This time, the imagery is more graphic. A hunter enters a forest, shoots, kills and eats a female pigeon but remains unable to quench his hunger. Falling at the foot of a tree, he calls out to the forest spirit (*vanadevatā*) for protection (*śaraṇam*) with his hands folded in supplication. By chance, this tree happens to be the same one in which the pigeon's male partner resides. This pigeon, hearing the hunter's call for protection, offers himself into fire so the hunter may eat him, despite the fact that this same hunter killed his own partner. The story resembles Buddhist gifts of the flesh and presents a striking contrast to the parallel incident of a hunter killing one among a pair of cranes culminating in the inaugural *mā niṣāda* verse, 1.2.15 (1.2.14), discussed at length in the next chapter. In the *mā niṣāda* verse, Vālmīki's curse of the hunter symbolically prefigures the epic emplotment of the separation of the two protagonists, Rāma and Sītā. A similar set of homologies involving relations between characters is set up here, with the female bird slain clearly standing in place of Sītā and the hunter in place of Rāvaṇa. The homologies resonate with Rāma's own statement in 6.18.36 (6.12.21) that he accepts whomever may have come to seek protection, 'whether he be Rāvaṇa himself' (*yadi vā rāvaṇaḥ svayam*). The interaction between Rāma and Vibhīṣaṇa is thereby cast by Śrīvaiṣṇavas in contrast to the battle with Rāvaṇa that culminates the epic story. As with the story of the bear, the pigeon story structurally resembles a parable – as a narrative of comparison told by one character to another. According to Govindarāja, Rāma demonstrates the fourth valid means, benefit to himself, through his pragmatic political argumentation with the monkeys. And the fifth valid means, his own desire, is apparent in the protection-granting verse with the reference to a previous vow.

A last dimension of Govindarāja's translation from Maṇipravāla, which stands in contrast to his direct incorporation of colloquial expressions, is his reluctance to include explicit references to the oral history of Maṇipravāla interpretations, as is apparent in his treatment of the word 'once' (*sakṛd*) in the protection-granting verse. This single word is given great significance in the two *Abhayapradānasāras*, with Periyavāccān Piḷḷai charting an oral tradition of interpretations dating back to Rāmānuja's original core disciples.[124]

The first cited by Periyavāccāṉ Piḷḷai is that of Kūreśa, Rāmānuja's scribe, according to whom the word *sakṛd* functions as the substitute (*ādeśa*) for 'immediately,' *sahasā*; hence the sense is that protection ought to be granted to one who approaches straight off like Vibhīṣaṇa. Next come the views of Empār, Rāmānuja's cousin, a significant figure in the line of succession but the author of no known works; for Empār, *sakṛd* means *only* once, since before performing surrender one is forever immersed in transmigratory existence and afterwards enjoys eternal happiness. And according to Parāśara Bhaṭṭar, son of Kūreśa and student of Empār, the restrictive pronoun *eva* which follows *sakṛd* means that repeated performances are in fact prohibited (with any semblance of repetition involving only the pleasure of remembering the original event). Vedānta Deśika, in his *Abhayapradānasāra*, interestingly enough, adopts this last position, which is especially notable given the standard Vaṭakalai view concerning the status of secondary acts of surrender. Whereas Teṅkalais adhere firmly to the principle that surrender may be performed only once, Vaṭakalais also consider surrender to function as a repeatable form of penance (*prāyaścitta*). Periyavāccāṉ Piḷḷai's attribution of alternative views represents an unusually explicit presentation of the transmission of esoteric readings through successive generations of teachers and students prefiguring subsequent sectarian conceptions of surrender, even though there is little substantive disagreement between them. It is a mark of Govindarāja's effort to shroud the esoteric interpretations of Vibhīṣaṇa's surrender in a universal idiom that he elides these rival interpretations of *sakṛd* entirely, though they are central to an understanding of the verse most well known to Śrīvaiṣṇavas in these chapters.

Translation between objects, texts and cultures is never a question of mere equivalence between source and target languages, but involves various degrees of refraction. As we have seen, translation from Maṇipravāla to Sanskrit generated very specific distortions: in the *Haṃsasandeśa*, composition in a mode of oral exegesis, adaptation of Tamil devotional styles to the dictates of a Sanskrit classical genre and an idiosyncratic patterning of regional space around religious institutions; in Govindarāja's *Rāmāyaṇa* commentary, the appearance of performative and colloquial elements in Sanskrit scholastic writing and the creative exploitation of Sanskrit grammatical analysis. Absorbing vernaculars into Sanskrit was not seamless but involved suturing and dislocation, creating an effect of 'haunting,' as Jesse Knutson has put it with respect to the incomplete approximation of vernacular prosody in the *Gītagovinda*, and this very incompleteness drew greater attention to the evocation of the vernacular.[125] In this chapter, we have been able to examine the historical pattern of crafting vernacular devotional Sanskrit poetry and commentary through the very broad lens of a wide array of Tamil, Maṇipravāla, and Sanskrit sources; in the next chapter, the lens is narrowed dramatically to focus on a single verse, perhaps the most famous in all of Sanskrit literature.

3 Double reading

In perhaps his most radical interpretive act, Govindarāja uses the trope of *śleṣa*, or double entendre, as a reading practice reconfiguring the verse that is considered to be the origin of poetry itself. Govindarāja stretches the application of Sanskrit aesthetic categories to the epic to the extreme, with the result that this famous verse, the prototype for Sanskrit poetic composition and standard example for definitions in Sanskrit aesthetic theory, is transformed into a Śrīvaiṣṇava benediction. The hermeneutic pyrotechnics involved here – the phonic and semantic doubling of the text into multiple levels, even as interpretation is simultaneously fused with the source – seem to destabilize meaning itself. In this chapter, I engage with this challenging interpretation by exploring a number of related questions. What is distinctive about Govindarāja's doubling of the inaugural verse through *śleṣa* as compared with other forms of figural reading? What factors limit his reading? Are there implicit or explicit norms governing *śleṣa* reading, or is it a total free for all, where one might, in theory, similarly double any text according to whim (and the technical virtuosity of the interpreter)? What are the implications for agency and the Śrīvaiṣṇavas' project of engaging the prior history of reception of the epic? In addressing these questions, I seek to uncover what appears to be a distinct logic behind Govindarāja's interpretation of *mā niṣāda*, predicated on a set of readerly expectations regarding the status of the poem as a work of remembered tradition or *smṛti* and, more generally, on an understanding of the poem's aesthetics of holism and plenitude, where parts and the whole closely reflect each other.

The inaugural verse (known simply as *mā niṣāda*) occurs in the *Rāmāyaṇa*'s frame narrative in the early chapters of the Bāla Kāṇḍa. The immediate setting is as follows. The divine sage Nārada has just visited the poet Vālmīki, recounting to him in brief the story of the acts of Rāma, best among men. Thinking about what he has heard while returning to his hermitage, Vālmīki beholds a painfully disturbing sight: a hunter kills one of a pair of cranes right before his eyes while they are in the act of love. The scene is violent and poignant: the female bird sees her mate writhing on the ground before her while still bearing the marks of their sexual union, and she utters a piteous cry. Vālmīki curses the hunter:

mā niṣāda pratiṣṭhāṃ tvam agamaḥ śāśvatīḥ samāḥ/
yat krauñcamithunād ekam avadhīḥ kāmamohitam//

Hunter, may you never attain stability,
since you killed one among the pair of cranes
engrossed in sexual desire.[1]

To Vālmīki's amazement, these words issue forth from him in metre, with four feet each containing an even number of syllables set to the melody of an instrument and musical time, as he himself remarks to his student three verses later. As we learn, the god Brahmā has just bestowed on Vālmīki the gift of poetic composition.

3.1 The aesthetics of the first verse

Mā niṣāda is taken by Sanskrit literary tradition to be the very first instance of poetic composition, and it is clear that much of its significance stems from the very fact of its firstness, as described in chapters two to four of the Bāla Kāṇḍa. The verse exerted a great deal of influence over the later history of Sanskrit literature, as poets from Aśvaghoṣa on used it as a basis for their characterization of the *Rāmāyaṇa* as inaugural poem, or *ādikāvya*. Scholars have long noted the modelling of the *Buddhacarita* on Vālmīki's epic, evident in the parallels between Rāma's departure from Ayodhyā and the description of Siddhārtha's exit from the kingdom and battle with Māra.[2] The strongest evidence we have for the reception of the *Rāmāyaṇa* as *kāvya* is the plethora of Sanskrit *kāvya* versions of the epic, almost a category of literature unto itself, including some of the most famous works of Sanskrit epic poetry (Table 3.1).

Table 3.1 Sanskrit Rāma *kāvyas*

Author, title of work	*Date*	*Type*
Kālidāsa, *Raghuvaṃśa*	4th or 5th century	*mahākāvya*
Pravarasena, *Setubandha* (Prakrit)	5th century	*skandhaka*
Kumāradāsa, *Jānakīharaṇa*	6th century	*mahākāvya*
Bhaṭṭi, *Rāvaṇavadha*	6th or 7th century	*mahākāvya*
Bhāsa, *Pratimānāṭaka and Abhiṣekanāṭaka*	7th century (?)	*nāṭakas*
Yaśovarman, *Rāmābhyudaya*	8th century	*nāṭaka*
Bhavabhūti, *Mahāvīracarita* and *Uttararāmacarita*	8th century	*nāṭakas*
Śaktibhadra, *Āścaryacūḍāmaṇi*	9th century	*nāṭaka*
Abhinanda, *Rāmacarita*	9th century	*mahākāvya*
Murāri, *Anargharāghava*	9th or 10th century	*nāṭaka*
Rājaśekhara, *Bālarāmāyaṇa*	10th century	*nāṭaka*
Bhoja, *Campurāmāyaṇa*	11th century	*campu*
Hanumān Nāṭaka/ Mahānāṭaka	10th or 11th century	*nāṭaka*
Kṣemendra, *Rāmāyaṇamañjarī*	11th century	*mañjarī*
Jayadeva, *Prasannarāghava*	12th century	*nāṭaka*

Other lost Sanskrit *Rāmāyaṇa kāvyas* produced in this period, referred to in subsequent works of poetry or poetics, include *Kṛtyarāvaṇa*, *Calitarāma*, *Jānakīrāghava*, *Rāmānanda*, *Māyāpuṣpaka*, *Rāghavānanda*, *Svapnadaśānana*, *Abhijātajānakī*, *Abhinavarāghava*, *Mārīcavañcita* and *Rāmavikrama*.[3] These various Sanskrit *Rāmāyaṇas* were produced over a wide temporal and spatial expanse. None radically transforms Vālmīki's narrative structure, except occasionally to elide the events of the Bāla and Uttara Kāṇḍas (as is the case with Bhāsa, Bhaṭṭi and Murāri), revise ethically questionable scenes (as in Bhavabhūti's *Uttararāmacarita* or Murāri's casting of Vālin as the aggressor in his fight with Rāma) or foreground later events (such as Rāma and Sītā toying with asceticism in Bhāsa's *Pratimānāṭaka* or Mantharā as Śūrpaṇakhā in disguise in Bhavabhūti and Murāri). It was this conception of the *Rāmāyaṇa* as *kāvya* that the Śrīvaiṣṇavas sought to engage with in their counter-readings of *mā niṣāda* and other verses in the frame narrative.

Sanskrit Rāma *kāvyas* bore a close relationship with kingship, with historical kings associated with Rāma and the commissioning or composition of specific works by kings; for example, Pravarasena's *Setubandha* (fifth century), Yaśovarman's *Rāmabhyudaya* (eighth century), Bhīmaṭa's *Svapnadaśānana* (eighth century), and Bhoja's *Campurāmāyaṇa* (eleventh century).[4] The epic story's idealization of divine kingship and Rāma's ideal rule (*rāmarājya*) enabled these poems to serve as dynamic vehicles for conceptualizing and celebrating royal power. It is important to note that the production of Sanskrit *Rāmāyaṇa kāvya* continued unabated and was actually heightened after the beginning of the first millennium, when landmark works of devotional and regional *Rāmāyaṇas* were being composed and disseminated. At this time, there was a proliferation of hundreds of Sanskrit *Rāmāyaṇa mahākāvyas* and *nāṭakas*, with the development of novel compositional styles such as double-stream poems (*dvisandhānakāvya*) co-narrating the *Rāmāyaṇa* and *Mahābhārata* through the use of *śleṣa*, the trope under discussion in this chapter. The devotional traditions never replaced the composition of Sanskrit *Rāmāyaṇas*.

In addition to this history of Sanskrit *kāvya* composition, the story of the killing of the crane and the description of the characteristics of the verse that follows in the frame narrative provides the ground for all subsequent theorization of the poem's aesthetic significance. Two features of these earlier readings are especially relevant to Govindarāja's own treatment: first, the perceived symbolic, almost magical, value of the verse; and second, the treatment of the verse as a poetic kernel or *kāvyabīja*.

Beyond its firstness, and the frame narrative's remarkable self-presentation of the verse as the origin of poetic creation, it remains an important question what exactly constitutes the newness of *mā niṣāda*, and Sanskrit literary criticism offers two possible answers: either formal (i.e. metrical) innovation or the poetic transmission of emotion. The emphasis on metrical form has its obvious source in the *Rāmāyaṇa* itself – the description of the creation of verse and of the constitutive features of the *anuṣṭubh* metre in Bāla Kāṇḍa 1.2.18 (1.2.17) and 1.2.40 (1.2.39). Pollock argues that references to metrical innovation serve as a 'synecdoche for the formal innovations of the work as a whole, and these are indeed substantial,' including composition in writing for perhaps the first time after the invention of writing in South Asia in the third century BCE.[5] The position that formal features define the literary is encapsulated most famously by the seventh-century theoretician Bhāmaha's characterization of literature as 'the combination of word and meaning' (*śabdārthau sahitau kāvyaṃ*), often invoked even when repudiated by subsequent theorists.[6] The definition itself appears over-extensive – insufficient to distinguish literature from other forms of discourse – but Edwin Gerow has shown by analysis of the immediate context preceding this phrase that the reference is to literary form and tropology, specifically the joined use of figures of sound (*śabda*) and figures of sense (*artha*).[7]

But if we return to metre itself, the notion that metrical form originated with the *Rāmāyaṇa* appears to be directly contradicted by the existence of the eight-syllable *anuṣṭubh* metre as far back as a millennium before Vālmīki. This incongruity is neatly resolved by Sanskrit critics who delimit the metrical innovation to non-Vedic discourse, for example Bhavabhūti in his eighth-century drama, the *Uttararāmacarita*, and Rājaśekhara in his tenth-century work on literary theory, the *Kāvyamīmāṃsā*. In the *Uttararāmacarita*, a character recounting the curse describes it as 'a new non-Vedic form of verse' (*anāmnāyo nutanaś candasām avatāraḥ*).[8] Similarly, Rājaśekhara foregrounds the distinction from the Veda while linking poetic creation itself with metre. In Rājaśekhara's narrative reformulation, Vālmīki's act of creation is preceded by that of a Poetry Man (*kāvyapuruṣa*), son of the goddess of language, Sarasvatī. Sarasvatī marvels at Poetry Man's use of metre in everyday language (*bhāṣāviṣaye chandomudrāṃ* [*vācam*]), which was previously witnessed only in the Veda (*āmnāyadṛṣṭacarīm*), and calls her son the 'inventor of metrical speech' (*sacchandaskāyā giraḥ praṇetaḥ*). The qualification of non-Vedic discourse extends to the many subsequent references to metre – when Sarasvatī tells Poetry Man that metrical speech is his discovery (*upajñā*) and that earlier 'the learned were only aware of prose, not verse'; when Poetry Man teaches the sage Uśanas metrical speech; and when Sarasvatī later secretly gives Vālmīki metrical speech before he curses the hunter.[9] Here is evidence of the categorical distinction between the everyday discourse of literature and the Veda. As Pollock has argued, the emergence of Sanskrit out of its restricted Vedic liturgical context as a vehicle for imaginative literature, aesthetic experience and political discourse was a moment of historical rupture, where the 'Language of the Gods' entered the 'World of Men.'[10]

Śrīvaiṣṇavas directly challenged this distinction by asserting that the *Rāmāyaṇa* is both a *kāvya* and a work of remembered tradition or *smṛti*. To appreciate the significance of this position, it might be helpful to consider briefly how *smṛti* is defined as a category. While there are a number of criteria for categorizing a text as *smṛti*, the classical, orthodox theory of Mīmāṃsā explicitly ties the concept of *smṛti* to the Veda. As articulated by Śabara in his commentary on 1.3.1. of the *Mīmāṃsā Sūtras*, the Mīmāṃsā category of *smṛti* is based on a clear logical argument: (1) practitioners of Vedic *dharma* perform other acts not described in the Veda; (2) the authority for these other dharmic acts must be lost Vedic texts;

(3) these lost Vedic texts posited by inference are preserved by memory (hence, *smṛti* = remembered tradition).[11] An example of a perspective on the relationship between these discursive categories is that of Bhoja, who distinguishes Veda, *smṛti* and *kāvya* on the basis of the relative dominance of meaning (*smṛti*), wording (Veda) or both wording and meaning (*kāvya*).[12] According to Bhoja, the Veda retains its power even if it is not understood (as in the case of mantras, etc.), but in *smṛti* texts capturing the commands of lost Vedic texts, the wording itself is predominant. An example of an important Śrīvaiṣṇava text engaging these debates on textual authority is Yāmuna's *Āgamaprāmāṇya* (tenth century), which argues against a Mīmāṃsā interlocutor for the authority of Pāñcarātra texts as authored by God and hence an articulation of Vedic commands, though not part of the Veda.

Govindarāja makes his argument regarding the status of the *Rāmāyaṇa* in the general introduction as well as in his comments on 1.4.7 (1.4.6) and 1.5.1. He affirms that the *Rāmāyaṇa* is a *kāvya* (since it 'teaches like a lover' as per Mammaṭa's taxonomy of didactic forms), but he also suggestively extends its status by describing it as an 'expatiation on the Veda' or *vedopabṛṃhaṇam*, a phrase that conforms to the strong Mīmāṃsā position, in effect equating *smṛti* with the Veda.

The significance accorded the innovation in metre by Bhavabhūti and Rājaśekhara enhances the status of the verse. In the *Uttararāmacarita, mā niṣāda* is shrouded in mystery as 'divine speech' (*devīṃ vācam*) uttered by one for whom the universal principle as sound is manifest (*āvirbhūtaśabdabrahmaprakāśa*). For Rājaśekhara, the cosmic prehistory of the verse, now a second act of poetic innovation, removes it from its immediate emotional context and adds another layer of depth. After Rājaśekhara describes the composition of *mā niṣāda*, he adds that Sarasvatī specially blessed it and that any poet who recites it becomes a metaphorical son to the goddess herself. And so it was that, in fact, Vyāsa came to compose the Mahābhārata. *Mā niṣāda* attains the status of a kind of magical formula or *mantra*, carrying with it an intrinsic power to engender poetic creativity. No doubt Govindarāja and the other Śrīvaiṣṇava commentators saw an opening in this special status accorded the verse, whose innocuous content seems to suggest a deeper significance.

In contrast to Bhavabhūti and Rājaśekhara, the treatment of the verse by the early Kashmir aestheticians Ānandavardhana (ninth century) and Abhinavagupta (tenth century) was a crucial part of their argument that the essence of literature consisted not in formal features but the linguistic process of suggestion (*dhvani*), or, more specifically, the suggestion of poetic sentiment (*rasadhvani*). Ānandavardhana's famous *kārikā* on *mā niṣāda* is as follows:

> *kāvyasyātmā sa evārthas tathā cādikaveḥ purā/*
> *krauñcadvandvaviyogotthaḥ śokaḥ ślokatvam āgataḥ//*

> That very meaning (i.e. the suggestion of poetic sentiment, *rasadhvani*) is the essence of poetry. So long ago the grief (*śoka*) that arose on account of the separation of the two cranes became the poetry (*ślokatva*) of the first poet.[13]

The *kārikā* is clearly drawing on the folk etymology and word play of *Rāmāyaṇa* 1.2.18 (1.2.17), where Vālmīki terms his new composition '*śloka*' because it emerged from one overcome with grief (*śoka*) (*śokārtasya pravṛtto me śloko bhavatu nānyathā*).

Abhinavagupta elaborates on this *kārikā* and its auto-commentary in conceptually rich ways, sometimes overwriting ambiguities, substituting perceived ellipses or directly transforming the text. The most significant reversal involves the primary locus of poetic sentiment (*rasa*): whereas for Ānandavardhana, *rasa* (in this case, the *rasa* of pity, *karuṇa*) may be located either in the poet, the character or the audience, for Abhinavagupta, *rasa* is located exclusively in the audience. Ānandavardhana here follows closely the scenario laid out in the *Rāmāyaṇa* itself, with the sorrow of the poet Vālmīki forming the stable emotion (*sthāyibhāva*) of grief (*śoka*) that becomes manifest as the *rasa* of pity. For Abhinavagupta, however, it is the crane who experiences grief and the audience who experiences the tragic *rasa* of pity – not the poet Vālmīki. Abhinavagupta elaborates on the rationale for this position in his comment on *Dhvanyāloka* 2.4 and provides a succinct summary here in 1.5: if the audience were to actually experience grief, it would not enjoy the work of art and some might actually leave the theatre. Moreover, according to Abhinavagupta, it is not the case that poets are in pain when composing poetry. Aesthetic response itself – the experience of *rasa* – is bliss, regardless of the specific *rasa* involved (pity, heroism, passion, etc.).

In order to bring the *Dhvanyāloka* into conformity with his own position, Abhinavagupta contorts the second full sentence of Ānandavardhana's auto-commentary, which reads: 'And so Vālmīki's grief, born from the cries of the helpless crane now separated from its slain companion, became poetry' (*cādikaver vālmīker nihatasahacarīvirahakātarakrauñcākrandajanitaḥ śoka eva ślokatayā pariṇataḥ*). The crucial element is the phrase 'grief, born from the cries of the helpless crane now separated from its slain companion': according to Abhinavagupta, we must supply 'though being relished by him' (*carvaṇāgocaratvena*) as qualifying the word 'born' (*janitaḥ*).[14] The emendation is an explicit effort on the part of Abhinavagupta to exploit apparent ambiguities in the text to justify the identification of grief with the crane but not the poet, the poet being a transmitter and chronicler of emotions rather than someone who experiences them directly. Abhinavagupta applies the analytic categories of the *Nāṭya Śāstra* to the *Rāmāyaṇa* passage: the object of the *rasa* (*ālambanavibhāva*) is the slain bird, the stable emotion (*sthāyibhāva*) is the grief of the surviving bird, the external manifestation (*anubhāva*) is the wailing of the surviving bird and the *rasa* itself is the reception by the audience. By grafting this highly rarefied analysis onto the *Rāmāyaṇa*'s poignant vignette, Abhinavagupta constructs a theory of the communication of emotion through art that ironically denudes art of the actual experience of emotions.

Abhinavagupta here provides conceptual resources for Govindarāja's alternative conception of the functioning of *rasa* in the verse and in the poem as a whole. Drawing from *Nāṭya Śāstra* 6.45, Abhinavagupta argues that although grief as a stable emotion is the source for both the *rasas* of pity and of love-in-separation (*vipralambhaśṛṅgāra*), the grief of the crane is not the grief of love-in-separation because of its hopelessness (*nirapekṣabhāvatvāt*).[15] In his comment on 1.4.9 (1.4.8) Govindarāja first states that his position is that all the *rasas* are predominant in various parts of the poem. Here we begin to see how his sense of the fullness and completeness of the poem with respect to its aesthetic and theological dimensions enables him to apply a range of analytic categories believed to be simultaneously at play in this single text. This is one of several places where Govindarāja provides a perspicacious analysis of the plot structure of the *Rāmāyaṇa* (others include the eighteen esoteric meanings discussed in the last chapter and the various examples of 'indication of the contents of a poem' [*kāvyārthasūcana*] discussed later in this chapter), although here, unlike elsewhere, Govindarāja does not mention any events of special theological significance to Śrīvaiṣṇavas. Govindarāja divides the poem into a series of sections corresponding to each of the *rasas*: (1) passionate love (*sambhogaśṛṅgāra*), the time Rāma spends with Sītā prior to her abduction; (2) love-in-separation (*vipralambhaśṛṅgāra*), the time of separation thereafter; (3) the comic (*hāsya*), the events involving Śūrpaṇakhā; (4) pity (*karuṇa*), the death of Daśaratha, etc; (5) heroism (*vīra*), the events involving Lakṣmaṇa, etc; (6) wrath (*raudra*), the events involving Rāvaṇa; (7) horror (*bhayānaka*), the events involving Mārīca; (8) the disgusting (*bībhatsa*), the events involving Virādha and Kabandha; (9) wonder (*adbhuta*), the battle between Rāma and Rāvaṇa, and (10) peace (*śānta*), the events involving the female ascetic (i.e. Śabarī).[16]

Govindarāja applies aesthetic categories to the epic narrative with a level of detail and precision while seeking to subvert the earlier interpretations of the Kashmir aestheticians, dismissed as 'some' (*kecit*) who, on the basis of 1.2.18 (1.2.17) claim that the *rasa* of pity is predominant in the *Rāmāyaṇa*.[17] Although according to Govindarāja all the *rasas* are predominant, the most important is love-in-separation – precisely the *rasa* singled out and rejected by Abhinavagupta. By shifting the *rasa* of the *Rāmāyaṇa* from pity to love-in-separation, Govindarāja raises questions regarding the narrative structure of the epic: does the possibility of union entail a rejection of the authenticity of the Uttara Kāṇḍa, or does it merely indicate a predilection for theological use, love-in-separation conducing as it does to Tamil devotional poetics?

Govindarāja's reading is anticipated even more directly by a striking aspect of Ānandavardhana and Abhinavagupta's representation of the curse: the reversal of the gender of the slain crane. In the *Rāmāyaṇa* it is clearly the male crane that is killed by the hunter's arrow, but in the reading of both Ānandavardhana and Abhinavagupta the male crane instead laments the death of the female crane. Jeffrey Masson has convincingly demonstrated that the reversal of genders is not incidental but rather a direct re-writing based on a sophisticated understanding of *mā niṣāda* as poetic kernel (*kāvyabīja*), an epitome of the entire epic plot.[18] Scholars have tried to resolve this contradiction by unnaturally splitting the compound in Abhinavagupta's commentary or positing the existence of an alternate recension, but Masson points to the implausibility of the alternative analysis of the compound, the consistency of references to the male crane grieving in several places in both the *Dhvanyāloka* and the *Locana*, and the absence of any extant manuscripts corroborating the putative recension. What is more likely involved, argues Masson, is a parallel between the separation of the female bird from the male bird and the separation of Sītā from Rāma. It appears clear that Ānandavardhana and Abhinavagupta have connected the killing of the crane with what they believe to be the main thrust of the epic narrative – the abduction of Sītā and separation of Rāma and Sītā, the event that allows them to identify pity as the predominant *rasa* in the poem. As we will see, Govindarāja draws heavily on this idea of the verse as a *kāvyabīja* and develops it in such a way that it transcends the existing categories of Sanskrit aesthetics.

3.2 Govindarāja's *śleṣa* reading

We can now turn to Govindarāja's reading of *mā niṣāda* as a *śleṣa*, or double entendre. In order to gauge the novelty of Govindarāja's interpretive practice here, it will be important to identify what exactly *śleṣa* is and consider some of the salient features of its theory and practice in Sanskrit poetics.

Double entendre, or *śleṣa*, is a rhetorical trope in which a single phonemic sequence yields numerous meanings. As Appayya Dīkṣita (sixteenth century) defines it in his classic textbook on poetic figures, the *Kuvalayānanda, śleṣa* is 'the stringing together of multiple meanings' (*nānārthasaṃśrayaḥ śleṣo*).[19] Depending on the type of *śleṣa* and depending on one's language ontology, *śleṣa* may be said to involve homonyms or homophonemic utterances – in other words a complex form of paronomasia. A classic English example is when Mercutio in Shakespeare's *Romeo and Juliet* is stabbed, knows he is to die, and says: 'Ask for me to-morrow and you shall find me a grave man'; here the pun rests on the two meanings of the single word 'grave,' a serious person or a corpse in a grave.[20] *Śleṣa*, however, includes a much wider range of phenomena than such forms of paronomasia, not only multiple meanings of single words, but also alternative splitting of compounds, construing of syntax and even symbolic associations of morphological and phonemic elements. *Śleṣa* emerges as a major category of analysis in Sanskrit poetics and a distinctive mode of composition, with the development of an entire technical apparatus (including associative lexicons) and the production of 'double-stream' poems, *dvisandhānakāvya*, from the beginning of the second millennium. Yet despite this complex diversity, there are certain standard features of *śleṣa* theory and usage against which we may measure Govindarāja's *śleṣa* readings.

As an example, we can turn to a verse from Daṇḍin (eighth century), which Appayya Dīkṣita cites:

> *asāv udayam ārūḍhaḥ kāntimān raktamaṇḍalaḥ/*
> *rājā harati lokasya hṛdayaṃ mṛdubhiḥ karaiḥ//*
>
> Rising in fame, handsome,
> the circle of neighbouring rulers devoted to him,

this king captures the hearts of people
with his light taxes.
(Contextual meaning)

Rising atop the eastern mountain,
resplendent, having a red-hued orb,
the moon captures hearts
with its gentle rays.
(Non-contextual meaning)[21]

Here the *śleṣa* rests on the double meanings of several words: *udaya* (fame, the eastern mountain); *rakta* (devoted, red colour); *maṇḍala* (circle of neighbouring rulers, orb); *rājā* (king, moon); *mṛdu* (light, gentle); and *kara* (tax, ray). Even in this relatively straightforward example, where the doubling of meaning is produced through semantic polysemy rather than phonemic resegmentation, the sophistication necessary for both composing and identifying a *śleṣa* should be clear. *Śleṣa* is not merely a technical device but rather a carefully cultivated, learned compositional practice with identifiable features, and this king–moon verse of Daṇḍin involves a common form of *śleṣa*, with the eulogy of the king expressed through rhetorical comparison. What results is two stable levels of meaning simultaneously co-narrated, producing a verbal effect of doubling akin to the duck-rabbit icon Wittgenstein and others analysed. With this example in the background, I turn now directly to Govindarāja's *śleṣa* reading of *mā niṣāda*.

I cite the *mā niṣāda* verse in its entirety here again:

mā niṣāda pratiṣṭhāṃ tvam agamaḥ śāśvatīḥ samāḥ/
yat krauñcamithunād ekam avadhīḥ kāmamohitam//

Hunter, may you never attain stability,
since you killed one among the pair of cranes
engrossed in sexual desire.

Govindarāja first provides a literal gloss of the verse then explains a grammatical irregularity, focusing attention on elements that become the axis of the *śleṣa* reading.[22] Even though this grammatical problem is not directly connected to the *śleṣa* itself, Govindarāja meditates so microscopically on grammar that the broader context recedes from view. As we have seen, the prescriptive application of Sanskrit grammar to epic usage is a standard feature of epic commentary, but Govindarāja exploits this practice, it would seem, to provide an opening for his counterintuitive second reading of the negative particle, *mā*. The issue is that the verb in the aorist (*luṅ*) retains the augment '*a*,' even though this normatively should be elided to form the injunctive. First, he provides a fairly straightforward resolution by citing the seventh-century *Kāśikā* position that through a different morphological analysis of the negative particle (*mā* vs. *māṅ*), the augment would no longer be prohibited.

Then, as though this solution were unsatisfactory, Govindarāja next refers to another, more unusual explanation, that of the twelfth-century *Durghaṭavṛtti* by the Buddhist grammarian Śaraṇadeva.[23] Śaraṇadeva resolves the problem of the unwanted augment by providing an alternate break of the phonemic sequence. Significantly, this move involves taking the negative particle *mā* to mean *śrī* (or *lakṣmī*, i.e. 'fortune,' 'prosperity,' name of the goddess, wife of Viṣṇu), actually an attested lexical meaning. By avoiding the augment altogether, one may read the phrase as 'O hunter, unfortunate one, may you never attain stability' (*mā niṣāda pratiṣthāṃ tv-ama gamaḥ*). What Śaraṇadeva has done is replace '*tvam agamaḥ*' with '*tv-ama gamaḥ,*' '*ama*' being a *bahuvrīhi* compound meaning unfortunate (i.e. without *lakṣmī, alakṣmīka*). Although Śaraṇadeva's construal is unnatural in terms of word order, it is grammatically plausible. And, again, it serves Govindarāja by providing a precedent for taking the word *mā* to mean *śrī*, albeit in a different part of the verse. The stage is now set for the more dramatic readings to follow.

Govindarāja perceives in the verse the sort of bitextuality we normally associate with *śleṣa*, both the more straightforward kind that occurs in *śleṣas* such as the king–moon example cited earlier (based on semantic polysemy) and the more complex kind involving phonemic resegmentation.[24] An example of the latter, involving the exact same element referred to above upon which both the grammatical reading of Śaraṇadeva and Govindarāja's own *śleṣa* reading rest – the word, *mā*, as referring to the goddess Śrī – is found again in the *Kuvalayānanda*. I cite the half-verse twice to represent orthographically the two different ways it may be read:

(1) *sarvado mādhavaḥ pāyāt sa yo 'gaṃ gām adidharat/*

May the all-giver,
the husband of Śrī
who held up the mountain and the earth,
protect you.

(2) *sarvadomādhavaḥ pāyāt sa yo gaṅgām adidharat/*

May the husband of Umā
who held up the Gaṅgā river
always protect you.[25]

Here the doubling of meaning cannot be confined to a play on the polysemy of single words. Rather, the same sequence of sounds is divided, on the one hand, into the words 'all-giver' (*sarvada*) and 'husband' (*dhava*) of 'Śrī' (*mā*), and on the other, into the words 'always' (*sarvadā*) and 'husband' (*dhava*) of Umā (*umā*). This doubling is made possible by the rules for euphonic combination (*sandhi*) in Sanskrit. While other examples involving resegmentation similarly rest on features proper to the Sanskrit language such as the splitting of compounds, such resegmentable utterances, or oronyms, occur in almost all languages.[26] In English, we find this more frequently in speech than in writing, given the rigidity of writing conventions, in combinations such as 'bean ice'/'be nice.' With Udbhaṭa's (*c*.800) definition, this kind of *śleṣa* came to be known as a *śabdaśleṣa*, i.e. a *śleṣa* in which the phonemic dimension itself rather than meaning is predominant; Govindarāja's construal of *mā*, the crucial element in his reading, closely resembles a *śabdaśleṣa*. The previously cited king–moon example, however, is classified as an *arthaśleṣa*, a *śleṣa* based on meaning.

The *śleṣa* reading rests on both standard lexical meanings and more complex etymologies and derivations.

> The word *niṣāda* means place of residence, i.e. that in which one dwells, derived from the root *ni* + *sad* with the *ghañ* suffix. *Mā* is a name for Lakṣmī, therefore *māniṣāda* refers to the place where Lakṣmī resides, i.e. Śrīnivāsa.[27]

Replacing the negative particle *mā* with *mā* as the goddess Śrī (as taken by both Maitreya Rakṣita's grammatical explanation and in the *Kuvalayānanda*), Govindarāja combines it in compound with the next word, *niṣāda*. Based on the derivation of this word from the first-class root *sad* plus the prefix *ni*, he takes *niṣāda* to mean 'place of residence' (*nivāso*). The meaning for the newly formed compound is 'one in whom the goddess Śrī resides,' i.e. Viṣṇu. The entire verse is thereby transformed into the desired benediction. We should note that this reading, though grammatically plausible, is based on no attested sense of the word *niṣāda*, which is actually derived from a different verb – the fourth-class verb *sad* meaning to scatter or to finish rather than the first-class *sad*. But it is upon this foundation that the entire *śleṣa* reading rests. Govindarāja further glosses the compound as Śrīnivāsa, a common Śrīvaiṣṇava epithet for Viṣṇu.

With this vocative in place – *mā-niṣāda* as Śrīnivāsa – Govindarāja fills out the other details of the *śleṣa* reading.

> O Śrīnivāsa, may you attain eternal preeminence, i.e. may you achieve greatness, since you killed one among the pair of *krauñcas* (demons), Rāvaṇa, who filled with amorous desire abducted Sītā.[28] Here is the basic sense: you protected the three worlds by killing Rāvaṇa, may you always be victorious.

First, the verb, now an aorist and not an injunctive, is understood to function semantically like an imperative. Next, he reads 'stability,' *pratiṣṭhām*, as greatness (*māhātmya*), 'one among a pair of *krauñca* cranes' (*krauñcamithunād ekam*) as Rāvaṇa (paired with his demon wife, Mandodarī), and 'in the thrall of sexual desire,' *kāmamohitam*, as 'filled with desire,' i.e. Rāvaṇa's lusting for Sītā. The *śleṣa* reading in its entirety construes as: 'May you, O Śrīnivāsa, who killed the one among the pair of demons filled with lust, be forever victorious.' It is a virtuoso hermeneutic performance, which completely transforms the verse through the meticulous application of the rules of Sanskrit grammar.

3.3 How this reading differs from *śleṣa*

The way Govindarāja's reading of *mā niṣāda* appears to resemble *śleṣa* – construed bitextuality through both resegmentation (*śabdaśleṣa*) and double meanings (*arthaśleṣa*) – should be clear. I would now like to look at the primary ways this reading differs from the basic theory of *śleṣa*. The relationship between Sanskrit poetics and Sanskrit poetic composition is complex: theory does not involve a straightforward empirical analysis of practice, nor does practice invariably conform to the normative precepts of theory; each rhetorical category is contested and reworked by theorists in ways not reducible to innovations in practice, *śleṣa* more so than almost any other. Yet there appears to have been consensus regarding one dimension of *śleṣa*: the co-presence of *śleṣa* with other figures. For a given bitextual utterance to be characterized as a *śleṣa*, the two levels of meaning usually convey a relationship inherent in another figure (*alaṃkāra*). This second figure may be a simile (*upamā*), metaphor (*rūpaka*) or another of the sense-based figures (*arthālaṃkāras*); Udbhaṭa characterizes this relationship as the appearance (*pratibhā*) of the second figure. The exact nature of this relationship constitutes one of the major points of debate in the poetic tradition, and the central issue is a taxonomical one: if *śleṣa* is co-present with other figures, what determines its autonomy vis-à-vis these figures? Answers to this question range from subsuming all other figures involving *śleṣa* under *śleṣa* itself, as Udbhaṭa does, to taking *śleṣa* itself to be a mere mode of these other figures, as Daṇḍin does.[29]

To illustrate how such a tropic relationship functions in a *śleṣa*, we can return to the king–moon example cited earlier. Here, the relationship between the king and the moon is a metaphor (*rūpaka*), which we might rephrase: the king *is* the moon. This metaphor also governs the double meanings of the other elements of the verse such as fame/the eastern mountain (*udaya*) and taxes/rays (*kara*). Such tropic relationships are easily identifiable wherever *śleṣas* occur in Sanskrit poetry and are in fact often marked by the presence of explicit indicators (*iva* for *upamā*, *eva* for *rūpaka*, *api* for *virodha*, etc.).

One notable exception to this rule, which would seem to provide an opening for Govindarāja's reading to be classified as a *śleṣa*, is Ānandavardhana's distinction between *śleṣa* and suggestion based on the denotative capacity of sound (*śabdaśaktimūladhvani*). In demarcating the domain for this category, Ānandavardhana must differentiate it from *śleṣa* which it closely resembles. A major problem for Ānandavardhana is to integrate the new concept of suggestion to existing categories of rhetoric that he inherits. According to Ānandavardhana, most previous examples of *śleṣa* may now be subsumed under the new rubric of *śabdaśaktimūladhvani*. If the figure related to the bitextual expression is merely implied (*ākṣipta*), it is a case of suggestion; if this figure is directly expressed (through the presence of words such as *api* for contradiction, or *virodha*, and *adhika* for distinction, or *vyatireka*), it is a case of *śleṣa*. Even more apposite to Govindarāja's reading is Ānandavardhana's identification of a variety of *śleṣa* in which no separate figure is present at all: the co-narrating of multiple plot elements (*vastus*). This category would seem to correspond better to the *mā niṣāda* reading than a *śleṣa* requiring the presence of another figure, not only because it is difficult to conceive of a tropic relationship between the two levels as Govindarāja lays them out, but also because it is not clear what could provide the focus of comparison as the word *rāja* does in the king–moon example. Govindarāja's reading could in theory be classified as a *śleṣa* if *śleṣa* were characterized merely as bitextual utterance.

The actual example Ānandavardhana provides, however, is not so straightforward. The verse simultaneously describes the exploits of Viṣṇu and Śiva using the exact same phrase from the earlier example of *śabdaśleṣa* ('the all-giver, lord of Śrī,' *sarvado mādhavaḥ*, and 'always, the husband of Umā,' *sarvadomādhavaḥ*):

> *yena dhvastam ano 'bhavena balijitkāyaḥ purā strīkṛto*
> *yaś codvṛttabhujaṅgahā ravalayo agaṃ gāṃ ca yo 'dhārayat/*
> *yasyāhūḥ śaśimacchirohara iti stutyaṃ ca nāmāmaraḥ*
> *pāyāt sa svayam andhakakṣayakaras tvāṃ sarvado mādhavaḥ//*
>
> May the all-giver, husband of Śrī, protect you.
> He is the eternal one who destroyed the cart,
> who once made his very body that conquered the demon Bali
> into a female form, who killed the raised serpent.
> That one who resides in sound
> upheld the mountain and the earth.
> The immortals praise him as, 'destroyer of the head of Rāhu.'
> He himself gave a home to the Andhakas.
>
> *yena dhvastamanobhavena balijitkāyaḥ purāstrīkṛto*
> *yaś codvṛttabhujaṅgahāravalayo gaṅgāṃ ca yo 'dhārayat/*
> *yasyāhūḥ śaśimacchiro hara iti stutyaṃ ca nāmāmarāḥ*
> *pāyāt sa svayam andhakakṣayakaras tvāṃ sarvadomādhavaḥ//*
>
> May the husband of Umā always protect you.
> He is the one who destroyed the god born of mind,
> who once made the conqueror
> of the demon Bali into his own weapon.
> His necklace and bracelets are serpents
> and he bore up the Gaṅgā river.
> The immortals praise him as, 'Hara,'
> the bearer of the moon on his head.
> He himself destroyed the demon Andhaka.[30]

It should be apparent that this example is not substantively different from the king–moon verse and that a similar metaphorical relationship between Viṣṇu and Śiva could be posited.[31] It seems that this category primarily allows Ānandavardhana to preserve some scope for *śleṣa*, now considerably marginalized by suggestion. So with the exception of this somewhat complex example of co-narrated plot elements, Govindarāja's reading would fail to qualify as a *śleṣa* due to the absence of another figure.

We should note that while Govindarāja's reading of *mā niṣāda* represents by far his most elaborate attempt to read a verse as a *śleṣa*, it is not his only such attempt. Govindarāja tries to read *śleṣas* elsewhere as well, invariably in combination with other forms of figural reading such as allegoresis. As I argued in the last chapter, these techniques were developed and adapted from Tamil Maṇipravāla commentary and oral performance, and their combination with *śleṣa* may involve a kind of concretion, or even literalization, and domestication to categories of poetics more familiar to Sanskrit readers. We saw in the context of Vedānta Deśika's *Haṃsasandeśa* that Śrīvaiṣṇavas read the entire Sundara Kāṇḍa narrative as an allegory, with Hanumān's journey to Laṅkā and the message he delivers to Sītā compared to that of a spiritual teacher (*ācārya*) to an individual soul (*jīva*); many other characters and details also gain an allegorical significance: Rāma is Viṣṇu; Hanumān the *ācārya*; Laṅkā the body; Rāvaṇa and Kumbhakarṇa are respectively ego (*ahaṃkāra*) and selfishness (*mamakāra*); Indrajīt and the other demons are desire (*kāma*), anger (*krodha*), greed (*lobha*), intoxication (*mada*), jealousy (*mātsarya*), ostentation (*dambha*); the *aśoka* grove is the mind or heart; and Sītā is the soul imprisoned in transmigration.

Govindarāja introduces these associations in *śleṣa* readings of two verses in the Sundara Kāṇḍa. The first is the very first verse in the book:

> *tato rāvaṇanītāyāḥ sītāyāḥ śatrukarśanaḥ/*
> *iyeṣa padam anveṣṭuṃ cāraṇācarite pathi//*
>
> Then the destroyer of enemies (Hanumān)
> went by the path of the celestial singers
> in search of the place where Sītā
> had been taken by Rāvaṇa.[32]

Govindarāja evokes the allegory by supplying double meanings for almost every word:

> Here what is described is the essence of being a teacher, that is, seeking out where the student is. 'Then' means after the teacher has obtained the lord's support by communicating secret *mudras*. 'Destroyer of enemies' refers to the teacher casting off ignorance as per the etymology of the word *guru: gu* means darkness and *ru* means to remove. 'The path of the celestial singers' is

> an allusion to previous *ācāryas* and the path they blazed. 'Rāvaṇa' means lack of discrimination, because the etymological meaning of the word is 'causing to roar,' i.e. spreading false speech, and 'taken' means brought under the power of. 'Sītā' is the soul who is dependant on the eternal lord. 'In search of the place' refers to the wheel of transmigration or to signs such as noble speech. Or, on the other hand, 'in search of the place' refers to the soul's determination to attain the lord.[33]

The 'destroyer of enemies' (*śatrukarśanaḥ*) is none other than the *ācārya*, since the synonym *guru* is derived from the syllables *gu* (meaning darkness) and *ru* (meaning destroying). Similarly, 'the path of celestial singers' (*cāraṇācarite pathi*) may be understood as the path of previous *ācāryas* due to the etymology of the word *ācārya* from the prefix *ā* plus the root *car* (hence '*cāranā*' means *ācārya* and '*carite*' means practiced). The rest of the verse similarly is seen as involving near *arthaśleṣas* and *śabdaśleṣas*, as in the commentary on *mā niṣāda*, although here many of the double readings rest on symbolic associations rather than direct bitextuality. In this verse, unlike *mā niṣāda*, however, a possible tropic relationship could be constructed between Hanumān and the *ācārya* (i.e. Hanumān is like an *ācārya*).

The second verse occurs much later in the Sundara Kāṇḍa. As Sītā is sitting forlorn in the *aśoka* grove, Trijaṭā has an ominous dream and exhorts the other female demons to propitiate Sītā. A bird calls out encouragingly from a nearby tree. The verse itself, identified by Govindarāja as an augur (*śākunanimitta*), is mysterious and, like *mā niṣāda*, seems to invite symbolic interpretations:

> *pakṣī ca śākānilayaḥ prahṛṣṭaḥ punaḥ punaś cottamasāntvavādī/*
> *susvāgatāṃ vācam udīrayānaḥ punaḥ punaś codayatīva hṛṣṭaḥ//*
>
> And a happy bird who made that branch his home,
> always chattering sweetly and speaking words of welcome,
> seemed to be eager to encourage her.[34]

The allegory here relates back to the Divyaprabandham commentarial associations of the names of *ācāryas* with specific birds, the apparent source for the allegory of the *Haṃsasandeśa*, as discussed in the last chapter. The immediate scenario directly parallels Hanumān's subsequent conversation with Sītā in the *aśoka* grove, and, as in the *Haṃsasandeśa* allegory, the verse outlines the distinguishing characteristics of an *ācārya*, according to Govindarāja. The word 'bird' ('winged,' *pakṣī*) figuratively means *ācārya* because the wings refer to movement (*gamana*), understood as movement along the spiritual path. The significance of other phrases is also impacted by this identification of the bird with the *ācārya*: the 'branch' (*śākhā*) where the bird is perched now refers to the Vedic branches; 'words of welcome' (*susvāgatāṃ vācam*) now refer to mantras passed down by tradition; the encouragement offered by the bird (*codayati*) now refers to the *ācārya*'s command.[35] In this verse as well, the comparison drawn between the bird and the *ācārya* seems to involve a tropic relationship, perhaps a reflection of broader affinities between allegory and *śleṣa* in terms of the relation between levels of meaning.

3.4 Govindarāja's first *kāvyārthasūcana* reading

Innovative as the *śleṣa* reading of *mā niṣāda* is, it does not exhaust the fecundity of meaning at play in the verse for Govindarāja; rather it is only the first of a series of interpretations which multiply readings for the entire preceding ten-verse passage. Through the rubric of 'an indication of the contents of a poem' (*kāvyārthasūcana*), Govindarāja's interpretive pyrotechnics reaches bewildering levels, with the single word *krauñca* made to yield as many as six different senses. These multiple transmutations of *mā niṣāda* are, however, governed by an observable logic and are directed toward specific hermeneutic objectives.

Govindarāja's *kāvyārthasūcana* readings creatively combine the types of Sanskrit poetic introductory verses—blessing (*āśiḥ*), invocation (*namaskriyā*), and indication of the contents of the poem (*vastunirdeśa*)—a typology first laid out by Daṇḍin and more reflective of *alaṃkāraśāstra* conceptions of the purpose of a preamble than of Sanskrit poetic compositional practice. Govindarāja cites a rule for the two basic forms of the indication of contents in benedictory verses: 'Whether through meaning or sound, there should be some indication of the contents of the poem' (*arthataḥ śabdato vāpi manāk kāvyārthasūcanam*).[36] An apposite example of *kāvyārthasūcana* by sound is the first verse of the *Pratimānāṭaka* attributed to Bhāsa, an important Sanskrit Rāma drama:

> *sītābhavaḥ pātu sumantratuṣṭaḥ sugrīvarāmaḥ sahalakṣmaṇaś ca/*
> *yo rāvaṇāryapratimaś ca devyā vibhīṣaṇātmā bharato 'nusargam//*
>
> May the god of the furrow,
> pleased with good verse, alluring with a beautiful neck,
> and bearing auspicious marks,
> protect us in life after life.
> That awe-inspiring lord is the unmatched enemy
> of the one who caused the goddess to cry.[37]

The verse is framed as a benediction to the god of the furrow, but it also indicates the names of various characters from the *Rāmāyaṇa* including Sītā, Sumantra, Sugrīva, Lakṣmaṇa, Rāvaṇa, Vibhīṣaṇa and Bharata, as well as the title of the play, *Pratimā*. The figurative effect is accomplished primarily by taking literally the names for these characters (e.g. Vibhīṣaṇa as 'awe-inspiring').

Govindarāja's reading projects both the blessing and indication of contents through meaning (*arthataḥ*) rather than sound. With *kāvyārthasūcana* by meaning, there is a doubling of the referents of the meanings of words, rather than words with two separate senses. An example of *kāvyārthasūcana* by meaning is the invocatory verse from Kālidāsa's *Abhijñānaśākuntala*.

> *yā sṛṣṭiḥ sraṣṭur ādyā vahati vidhihutaṃ yā havir yā ca hotrī*
> *ye dve kālaṃ vidhattaḥ śrutiviṣayaguṇā yā sthitā vyāpya viśvaṃ/*
> *yām āhūḥ sarvabījaprakṛtir iti yayā prāṇinaḥ prāṇavantaḥ/*
> *pratyakṣābhiḥ prapannas tanubhir avatu vastābhir aṣṭābhir īśaḥ//*
>
> May the lord who has taken on these eight visible forms protect you.
> He is the first creation of the creator.
> He carries the oblation that is offered according to rites.
> He is the sacrificer.
> He is the two entities that apportion time.
> He pervades space and is heard.
> He is called the root seed of all and
> that by which living beings breathe.[38]

The verse is addressed as an invocation to Śiva, in his eight manifest forms (*aṣṭamūrti*): the sun, the moon, water, fire, earth, air, ether and the officiating priest. As Guy Leavitt shows, each of the seven clauses in which these eight forms are described (the sun and the moon being included in a single clause) respectively correspond to the seven acts of the drama, with the specific form of Śiva and the content of the act of the drama often drawn together by multiple references for the specific terms used.[39] Leavitt argues that the structuring of these indications in the benediction chart a series of concentric responsions, with Act One mirroring Act Seven, Act Two mirroring Act Six, and so on. Leavitt's work has focused on these responsions, which are also found in the poems of, for example, Bhavabhūti, Ratnākara and Maṅkha, as an adaptation of the practice of ring composition which is common in folklore traditions around the world. The combination of benediction and plot structuring, in dramas at least, may also involve a ritual dimension in the relation of the verse to the performance of the *nāndī* at the commencement of the performance.[40] While ring composition is common in literary works, it is also found in Vedic texts and perhaps even the *Bhagavad Gītā*, based on Dennis Hudson's analysis of its 'barley-corn structure.'[41] Drawing on Goldman and Sutherland Goldman's detailed study of responsions in the Sundara Kāṇḍa, Leavitt also persuasively demonstrates that the *Rāmāyaṇa* is *itself* an extended ring composition, and so Govindarāja may very well be tapping into a basic structure of the epic.[42]

The examples cited show that the practice of composing a benedictory verse as a *kāvyārthasūcana* was common, but the rhetorical process involved in such verses was not deeply theorized as was the case with *śleṣa*. The figure that *kāvyārthasūcana* most resembles is the figure of signing (*mudrālaṃkāra*), defined in the *Kuvalayānanda* as the 'indication of the meanings to be indicated' (*sūcyārthasūcana*).[43] *Mudrālaṃkāra* occurs not only in the benedictory verses at the beginning of plays but also in other modes of composition, such as the *Vṛttamaṇimālā*, a work where the names of metres are indicated in each verse, and texts on gemology and astronomy. Appayya sees this same rhetorical process involved 'in dramas in the indication of meanings to be articulated.'[44] The mechanics of this figure are distinct from *śleṣa* in that the double meanings (usually names or titles) are merely *indicated* by the words of the verse and form no secondary level with a coherent syntax. So in the *Pratimānāṭaka*, the names Sītā, Sumantra, Sugrīva, Lakṣmaṇa, Rāvaṇa, Vibhīṣaṇa and Bharata do not come together as a second coherent level of meaning but appear just as individual signposts for the content to come. The same effect of signposting is achieved in *kāvyārthasūcana* by meaning, though the examples and analysis of *mudrālaṃkāra* in the *Kuvalayānanda* more closely resemble *kāvyārthasūcana* by sound.

Another option for classifying *kāvyārthasūcana* by meaning is *samāsokti*, or collapsed expression. *Samāsokti*, discussed briefly in the last chapter, involves an implicit comparison between a contextual object actually described and a non-contextual object based on the presence of shared qualifiers (*samānaviśeṣaṇāḥ*). Some aspects of this figure would seem to correspond to *kāvyārthasūcana* on the level of meaning, specifically the doubling of reference rather than the senses of words. The close relationship between *samāsokti* and *śleṣa* is evident in the fact that it is often the case that the adjectives describing the two objects (the contextually described object and the non-contextually inferred object) in *samāsokti* often bear double meanings and therefore may be said to involve *śleṣa*. The relevance of this theory of the rhetorical effect of *samāsokti* to our understanding of Govindarāja's reading practice is, however, restricted by the considerable differences with the actual practice of *samāsokti*, which is usually limited to obvious parallels between specific objects (e.g. the heroine and a creeper, the hero and a tree, etc.).

Govindarāja's first *kāvyārthasūcana* reading involves an indication of each of the seven books of the *Rāmāyaṇa* (through meaning rather than sound, since the titles of the books are not directly stated):

Table 3.2 Indication of books in the first *kāvyārthasūcana* reading

Phrase	*Meaning*	*Indicated book*
mā-niṣāda	'Śrīnivāsa'	Bāla Kāṇḍa.
pratiṣṭhāṃ tvam agamaḥ	'keeping one's vow'	Ayodhyā Kāṇḍa
śāśvatīḥ samāḥ	'for all time'	Āraṇya Kāṇḍa
krauñca and *kāmamohitam*	'crooked, small' and 'filled with desire'	Kiṣkindhā, Sundara, Yuddha, Uttara Kāṇḍas

So '*mā niṣāda*' indicates the Bāla Kāṇḍa culminating in Rāma's marriage to Sītā.

> '*Pratiṣṭhāṃ tvam agamaḥ*' expresses Rāma honouring his father's vow and indicates the Ayodhyā Kāṇḍa. '*Śāśvatīḥ samāḥ*' is a reference to Rāma honouring the promise made to the sages and indicates the Āraṇya Kāṇḍa. The root *kṛñca* can mean to go crookedly or to be small. Therefore the pair of *krauñcas* is Tārā and Vālin, '*kāmamohitam*' describes Vālin, who abducted Sugrīva's wife, and the Kiṣkindhākāṇḍa is indicated. Or if *krauñca* means small, the *krauñcas* are Sītā and Rāma, emaciated from mutual separation. '*Kāmamohitam*' would then mean Rāvaṇa's 'killing,' i.e. hurting one of them, Sītā, excessively. Or if *krauñca* means crooked in character, the *krauñcas* are Rāvaṇa and Mandodarī and the Yuddha Kāṇḍa is indicated. The Uttara Kāṇḍa is also indicated here, since Sītā was frustrated and hurt in her desire to see the sages' wives.[45]

It is significant that several elements of this first *kāvyārthasūcana* are built around the *śleṣa* reading generating the benediction, with *mā niṣāda* indicating the Bāla Kāṇḍa only when *mā* and *niṣāda* are combined to form the compound meaning 'Śrīnivāsa.' The *śleṣa* reading therefore relates closely to a specific conception of the structural and thematic unity of the poem as a whole.

The individual phrases sequentially lay out this understanding of structure. *Mā-niṣāda* as 'Śrīnivāsa' refers to the union of the goddess Śrī (the meaning of *mā*) and Viṣṇu and therefore also refers to the Bāla Kāṇḍa and the union between Rāma and Sītā. Here, as in the phrases that follow, the events of an entire book are reduced to a single event, the marriage of Rāma and Sītā, in a way that is reminiscent of the weaving of plot elements in the *Abhijñānaśākuntala* benediction, where the responsions do not always correspond to the surface logic of the narrative. With *pratiṣṭhāṃ tvam agamaḥ* the connection to the Ayodhyā Kāṇḍa is developed from the meaning of the word *pratiṣṭhā* as 'completion of a vow,' which Govindarāja associates with Rāma's protection of his father's vow. Here, the shift of the injunctive in the verse to the imperative of the benediction is reversed in favour of the aorist as simple past. The third phrase, '*śāśvatīḥ samāḥ*' as eternal years relates to duration of time; hence the phrase, in combination with the previous one, indicates the Āraṇya Kāṇḍa through an allusion to the vow Rāma makes to the sages to defeat the demons. The idea is that Rāma was true to his word and that of his father through time.

The exploitation of serendipitous associations is evident in the way all the rest of the books – the Kiṣkindhā, Sundara, Yuddha and Uttara Kāṇḍas – are represented by the single word *krauñca*. Several of the meanings Govindarāja cites here are not attested lexical meanings, but rather loose associations based on the root from which the word is derived, *kruñc*: (1) to curve or to make or become crooked; (2) to be small, to shrink (*kruñca gatikauṭilyālpībhāvayoḥ*). The indication of contents of the poem now slides into the word play familiar from vernacular Maṇipravāla. Govindarāja has already squeezed extra meaning out of this word in the *śleṣa* reading by extending it beyond the contextual meaning of cranes to 'demon,' presumably on the basis of the name of the demon who obstructed Agastya and later became the Krauñca Mountain. Now the word *krauñca* is read as referring to the pair of Vālin and Tārā and thereby to the action of the Kiṣkindhā Kāṇḍa, by virtue of the etymological derivation from to go horizontally or obliquely, as animals do. But this polysemous word still has more work to do. With the sense 'small,' (or, by extension, 'emaciated,' *kṛśau*), both the Sundara Kāṇḍa and Uttara Kāṇḍa are indicated, alluding to the emaciation of Rāma and Sītā on account of their mutual separation. Finally, reverting back to *krauñca* as meaning 'demon,' Govindarāja believes the Yuddha Kāṇḍa is also indicated (bringing to mind the separation of the demons Rāvaṇa and Mandodarī as per the *śleṣa* reading).

The specific events conjured by the multifarious work done by this single word, *krauñca*, subtly illustrates how Govindarāja's first *kāvyārthasūcana* reading conforms to the approach of the Kashmir aestheticians. Each sense involves the separation of two lovers, just as the *mā niṣāda* verse itself refers to the separation of the two cranes: Tārā's separation from Vālin, Sītā's separation from Rāma and Mandodarī's separation from Rāvaṇa. The verse as *kāvyārthasūcana* therefore crafts a series of resemblances between characters revolving around tragic themes of loss and abandonment.

3.5 Govindarāja's second and third *kāvyārthasūcana* readings

Govindarāja's creative application of the idea of *kāvyārthasūcana* does not stop here but expands to include two additional readings each retrospectively generating new sets of meanings. In response to an objection regarding the propriety of Vālmīki representing his own experiences in the first fifteen verses of the chapter, Govindarāja develops these new, more elaborate *kāvyārthasūcana* readings. The objection provides Govindarāja with a convenient opening: he responds that the entire passage from verse three to *mā niṣāda* is yet again an indication of the meaning of the poem:

> But isn't describing his own actions like this after beginning by demonstrating his fitness for composing the poem like someone who follows a path to the Mandara Mountain while trying to go to the Malaya Mountains? All he needed to tell us was that Brahmā came and gave him the gift of poetry. Well, here's our response. Listen carefully. As per the quote, 'Whether by meaning or by sound, there should be some indication of the contents of the poem,' the entire passage is an indication of contents.[46]

It is important to note, in the context of Govindarāja's response to the objection, that the chapter in which the *mā niṣāda* verse occurs is actually the second in the Bāla Kāṇḍa, preceded by Nārada's brief recounting of the Rāma story. Since benediction and the indication of contents occur in the first verse of Sanskrit dramas, by identifying these with *mā niṣāda* and the passage preceding it,

Govindarāja is in effect locating the commencement of the poem with Vālmīki's own description of his act of poetic creation.

According to Govindarāja, in the passage beginning the second chapter, two central themes of the epic described in 1.4.7: (1.4.8), 'The Killing of Rāvaṇa' (*paulastyavadha*) and 'The Great Acts of Sītā' (*sītāyāś caritaṃ mahat*), are indicated. The theological significance, particularly of The Great Acts of Sītā, allows the *kāvyārthasūcana* to slide away from the aesthetic focus on the *rasa* of pity to more overtly Śrīvaiṣṇava themes. Just as the *śleṣa* reading generates theological meanings through hyper-aestheticization, so too *kāvyārthasūcana* provides the ground for a theological reconceptualization of the logic of the epic narrative. What Govindarāja does here seems to be unprecedented in Sanskrit criticism, a highly idiosyncratic extension of *kāvyārthasūcana* that often approaches *śleṣa* and yet does not adequately fit into any category of Sanskrit poetics. Both new *kāvyārthasūcana* readings rest on the presumption that Vālmīki's omniscient vision allows him to perceive distant events as if before his eyes, and hence his comments to his student and representation of his own witnessing of the killing of the crane convey prospectively subsequent events in the epic. This lends an additional texture of verisimilitude to the multiplication of meaning. Here Govindarāja's reading is wholly his own and not anticipated by earlier Śrīvaiṣṇava interpreters in Sanskrit or Maṇipravāla.

What Govindarāja accomplishes seems to be some kind of cross between the modes of figuration discussed so far – *mudrālaṃkāra, samāsokti*, allegoresis and *śleṣa*. As with *mudrālaṃkāra*, these new readings explicitly involve *kāvyārthasūcana* on the level of meaning anticipating the plot of the poem, but they are stretched out over several verses and are far more involved than a mere indication of plot elements. More so than in the first *mudrālaṃkāra* reading, the doubling of reference also resembles *samāsokti*. For example, the word *tīrtha* (river bathing or pilgrimage spot) refers in the Killing of Rāvaṇa reading to the sacred Rāma Setu site and on the Great Acts of Sītā reading to the Godāvarī River. But in both cases, the sense of the word *tīrtha* itself has not changed, as with *śleṣa* (e.g. *kara* as rays, taxes). The narrative element also resembles allegory, though the generation of multiple references through the poet's supernatural vision differs from the signifying process usually associated with allegory – signs standing for other signs through symbolic associations. (It also resembles Christian typological reading insofar as events portend other events.) Finally, both the Killing of Rāvaṇa and the Great Acts of Sītā readings approach *śleṣa* at several places. These dynamics may become clearer through an examination of the specific verses involved. Govindarāja does not spell out in detail the new meanings for every word of these verses, and we are left to extrapolate in places or presume that the multiple levels already identified continue. It is interesting that Govindarāja does not allude to the new *kāvyārthasūcana* readings in his commentary on the actual verses involved, but only in the long comment on *mā niṣāda*.

The second *kāvyārthasūcana* reading projects Vālmīki viewing the future event of the killing of Rāvaṇa. The passage begins with Vālmīki pointing out a bathing spot to his student:

akardamam idaṃ tīrthaṃ bharadvāja niśāmaya/
ramaṇīyaṃ prasannāmbu sanmanuṣyamano yathā//

Bharadvāja, look at this bathing spot
free from dirt, beautiful, with clear water
like the mind of a good person.[47]

With the second *kāvyārthasūcana* reading, Vālmīki is seen as viewing with his mind's eye the site of the bridge built over the ocean as described in the Yuddha Kāṇḍa, perhaps considered a sacred bathing spot (*tīrtha*) because of the contemporary pilgrimage site of Rāmeśvaram.[48] This doubling of meaning presumably applies to the intervening verses. Govindarāja next analyses the poet's sighting of the cranes four verses later:

tasyābhyaśe tu mithunaṃ carantam anapāyinam/
dadarśa bhagavāṃs tatra krauncayoś cāruniḥsvanam//

Nearby there, the sage saw a pair of cranes,
chirping sweetly,
moving inseparably.[49]

Govindarāja makes it clear that here and in the following verses, on this second *kāvyārthasūcana* reading the *krauñcas* are Rāvaṇa and Mandodarī as they are in the *śleṣa* reading:

> 'Nearby there,' etc.: with his divine eye, he saw on the bank of that river the 'pair of *krauñcas*,' i.e. demons, Mandodarī and Rāvaṇa, 'moving inseparably,' i.e. enjoying and long-lived on account of Rāvaṇa's boon, 'chirping sweetly,' i.e. taking pleasure in beautiful *vīṇā* music.[50]

Unlike the previous verse examined, here the doubling is not merely one of reference but resembles *śleṣa*. Once *krauñca* is read as 'demon,' other words also bear secondary meanings: *anapāyinam* no longer means 'inseparable' but refers to Rāvaṇa attaining long life through the boon received from Brahmā (*apāya* now meaning 'death' rather than 'separation'); similarly, *cāruniḥsvanam*, which on the literal level refers to the pleasing sounds of the cranes' lovemaking, now refers to Ravaṇa and Mandodarī's pastime of playing a beautiful *vīṇā* instrument (*ramyavīṇāvinodam*). The identification between the slain crane and Rāvaṇa applies throughout the rest of the passage, terminating in the original *śleṣa* reading of *mā niṣāda*:

> 'Among' etc.: 'determined in sin' means having determined that Rāvaṇa was sinful; 'a receptacle of enmity' refers to Hiraṇyakaśipu, Rāvaṇa and Śiśupāla following the lord as enemies in three births; the '*niṣāda*' (hunter) is Viṣṇu, for all worlds reside (*niṣīdanti*) in him; 'the male' is Rāvaṇa; 'killed.' 'His wife' refers to Mandodarī's lament. 'The bird' (*dvijena*) is Rāvaṇa on

> account of his being a Brahmin born in the Pulastya family. 'His head all red,' is a reference to Rāvaṇa wearing a gem-studded crown. 'With' refers to his having companions like Kumbhakarṇa, Indrajit, etc. 'Pity' means disgust, a definition for the word *jugupsā* in the *Amarakośa*. 'This is unjust' refers to the poet beholding with his divine eye Rāvaṇa's actions and then composing the poem, 'The Killing of Rāvaṇa.' Hence what we have here is a summary of the entire *Rāmāyaṇa*.[51]

According to Govindarāja, the epic is referred to as 'The Killing of Rāvaṇa' by unnamed interpreters who assert that it is in fact the heroic *rasa* (*vīra*) which is predominant in the Rāmāyaṇa.

The theological dimension is front and centre in the third, and final, *kāvyārthasūcana* reading. This reading proceeds along identical lines to the second reading, only this time involving another theme, The Great Acts of Sītā (*sītāyāś caritaṃ mahat*). Piḷḷai Lokācārya highlights this phrase in the *Śrīvacanabhūṣaṇa*, as does Parāśara Bhaṭṭar in the *Śrīguṇaratnakośa*. Again Govindarāja generates the new readings by positing shifts in reference and near *śleṣas*:

> Or 'free from dirt,' etc. refers to the Godāvarī River. Witnessing with his mind's eye wicked Rāvaṇa 'killing,' i.e. causing pain, to Sītā, who resided in the Pañcavaṭī on the bank of that river, the poet composed this poem about the life of Sītā. On this reading, 'inseparably' means without beginning or end. 'Chirping sweetly' means being the progenitor of all the Upaniṣads. 'Among the two *krauñcas*,' i.e. among the two emaciated ones, Rāma and Sītā, who were performing asceticism, 'the hunter,' i.e. the one hurting the world, Rāvaṇa, abducted Sītā, and she cried out. 'Bird' means warrior, 'his head all red' refers to his jewelled crown, 'wing' to his arrow, and 'with' to the fact that he intends good for all the world. The rest is the same. The meaning of *mā niṣāda* as a curse is thereby explicated.[52]

The future event Rāma sees and describes to his student this time is Rāvaṇa's abduction of Sītā. The bathing spot refers to the Godāvarī River, and its environs to the Pañcavaṭī hut where Rāma and Sītā resided during their forest exile. On this reading, the genders are reversed as with Ānandavardhana and Abhinavagupta: Rāvaṇa is the hunter, Sītā the 'slain' bird and Rāma the surviving, grieving bird. In this third *kāvyārthasūcana* reading, the parallel between Rāvaṇa's abduction of Sītā and the hunter killing the crane is loose and less dependent on *śleṣa*: e.g. we are told that the violence (*hiṃsanam*) of Rāvaṇa was his inflicting pain greater than death – i.e. the separation of Sītā from Rāma.

We have now covered a series of detailed, provocative readings on *mā niṣāda* and its immediate context in the Bāla Kāṇḍa. Given the numerous ways in which this series of readings breaks with or contorts prior readings, it would be of interest to gauge what the reaction was among other Sanskrit critics. There is some evidence that at a minimum the approach of the Śrīvaiṣṇava commentators appealed to *Rāmāyaṇa* commentators adhering to textual and theological traditions in other ways at odds with those of the Śrīvaiṣṇavas. Govindarāja's reading was appropriated by Kataka Mādhava Yogīndra (seventeenth century) and Nāgeśa Bhaṭṭa (eighteenth century), both of whom utilize a different version of the southern recension and often differ from the Śrivaiṣṇavas in their interpretations of specific verses. While Kataka's commentary clearly adapts the idea of *mā niṣāda* as the *kāvya bīja*, Nāgeśa Bhaṭṭa refutes both Kataka and Maheśvaratīrtha (who neatly summarizes Govindarāja) even as he usurps elements of Govindarāja's first *kāvyārthasūcana* reading.

The Śrīvaiṣṇava influence takes an interesting shape with Nāgeśa's direct critique of Kataka. The major issue Nāgeśa has with taking *mā niṣāda* to be an indication of the contents of the poem rests on temporal grounds: this verse occurs after the events of the *Rāmāyaṇa* are complete: how can it proleptically anticipate something that has already occurred?

> Now we should consider this carefully. Since it has already been explained that the killing of Rāvaṇa already occurred and that Vālmīki asked his question of Nārada after Rāma returned to Ayodhyā, the verse itself would be later. How then does Kataka's idea make sense? Or how would the omniscient poet project something that had already occurred as a future benediction?[53]

In this sense, the frame narrative is seen as occurring at the *end* of the *Rāmāyaṇa*, coterminous with events described in the Uttara Kāṇḍa. Nāgeśa is here demonstrating a literalism with regard to the *kāvyārthasūcana* which he carries one step further. According to Nāgeśa, the hunter who kills the bird does not stand for Rāvaṇa but, on the contrary, is Rāma – literally, not figuratively; Rāma has actually taken the form of the hunter. Why would Rāma do this? Nāgeśa argues that it is because Rāma wanted to test Vālmīki, since only someone full of compassion would be able to narrate the tragic story of the *Rāmāyaṇa*. In addition, in this way Vālmīki's curse serves as a repetition of Bhṛgu's curse of Viṣṇu, as described in *Matsya Purāṇa* 47.100–110.[54]

It is clear that whatever differences other commentators had with the details of Govindarāja's and Maheśvaratīrtha's readings, and despite the significant divergence in their own theological approaches to the epics, the basic shape of the *śleṣa* and *kāvyārthasūcana* readings of *mā niṣāda* was viewed as largely syntonic with assumptions regarding the way the verse embodied the theological significance of epic in an extension of the perspectives of the earlier aestheticians.

3.6 Interpretive bet on the kernel of the poem

We are now ready to return to the questions posed at the beginning of the chapter. Can any verse be doubled in this way as a *śleṣa* or read in manifold ways through the application of *kāvyārthasūcana*? The radical dimension of the discursive effect of these readings intensifies more general hermeneutic questions. What validates interpretation? How do we know, for example, that the *śleṣa* is a constitutive feature of the text or the projection of the reader?

There *are* limits to reading a verse as a *śleṣa* according to the standard practices of Sanskrit literary criticism. Identifying a *śleṣa* is generally uncontroversial because of the presence of one or more features in the textual apparatus, as Bronner has shown, including: (1) the existence of auto-commentaries, explicating the double meanings; (2) specific titles (e.g. on Rāma and Nala or on Kṛṣṇa and Rāma); (3) explicit descriptions of the method of conarration; (4) specific plot junctures where blocks of *śleṣa* alternate with other figures; (5) the existence of words like *iva* or *api*, which are linguistic cues (*nibandhanas*) for the propositional structure of *śleṣa*; or (6) the use of homonyms prone to *śleṣa*; e.g. *kara* (hand, ray, tax), *hari* (lion, Viṣṇu, Indra, yellow), etc.[55] These various factors are conspicuously absent in the *śleṣa* reading of Govindarāja, though like other *śleṣa* readers, Govindarāja does not present his reading as an innovation, as supplementary to the original text.

Śleṣa reading is validated through appeal to authorial intention. Sanskrit criticism is unconcerned with the epistemological problems associated with recovering an author's intention, even if the category of intention (*vivakṣā*) is itself a complex one, as evident in the attribution of intentionality to the authorless Veda in Mīmāṃsā. For Mīmāṃsākas, intention is equated with 'expression' (*abhidhā*) in language itself, voiced paradigmatically by the optative verbal tense. And while *vivakṣā* in literary criticism is usually associated with an empirical author, the term is also used broadly and becomes roughly synonymous with semantic content (*abhiprāya*). The potential circularity of appeals to authorial intention is evident in the examples used to define faults (*doṣas*) of poetry in Mammaṭa's eleventh-century textbook on aesthetics, the *Kāvyaprakāśa*. All of these, as noted by Bronner, involve *śleṣa*, however although the *śleṣa* meanings appear 'intended' by the standard criteria, they are rejected on non-textual grounds such as obscenity.[56] It is perhaps because of the importance of the appeal to authorial intention that Ātreya Ahobila, a commentator writing within a generation after Govindarāja, sees the *śleṣa* meanings as intended by Brahmā (who after all bestowed the gift of poetic composition) and not Vālmīki. For Ātreya Ahobila, two levels of meaning indicate the existence of two separate authors. (Similar strategies are employed for other extravagant examples of *śleṣa* reading, such as Ravicandra's justification of ascetic meanings for verses in the erotic collection, the *Amaruśataka*, through the hagiographical story of the out-of-body authorship of the collection by Śaṃkara.)[57] But Govindarāja does not go down this path.

We may gain another perspective of the limits of Govindarāja's *śleṣa* and *kāvyārthasūcana* readings by comparing the notion of *kāvyabīja* with what Greimas calls isotopy, 'a complex of manifold semantic categories making possible the uniform reading of a story,' also defined by Umberto Eco as 'constancy in going in a direction that a text exhibits when submitted to rules of interpretative coherence.'[58] Eco provocatively brings out the relevance of isotopy to literary hermeneutics through an analysis of an interpretation of one of Wordworth's Lucy poems by deconstructionist critic Geoffrey Hartman:

> A slumber did my spirit seal;
> I had no human fears:
> She seemed a thing that could not feel
> The touch of earthly years
> No motion has she now, no force;
> She neither hears nor sees,
> Rolled round in earth's diurnal course
> With rocks and stones and trees.[59]

Hartman's reading invokes Freud's dream analysis – not the rationalist analytical reduction of the dream, but the indeterminate associations supplying the commentary built up around dreams. Based on linguistic echoes, Hartman perceives 'a series of funereal motifs under the surface of the text':[60]

> Wordsworth's language is penetrated by an inappropriate subliminal punning. So 'diurnal' (line 7) divides into 'die' and 'urn,' and 'course' may recall the older pronunciation of 'corpse.' Yet these condensations are troublesome rather than expressive; the power of the second stanza resides predominantly in the euphemistic displacement of the word *grave* by an image of *gravitation* ('Rolled round in earth's diurnal course'). And though there is no agreement on the tone of this stanza, it is clear that a subvocal word is uttered without being written out. It is a word that rhymes with 'fears' and 'years' and 'hears,' but which is closed off by the very last syllable of the poem: 'trees.' Read 'tears,' and the animating, cosmic metaphor comes alive, the poet's lament echoes through nature as in pastoral elegy. 'Tears,' however, must give way to what is written, to a dull yet definitive sound, the anagram 'trees.'[61]

Eco views Hartman's mild punning as an example of 'overinterpretation' because '"grave" is suggested by a "gravitation" that does not appear in the text; "tears" is not the anagram of "trees"'; there is an 'oscillation between phonic similarity of terms *in praesentia* and the phonic similarity of terms *in absentia.*'[62] Yet Hartman's interpretation is potentially legitimate because it is based on a harmonics or echo effect to the main theme or semantic isotopy, and so Eco concludes that 'the evidence may be weak, but it does fit in.'[63] Though deciding on semantic isotopy – the *aboutness* of a text – involves an 'interpretive bet,' the decision cannot be random or overly vague in order for it to be persuasive but must be based on a context and a conception of the text as a coherent whole.

We can see similar merits in Govindarāja's reading of *mā niṣāda*. The symbolic mysteriousness of the verse and its centrality in the frame narrative virtually begs the question of its relation to the *aboutness* of the poem. These aspects also support Ānandavardhana and Abhinavagupta's analysis of the verse as poetic kernel encapsulating the dominant *rasa* of the poem. The verse may easily be seen as syntonic with other thematic elements in the plot; for example, the hunting accident involving Daśaratha, which bears its own symbolic relationship to events that follow, as pointed out by Wendy Doniger;[64] or the ordeals Sītā is forced to undergo as a result of challenges to her chastity, as well as the overall gendered conceptions of space in the Bāla Kāṇḍa, as Sally Sutherland Goldman has shown.[65] These connections are powerful examples of Ramanujan's notion of textual self-reflexivity. The effort to identify a coherent conception of the whole and its related parts is especially apparent in Govindarāja's *kāvyārthasūcana* readings. The syntactic and semantic reversal involved in Govindarāja's *śleṣa* reading also involves an amplification of a basic feature of the narrative, the identification of Rāma with Viṣṇu (though the conception of divinity has been transformed, as discussed in the first chapter). As with Hartman's reading of Wordsworth, the over-interpretation involved in the *śleṣa* reading benefits from the fact that 'though on the one hand nothing proves that the text suggests' the lexemes *in absentia*, 'on the other hand nothing excludes it.'[66]

One measure of the distance travelled in the *Rāmāyaṇa*'s receptive history is the difference between these various images of what holds the poem together and recent scholarship on the poem's compositional history. Leavitt has focused on the ring compositional structure of the five central books, widely perceived to be older than the first and last books. In the 'major' ring (consisting of the Ayodhyā, Kiṣkindhā and Yuddha Kāṇḍas) the core narrative sequence centres on parallels between Rāma, Sugrīva and Vibhīṣaṇa and themes of royal succession, political intrigue and fraternal conflict.[67] On the other hand, the work of Indologists suggesting that the *Rāmāyaṇa*'s current form represents a fusing of two narratives, each epitomizing the romance and heroic genres, dovetails with Govindarāja's double perspective on the main action of the *Rāmāyaṇa* – as 'The Great Acts of Sītā' and 'The Killing of Rāvaṇa.' And it appears that Goldman and Sutherland Goldman's characterization of the centrality of the Sundara Kāṇḍa's ring-composition to the overall structure of the epic may be supported by a devotional tradition popular among Śrīvaiṣṇavas—the recitation of a 'Gāyatrī *Rāmāyaṇa*.' Through this recitational practice, each of the twenty-four syllables of the Vedic Gayatrī hymn are matched with verses from the *Rāmāyaṇa* spaced into roughly one-thousand-verse intervals. As Goldman and Sutherland Goldman show, Govindarāja and others thereby place the first verse of the Sundara Kāṇḍa at exactly the midpoint of the entire epic.[68]

Yet while the *śleṣa* reading is therefore limited by the need to persuasively demonstrate a relationship between the verse and the overall thematics of the poem, it is also clearly a radical practice placing extreme power in the hands of readers. If we adopt a hermeneutics of suspicion regarding the claimed identity between the *śleṣa* reading and authorial intention, the reading appears to both double the text into literal and figurative levels and at the same time fuse interpretation with the source. Such a practice moves beyond, for instance, Derrida's respect for the doubling or reproduction of the author's act of creation as an 'indispensible guardrail' that precedes any deconstructive reading identifying textual aporias.[69] If, as appears to be the case, Govindarāja is himself supplying the second, *śleṣa* level of meaning, this guardrail has in a sense been cast aside, for the *śleṣa* is presented on the level of denotation as part and parcel of the text itself.

We can further flesh out dimensions of *śleṣa* reading by comparing it with other types of figural reading employed by Govindarāja, such as allegoresis. As discussed in the last chapter, allegory is unknown to the Sanskrit aesthetic tradition. Govindarāja himself does not use the category of poetics sometimes used by Sanskrit critics to incorporate allegory, collapsed expression (*samāsokti*), instead classing it as a subset of 'suggestion on the scale of the entire text' (*prabandhagatadhvani*, contrasted with suggestion on the level of the word, *padagatadhvani*, and suggestion on the level of the sentence, *vākyagatadhvani*) in his commentary on 5.27.61 (5.25.38). This is an interesting perspective, because suggestion in which the literal meaning conveys another meaning (*vivakṣitānyaparavācyadhvani*) seems an accurate way of describing what occurs in allegory, but Govindarāja does not elaborate. And *prabandhagatadhvani* is a term used in Sanskrit aesthetics exclusively for *rasa*.

Govindarāja's allegoresis resembles a form of biblical figural interpretation – termed allegory by Augustine in *On Christian Doctrine* in contradistinction to typology. The difference is between interpretive codes or levels rather than the later fourfold classification designating categories of meaning (history, anagogy, typology, allegory); whereas in typology, the referents or events themselves signify real events in the future, in allegory the meanings of words signify other concepts. So, for example, commentators read the crossing of the River Jordan typologically as indicating something occurring in the future, while meanings like 'lamb' or 'winds' allegorically indicate other meanings like 'Christ' or 'souls.' Martin Irvine summarizes this difference:

> On the semantic level, allegory and typology are distinct: allegory functions on the vertical axis of signification and the correspondences among general terms, whereas typology operates on the horizontal axis of reference and the contiguity of distinct agents and events in sacred history considered as proper names or unique referents.[70]

Govindarāja's allegorical reading closely resembles Augustine's allegory and not typology. (Note that, on the other hand, Govindarāja's idiosyncratic second and third *kāvyārthasūcana* readings do resemble typology.) Not only do the allegorical meanings not signify events, they are not ontological, but rather are embedded in the immediate plot structure. Govindarāja's allegoresis is relatively stable in terms of levels of signification; the semiotic relationship between signifier and signified becomes the new signifier for another signified, along the lines of Barthes's study of second-order semiotic systems.[71]

In *śleṣa* reading, on the other hand, the secondary level of meaning arises from the splitting of the signifier itself (or the relation between signifier and signified, in the case of *arthaśleṣa*). So, whereas the signifier '*ha-nu-mān*' yields the signified, the monkey Hanumān, and this signified in turn produces the allegorical meaning *ācārya*, '*mā-ni-ṣā-da*' itself is split into two meanings. This comparison is made more complex by the many views of language ontology in Sanskrit philosophy (whether a word is defined by sound or meaning; orthography in Sanskrit is not differentiated from sound). But the contrast with allegory should be clear: whereas in allegory a stable literal level remains intact, in *śleṣa* reading the text itself is phonologically and semantically split open. It is this dimension that leads Bronner to argue that '*śleṣa* readers were empowered, perhaps more than any other group of readers in human history, to regenerate and mold a text at will.'[72]

Commentaries such as Govindarāja's have generally been valued by Indologists merely as a heuristic for translation insofar as they reflect the original and narrow the distance between the contemporary reader and the text itself. Such an approach fails to account for the supplementarity involved in any act of interpretation, the absence of hermetic closure in a text, and the productive work of commentary as a concrete intervention in the world. This supplementary distance is especially pronounced when Śrīvaiṣṇava metaphysics are projected back onto a poem composed more than a millennium earlier. Sanskrit commentaries vary widely in terms of purpose and level of interpretive engagement with the source, and it may be useful to compare Govindarāja's commentary with established genres of commentary, as differentiated by Rājaśekhara:

> *vṛtti* (explicating the essence of the source text), *paddhati* (a subcommentary), *bhāṣya* (a polemical commentary), *ṭīkā* (occasional comments), *pañjikā* (grammatical gloss on difficult words), *vārttika* (supplements or corrects the source text).[73]

Rājaśekhara presents a normative rather than descriptive taxonomy, and there is no indication that the composers of commentaries similarly conceived of their works as falling within such categories. But it is interesting how the *Rāmāyaṇa* commentaries straddle these categories: they include simple grammatical gloss, literary criticism and more elaborate theological figurative reading, enabling radical interpretations like Govindarāja's *śleṣa* reading to remain insidious under the cover of more straightforward glossing. (Although the *Rāmāyaṇa* commentaries are characterized as either *vyākhyās* or *ṭīkās* in modern editions, they neither conform to Rājaśekhara's idea of *ṭīkā*, since they include comments on nearly every verse, nor to other *vyākhyās*, which are generally subcommentaries).

These aspects of *śleṣa* reading powerfully bring into focus the historical agency involved in *Rāmāyaṇa* commentaries. Various forms of commentarial literature in many periods constitute a primary mode of intellectual activity in South Asia – examples of the way premodern readers actually read texts – yet we have very few studies of commentary as a historical phenomenon in South Asia. Ron Inden focuses on agency in his discussion of commentary as a way of acting upon the world purposefully and remaking that world, with agents themselves being complex, shifting, overlapping, and often, compounded. Compound agency is an excellent way of describing Govindarāja's incorporation of the amalgam of previous Śrīvaiṣṇava comments on the verse, as well as the intersubjectively shared metaphysics and epistemological commitments of Śrīvaiṣṇava theology. Inden's approach is especially helpful in emphasizing how power is involved in any act of interpretation:

> It calls on its readers as they read the text not only to engage in (or refrain from) textual activity but to engage, to some degree, in other acts as well. The very composition (and reiteration) of a text, the placement of it in relation to other texts, is itself an assertion of relative power.[74]

There is a playfulness involved in the *śleṣa* readings that resembles the performative quality of Maṇipravāla commentaries discussed in the last chapter. As I have tried to point out, this mode of creative engagement with the text also had a distinct logic and was highly purposeful – aimed at credibly challenging one established interpretation and replacing it with another. Govindarāja's counter-reading intended nothing less than to take control over the text, wresting it away from a rival interpretive community. Given the centrality of the frame narrative to the idea of literary origins and the theory of *rasa* in literary art, this was a highly provocative intellectual and theological project accomplished with respect to the *mā niṣāda* verse from within the very categories of the system Śrīvaiṣṇavas sought to subvert.

4 Rāma in the imperial capital

The historical agency evident in the composition of Rāma poems and *Rāmāyaṇa* commentaries may help explain the motivations of agents involved in a parallel project at the same time and place: the construction of the first-ever royal Rāma temples in the imperial capital of the Vijayanagara Empire. Evidence for Śrīvaiṣṇava involvement in the development of Rāma worship challenges causal accounts of Rāma worship as a reaction to Islamic rule in South Asia, which are incompatible with the basic dynamics of the Śrīvaiṣṇava theological appropriation of the epic, as is evident for example in the treatment of Rāvaṇa at junctures in the basic narrative of greatest significance to Śrīvaiṣṇavas. In addition recent studies of the Islamicization of political culture at Vijayanagara erode the idea that Vijayanagara and the sultanates to the north represented oppositionally related civilizational spheres. While scholarly attention has focused almost exclusively on the Rāmacandra temple, the earliest and most well-known Rāma temple at Vijayanagara, less attention has been directed to the existence of at least three other monumental Rāma temples of the fifteenth and sixteenth centuries, whose affiliation is clearly Śrīvaiṣṇava. Moreover it appears that Śrīvaiṣṇavas at some point took over the Rāmacandra temple itself. The Śrīvaiṣṇava association with the emerging Rāma cult coincided with their increasing influence at the Vijayanagara court during the empire's second, third and fourth dynasties, including their service as royal preceptors (*rājagurus*) to Vijayanagara kings.

In light of Pollock's influential characterization of the origins of Rāma cultic worship as linked to epigraphic and literary sources marking the expression of a Hindu identity developed in the face of the challenge posed by the presence of Muslim Others, whose ideology may have represented what he has called an 'unprecedented unassimilability,' the implications of this new perspective regarding the relationship between Śrīvaiṣṇavas, royal agents and the building of Rāma temples has significance for our understanding of the history of communalism in India.[1] Did colonialism construct communalism? Or do communal relations have a history antedating colonialism? Were there in fact proto-communal forms of identification prior to the advent of the British? An alternative analysis may call into question the rigidity of this set of oppositions (presupposing an implicit civilization concept), as well as the isolation of particular institutions (e.g. Islam) over and against others in South Asia during the early second millennium.

4.1 Vijayanagara and other sites

Pollock's argument, developed in his article, 'Rāmāyaṇa and Political Imagination in India,' is as follows. The early second millennium (twelfth–fourteenth centuries) witnessed a sudden revaluation of the *Rāmāyaṇa* narrative in the public discourse of kingdoms throughout the subcontinent. Whereas the *Rāmāyaṇa* was previously an important source for the conceptualization of divine kingship, now for the first time historical kings identified themselves with Rāma; kings actually *became* Rāma, as is demonstrable from temple remains, inscriptions and historical narratives. Texts and ritual practices transformed the *Rāmāyaṇa* into a vehicle for rhetorical othering through the strategic deployment of imaginative resources in the narrative: just as the king was now identified with Rāma, so too demonized Others were identified with the epic antagonist, Rāvaṇa. According to Pollock, this appropriation of the *Rāmāyaṇa* narrative in political symbology was directed towards Muslims and the historically imminent threat of Indo-Islamic rule.

Pollock directly correlates the new centrality for the *Rāmāyaṇa* with the dates of Muslim invasions and the rapid expansion of the Delhi Sultanate. This is tantamount to a *causal* argument. By causal I mean an argument that posits an asymmetric relation between prior and subsequent events and ascribes motives to historical agents.[2] Pollock describes how the use of the epic in public discourse and the resulting royal patronage of Rāma temples occurred 'in reaction to the transformative encounter with the polities of Central Asia . . . and the resultant new social and political order instituted by the establishment of the Sultanate.'[3] The evidence for this conclusion is the concomitance – both spatial and temporal – between events: the raids of Maḥmūd of Ghazna in early eleventh-century Punjab and eastern Rajasthan with the rise of Ayodhyā as a Vaiṣṇava pilgrimage centre; 'Alā al-Dīn Khalji's subjugation of kings in what is now Rajasthan, Madhya Pradesh and Maharashtra with the construction of temples at Rāmtek by the Yādavas; and the appointment of governors of the Delhi Sultanate in the Deccan with the establishment of Vijayanagara with a Rāma temple at its core.

Among the temple sites examined by Pollock, the Vijayanagara Empire (1336–1565 CE) and its capital in the Deccan warrant special attention for several reasons. Vijayanagara was *the* central locus for Rāma worship on an imperial scale. Based on a variety of data, which I detail in what follows, it appears that members of the Śrīvaiṣṇava order were primary players in institutionalizing Rāma worship at Vijayanagara. If I am correct, this may suggest an alternative causal explanation to the concomitance argument. The question I would like to pose is: to what degree is what occurred at Vijayanagara in part the culmination of developments within the Śrīvaiṣṇava order (beginning with the treatment of the Rāma story in temples and devotional poetry from as early as the ninth century) and partnership between Śrīvaiṣṇavas and the Vijayanagara royal elite? While there is no explicit connection between the Vijayanagara temples and the epigraphic and poetic discourses of othering, the extensive corpus of Tamil and Sanskrit poetry and Maṇipravāla and Sanskrit commentary on the *Rāmāyaṇa* examined in the previous chapters may help us infer the motives of Śrīvaiṣṇavas who appropriated the Rāma cult. This literature presents a theological engagement with the epic narrative totally unrelated to the political demonizing of Muslims.

Excepting an uncertain fifth-century Vākāṭaka sanctuary at Rāmagiri, there are no traces of Rāma worship until at least the tenth century, where some notable Cōḻa bronzes provide the first, weak, evidence.[4] These bronzes, which Barrett (1965) and Nagaswamy (1980) examined, are almost identical in appearance, with bow-bearing Rāma (Kodaṇḍa Rāma) accompanied to the right and left by Lakṣmaṇa and Sītā. The bronzes are not attached to existing temples, and their historical significance is unclear. There is also evidence of Cōḻa patronage of temples in Uttaramerūr and in the vicinity of Kāñcī bearing names associated with Rāma, but the actual icon in these temples is Viṣṇu. Although there are descriptions of Rāma iconography in Vaikhānasa Āgamas and the *Viṣṇudharmottara Purāṇa*, these occur in the generic context of the ten incarnations of Viṣṇu, and it is doubtful that the references are to worshipped icons.

Whereas scenes from the *Rāmāyaṇa* appear in temple wall friezes from at least the fifth century CE, the figure of Rāma was not the object of veneration, the actual installed icon, until the sudden emergence of a number of temples coinciding with the expansion of Muslim political power in South Asia. Pollock examines three sites in detail: Ayodhyā, Rāmtek and Vijayanagara, but of these it is only at Vijayanagara that we find a Rāma temple as a state sanctuary and the performance of major royal rituals associated with Rāma. Although Ayodhyā became a Vaiṣṇava centre from the eleventh century with the Gāhaḍavālas, it is not clear that a Rāma temple existed there during the period in question (twelfth to fourteenth centuries). The development of the putative birthplace of Rāma into a place of pilgrimage need not entail a Rāma cult; there is no textual or epigraphic link between these temples and the figure of Rāma. And the complex of four dry masonry temples at Rāmtek is located more than five hundred kilometres from the Yādava capital, with no indication of its centrality to Yādava kingship. There are strong mythic associations for Rāmtek: it is believed to be both the place where Rāma killed the Śūdra ascetic Śambūka and the Rāmagiri where the semi-divine *yakṣa* in the *Meghadūta* is exiled. Besides the Rāma temple, the site includes the surrounding Ghaṭeśvara, Śuddheśvara, Kedāra and Āñjaneya (Hanumān) temples. Rāmacandra dedicated these temples in a stone inscription datable to the last quarter of the thirteenth century.[5]

Hemādri, *rājaguru* of the Yādava rulers Mahādeva (1261–1271) and Rāmacandra (1271–1312), who oversaw the construction of these temples at Rāmtek, was the first to describe Rāma liturgies in his compendium, the *Caturvargacintāmaṇi*, but these appear to be minor domestic rituals, not royal ceremonies. Although Hemādri quotes from a Pāñcarātra source, the *Agastyasaṃhitā*, it seems that this text is likely apocryphal. The *Agastyasaṃhitā* describing Rāma rituals is not among the Pāñcarātra manuscripts H. Daniel Smith collected for his descriptive catalogue more than thirty years ago; instead, he includes an altogether different text bearing the same title.[6] Since the longer version of the *Agastyasaṃhitā* was likely compiled subsequent to Hemādri's citation, we can therefore say that, in effect, Hemādri invented the Rāma liturgies. *Caturvargacintāmaṇi* describes three separate festivals relevant for our discussion: the Rāmanavamī, the Rāghavadvādaśīvrata and the Mahānavamī. Rāmanavamī, the earliest of the three in the calendar during the month of Caitra, marks the birth of Rāma. Occurring during the ritually inactive period of the spring, it could not have been a large-scale royal ceremony; Hemādri's description indicates instead a domestic service. The worshipper is enjoined to fast and sleep on the ground the previous night thinking of Rāma, worship Rāma in the morning, and then dispense gifts to Brahmins. The martial account of the Mahānavamī and Vijayadaśamī is an important precedent for the Vijayanagara royal festivals, but in the *Caturvargacintāmaṇi* they are not explicitly connected to the *Rāmāyaṇa*.

Only during the Vijayanagara Empire, founded in 1336, did the cult of Rāma become significant at the level of an imperial order. Built on a site associated in inscriptions from the eleventh century with the events of the *Rāmāyaṇa*, the city was oriented towards the private royal shrine, the Rāmacandra temple. The geo-mythic associations of the Vijayanagara site are all from the Kiṣkindhā Kāṇḍa, including Lake Pampā (also the name for the consort of Virūpākṣa, the city's Śaiva tutelary deity), the Mālyavanta Mountain, the Ṛṣyamūka Hill and the Añjanādri Mountain, several of which later became the locations for important Rāma temples. While a few pre-Vijayanagara inscriptions refer to these associations from the eleventh century, there is no evidence of pre-existing Rāma worship, barring an isolated twelfth- or thirteenth-century Hoysaḷa *kodaṇḍa* temple.[7] On a special platform at the centre of the city during the nine-day Mahānavamī festival (today called Daśera), Vijayanagara rulers self-consciously identified themselves with Rāma in his triumphant return to Ayodhyā as described at the end of the epic. Archaeologists and historians working on Vijayanagara have never previously considered the role of Śrīvaiṣṇavas in developing the Rāma cult. While the large temple at the heart of the royal centre of the capital, the Rāmacandra temple, has received a great deal of attention, almost all of this scholarship focuses on the structure of the temple and its significance for Vijayanagara kingship, without any consideration of the character of Rāma worship therein.[8] In what follows, I will show that the connection between Śrīvaiṣṇavas and Rāma worship was not an insignificant one but rather the result of strategic partnership between Vijayanagara kings and members of the Śrīvaiṣṇava order.

Existing studies of Vijayanagara present a static, synchronic picture of Rāma worship that does not take into account the shift in royal dynasties from the Saṅgamas, with their Śaiva Kālāmukha affiliation, to the Śrīvaiṣṇava Sāḷuvas and Tuḷuvas. In the next section I therefore examine two phases of Rāma worship: Rāma worship in Vijayanagara as a Śaiva kingdom and Rāma worship in Vijayanagara as a Vaiṣṇava kingdom. In fact, it would be helpful to distinguish between three relevant blocks of time: (1) 1336 to the reign of Devarāya I (1406–1422), a period of eighty to ninety years when no Rāma temple at Vijayanagara existed; (2) the reign of Devarāya I to the reign of Sāḷuva Narasiṃha (1486–1491), a period of seventy to eighty years likely witnessing distinctively Śaiva performances of the Mahānavamī festival; and (3) the Sāḷuva, Tuḷuva and Aravīḍu periods during the fifteenth and sixteenth centuries, when Vijayanagara rulers patronized temples bearing the Śrīvaiṣṇava insignia and had images of the Āḻvārs and Rāmānuja installed in the Rāmacandra temple itself. I focus on the latter two periods, and especially on the last, because this is when both the rapid growth of Śrīvaiṣṇava influence at Vijayanagara and the construction of the majority of Rāma temples occurred.

I support my argument with concrete evidence, as well as a diachronic delineation of periods of Vijayanagara rule. The evidence includes: (1) the dating of accounts describing the Mahānavamī; (2) documentable stages of accretion and augmentation to the Rāmacandra temple and the Mahānavamī platform; and (3) the Śrīvaiṣṇava affiliation of significant temples located along the so-called 'axial systems.' I conclude with a discussion of how this analysis establishes the viability of an explanation of the establishment of Rāma worship independent of any possible reaction to Muslim rule.

4.2 Two phases of Rāma worship at Vijayanagara

Vijayanagara was a Śaiva (likely Kālāmukha) kingdom during the first dynasty of the Saṅgamas. The ensign of the Vijayanagara rulers remained the local form of Śiva, Virūpākṣa, until it was replaced by the Aravīḍu king Veṅkaṭa II (1586–1614) with Veṅkaṭeśvara, long after the kings Sāḷuva Narasiṃha, Kṛṣṇadevarāya and Acyutarāya had replaced Śaivism with Vaiṣṇavism – more specifically Śrīvaiṣṇavism – as the state religion.

The construction of the Rāmacandra temple at the heart of the city, probably during the reign of Devarāya I (1406–1422), marks the first significant step towards the conceptualization of Vijayanagara kingship around the figure of Rāma. It appears clear that Devarāya I and the other Saṅgamas retained the Śaiva form of Virūpākṣa as the dynastic deity for the empire, despite the new association with Rāma. The famous inscription of Devarāya I commemorating the Rāmacandra temple mentions Virūpākṣa's consort, the goddess Pampā: 'Just as Vāṇī supported King Bhoja, Tripurāmbā King Vatsa, and Kālī King Vikramāditya, so Pampā now supports King Devarāya' (*śrī vāṇīva bhojarājaṃ tripurāmbā vatsarājam iva kālīva vikramārkaṃ kalayati pampādya devarāyanṛpam*).[9]

This central place for Rāma in a Śaiva kingdom may be congruent with a peculiarly Śaiva division of labour: while the Śaiva king orients himself soteriologically towards Śiva as ideal devotee, he represents in his own person Rāma the ideal king on earth. The division is exemplified by the respective locations of the Rāmacandra and Virūpākṣa temples. Whereas the Virūpākṣa temple was a public building, the restricted space of the inner sanctum of the Rāmacandra temple indicates that only the king and his priests would have been present at ceremonies conducted therein. According to Fritz, Michell and Rao, 'the limited space within the principal shrine suggests a restricted use (for the kings, his priests, and, perhaps, also his ministers and high officials?).'[10] In addition to the Rāmacandra temple, there are records of grants by Devarāya II (1423–1446) to a few other Rāma temples, including the Rāma temple in the Advaita Raghūttama Maṭha at Gokarṇa. The relationship between Śaivism and the nascent Rāma cult (corroborated by the presence of the early *Rāmāyaṇa* friezes in predominantly Śaiva temples) means that Śrīvaiṣṇavas likely appropriated and adapted existing forms of Rāma worship, perhaps in part to stake a claim on the religious affiliation of the empire by transforming a practice that had become critical to the self-understanding of Vijayanagara kingship. The early Rāma cult could be seen in this sense as the merging of an earlier conception of divine kingship with a new definition of royal sovereignty through endowments to temples and, in the case of Vijayanagara, increasingly at the expense of grants to Brahmin communities (*brahmadeyas*).[11]

The most important festival at Vijayanagara, the Mahānavamī, at some point came to be associated with the figure of Rāma. But what is unclear is *when* exactly this occurred. This festival took place in the month of Śrāvaṇa during the crucial transition from 'passive' to 'active' periods in the ritual cycle. According to Fritz, Michell and Rao, 'At Vijayanagara periods of rest alternated with periods of movement. For part of each year, the king, court, and army resided at the capital; the other part of the year was set aside for pilgrimage and war.'[12]

Our knowledge of the martial and celebratory character of this festival derives almost wholly from the accounts of four foreign visitors: Nicolo Conti, 'Abd al Razzāq, Domingo Paes and Fernão Nuniz.[13] The first two, those of the Italian Conti and Persian 'Abd al Razzāq, are incomplete; in fact, 'Abd al Razzāq describes a festival spread over only three days, occurring at a different time during the year. The Portuguese visitors who provided more complete accounts visited Vijayanagara only in the sixteenth century, at the height of Śrīvaiṣṇava influence in Vijayanagara. It therefore remains entirely possible that the performance of the Mahānavamī transformed from the time of the Śaiva Saṅgama dynasty to that of the Śrīvaiṣṇava Sāḷuva, Tuḷuva and Aravīḍu dynasties. We can note the divergences even in pre-Vijayanagara liturgical descriptions of the Mahānavamī from Śaiva sources to Vaiṣṇava sources, particularly in the addition of a tenth day, Vijayadaśamī, commemorating Rāma's victory in a celebratory public display of power. While in the *Devībhāgavata Purāṇa*, the Mahānavamī ends after nine days, Hemādri's *Caturvargacintāmaṇi* adds the tenth day which became so significant in Vijayanagara.[14] Also consider the Jaina transformation of the Navarātra under the Cālukya king Kumārapāla of Gujarat (1143–1174), who prohibited the sacrificial animal offering (*balidāna*) upon conversion from Śaivism to Jainism.[15]

Given the paucity of evidence corroborating the performance of this festival before the sixteenth century, the *Rāmāyaṇa* association of the Vijayadaśamī, which directly followed the Mahānavamī – the central public festival of the goddess – could itself have been a late development.[16] According to the sixteenth-century accounts of Paes and Nuniz, after the lustration of weaponry on the ninth day, during this tenth day, on a central platform in front of the Rāmacandra temple the king identified himself with Rāma, granted honours and reviewed the army in an ostentatious exercise of military and political power. We know that the Mahānavamī Dibba, the platform just described, was constructed in three stages, the last in the sixteenth century (again, the period of Śrīvaiṣṇava influence at Vijayanagara).

With the end of the Saṅgama dynasty, a discernible ideological shift favoured Śrīvaiṣṇavas and the pilgrimage centre of Tirupati, first with Sāḷuva Narasiṃha (1486–1493) and later with the Tuḷuva kings Kṛṣṇadevarāya (1509–1530) and Acyutarāya (1530–1542). In all periods of Vijayanagara history, kings patronized a wide variety of Śaiva, Vaiṣṇava, Jaina and Islamic institutions; in this sense, the shift was not an absolute one. The close relationship between Vijayanagara royal agents and Śrīvaiṣṇavas is already evident in the Saṅgama period in the response to the sacking of Śrīraṅgam in the fourteenth century by armies of the Delhi Sultanate headed by Malik Kāfūr, when the Vijayanagara general Gopanārya triumphantly reconsecrated the moveable icon protected in Tirupati. As the work of Rangachari (1914–1915, 1917), Viraraghavacharya (1953), and Appadurai (1981) has shown, Vijayanagara royal agents played a key role in institutionalizing the divide between the southern (Teṅkalai) and northern (Vaṭakalai) Śrīvaiṣṇava schools. While the emergence of Teṅkalai institutionalism can be traced to the formation of the Śrīraṅganārāyaṇa Cīyar Ātinam in the fourteenth century at Śrīraṅgam through the partnership between Vijayanagara generals Gopanārya and Sāḷuva Kuṇṭa and Periya Kṛṣṇarāya Uttamanāmbi, Vaṭakalai institutionalism began after 1500 with Kantāṭai Rāmānuja Ayyaṅkār.

During the Sāḷuva and Tuḷuva dynasties, the same period in which monumental post-Rāmacandra Rāma temples were built, Śrīvaiṣṇavas (and Mādhvas) attained unprecedented influence at Vijayanagara. Almost all new temples were Śrīvaiṣṇava, often bearing the Teṅkalai or Vaṭakalai insignia, and several were dedicated to Srīvaiṣṇava deities: Raṅganātha, Veṅkaṭeśvara and Varadarāja, along with images of the Āḻvārs, the saintly figures of the tradition. It was also at this time that the temple of Tirupati began to become an important locus of cultural power, beginning with the change in dynasty with Sāḷuva Narasiṃha. Sāḷuva Narasiṃha had been a patron of Tirupati even before becoming king with endowments through his chosen intermediary, the influential Kantāṭai Rāmānuja Ayyaṅkār. Through his affiliation with the Vijayanagara king, this Kantāṭai Rāmānuja Ayyaṅkār was able to take charge of a Rāmānuja Kūṭa established for the benefit of non-Brahmin Śrīvaiṣṇavas and became the guardian of the gold treasury at Tirupati.[17]

The status of Tirupati continued to rise with the Tuḷuva emperors Kṛṣṇadevarāya and Acyutarāya; Anila Verghese points out that

> out of the 1250-odd epigraphs published by the [Tirupati] Devasthānam there are fewer than 150 records of the pre-Vijayanagara period, while 59 records are of the Saṅgama period, 168 of the Sāḷuva period, 229 of the reign of Kṛṣṇadevarāya, 251 of Acyutadevarāya's period, 176 of Sadāśiva's reign and 192 of Veṅkaṭa II's period.[18]

Kṛṣṇadevarāya made Veṅkaṭeśvara his patron deity, visited Tirupati seven times, and composed the *Āmuktamālyada* in Telugu narrating the life of the Tamil saint

Āṇṭāḷ, an important figure in the Śrīvaiṣṇava canon. Acyutarāya's regard for Tirupati was so great that he had himself crowned emperor first in the presence of Veṅkaṭeśvara at his temple before doing so again at Kālahasti and at Vijayanagara. With the Aravīḍus, Śrīvaiṣṇava influence reached its apogee, with the aforementioned replacement of the ensign of Virūpākṣa with that of Veṅkaṭeśvara.

The construction of Rāma temples at this time and the simultaneous shift in the religious affiliation of Vijayanagara kings were not merely accidental, concurrent events. My claim that the sudden growth of the royal Rāma cult is related to Śrīvaiṣṇava influence rather than to the narratives of othering is based primarily on an understanding of the relationship between these two sets of circumstances. Key to our understanding of this relationship is the identity of those who held the all-important position of Vijayanagara's *rājaguru* in the fifteenth and sixteenth centuries. During this crucial period several *rājagurus* belonged to the Śrīvaiṣṇava Tātācārya family, which descended from Śrī Śaila Pūrṇa, Rāmānuja's maternal uncle who, as discussed in Chapter 2, instructed him in the special meanings of the *Rāmāyaṇa*. These Tātācāryas remained expert redactors and exponents of the *Rāmāyaṇa*. The *Prapannāmṛta*, authored by Anantācārya (also a Tātācārya), recounts the story of two members of this family from Eṭṭūr converting the last Saṅgama king to Vaiṣṇavism through their recitation of the *Rāmāyaṇa*.[19] If scholars have paid any attention to this remarkable account, they have done so in order to refute its historical veracity, due to the absence of any corroborating epigraphic evidence.[20] But the status of *Prapannāmṛta* as a historical document may be more indirect and, in fact, deeper: this account, whatever its accuracy may be, provides valuable insight into Śrīvaiṣṇava conceptions of the role of the *Rāmāyaṇa* narrative as a powerful means for promulgating theology and securing the support of Vijayanagara rulers. Influential Tātācāryas at Vijayanagara included Kṛṣṇadevarāya's *rājaguru* Veṅkaṭa Tātācārya and Rāmarāya's (1542–1565) *rājaguru* Pañcamatabhañjanam Tātācārya.

Along with the Śrīvaiṣṇavas, members of the Mādhva order were critically involved in the intensified Vaiṣṇava influence at Vijayanagara, and they were likely instrumental in spreading the popularity of Hanumān. The height of Mādhva influence at Vijayanagara is observable in the close relationship between the Mādhva leader Vyāsatīrtha and two of Vijayanagara's most influential kings, Kṛṣṇadevarāya and Acyutarāya (though given the lack of supporting epigraphic evidence it appears that the claim of the *Vyāsayogicarita* that Vyāsatīrtha was the actual *rājaguru* of Kṛṣṇadevarāya is hyperbolic).[21] Hanumān figures prominently in Mādhva theology, a fact that may be connected to the ubiquity of iconic representations of Hanumān in Vijayanagara; these are carved onto boulders around the city and are neither found in temples nor accompanied by inscriptions.[22]

Among the Rāma temples of fifteenth- and sixteenth-century Vijayanagara, four in particular merit consideration: (1) the aforementioned Rāmacandra temple (early fifteenth century) (Figure 4.2), (2) the Mālyavanta Raghunātha temple (sixteenth century), (3) the Paṭṭābhirāma temple (sixteenth century, during the reign of Acyutarāya) and (4) the Kodaṇḍarāma temple (early seventeenth century) (Figure 4.1).

Figure 4.1 Śrīvaiṣṇava insignia at the Kodaṇḍarāma temple.

Figure 4.2 Śrīvaiṣṇava insignia at the Rāmacandra temple.

While the fifteenth-century Rāmacandra temple almost certainly did not bear the Śrīvaiṣṇava insignia at its inception, I have observed it on pillars of the walls subsequently constructed around the central structure (see Figures 4.1 and 4.2). Note the similarity between the insignia in a universally recognized Śrīvaiṣṇava temple (Kodaṇḍarāma) in Figure 4.1 and the Rāmacandra temple itself in Figure 4.2. The Rāmacandra temple was the first temple built ornately in the distinctive Tamil style. In the mid-fifteenth-century temple added to the Rāmacandra complex during the reign of Mallikārjuna (1447–1465), images of the Āḻvārs and Rāmānuja appear in the reliefs of the pillars.[23] If the Rāmacandra temple was not explicitly Śrīvaiṣṇava at its inception, it became so within a mere quarter of a century. In the sixteenth century Āravīḍī Veṅgaḷarāju (likely another name for the younger brother of Rāmarāya, Veṅkaṭādri) made this affiliation within the primary temple itself by installing icons of the Āḻvārs, as recorded on an undated inscription on the west wall of the north gateway.[24]

What are we to make of this set of facts? Such explicit markers indicate that at some point in time Śrīvaiṣṇavas likely took control of the Rāmacandra temple, which earlier may not have been closely affiliated with a particular order, or may even have had a Śaiva orientation given the centrality of Virūpākṣa and the centrality of the goddess to the Mahānavamī festival during the Saṅgama period. This fact in and of itself may have far-reaching implications for our understanding of Rāma worship at Vijayanagara. All of the archaeological research on Rāma worship at Vijayanagara, including Pollock's sources, rests on the Rāmacandra temple alone (ignoring the other temples examined below). That this monumental temple eventually became a Śrīvaiṣṇava temple (corroborated by the Śrīvaiṣṇava insignia in Figure 4.2) dramatically demonstrates the close association between Śrīvaiṣṇavas and the Rāma cult in what I have called the second phase.

In contrast to the Rāmacandra temple, other Rāma temples at Vijayanagara have never been carefully studied. All bear either Teṅkalai or Vaṭakalai Śrīvaiṣṇava insignia, and many of them are built on sites bearing associations with events from the *Rāmāyaṇa*. The Mālyavanta Raghunātha temple (Figure 4.3), believed to be situated on the mountain where Rāma stayed before the campaign for Laṅkā, contains a core built around a large boulder dating to the Saṅgama period, but the temple structure itself is from the sixteenth century. In this large complex, images of the Āḻvārs, Rāmānuja and the Teṅkalai insignia appear in several places on the pillars. The Paṭṭābhirāma temple, actually the largest extant Rāma temple in the city, was likely dedicated by Acyutarāya, as inscriptions in the temple are datable to his reign.[25] Another example is the Kodaṇḍarāma temple which, unlike the previous two temples, bears the Vaṭakalai insignia and dates to an even later period. Although here too the images were carved from a boulder, the temple itself is likely from the very last period before the collapse of the empire; it is said to be the site for the coronation of the monkey king Sugrīva, who secured his throne with the aid of Rāma. In total there are eight extant Rāma temples at Vijayanagara. They appear to have been endowed by a variety of groups, including royal agents, subordinate rulers, private citizens and merchant guilds, indicating

Figure 4.3 Mālyavanta temple.

that the cult of Rāma had a life of its own in addition to its significance for the ideology of kingship.

One feature of these newly built temples – their location – may provide an especially telling sign of the relationship between the Śrīvaiṣṇavas and Rāma worship at Vijayanagara. Fritz, Michell and Rao have suggested that the arrangement of temples was organized into axial systems and circumambulatory routes establishing 'the importance of the Rāmacandra Temple as the nucleus of the royal centre,' in effect, transforming the geography of the city itself into an emblem of the identification between king and god.[26] I would like to point out that the surrounding points – the Tuṅgabhadrā River, Mātaṅga Hill and Mālyavanta Hill – gained special prominence in the fifteenth and sixteenth centuries as Śrīvaiṣṇava temples, heightening the mythic associations of these sites dating to pre-Vijayanagara times. Śrīvaiṣṇavas, therefore, would have been agents in the construction of the landscape of the Vijayanagara capital into a virtual theophany of Rāma. The mapping of the identification of Rāma and the Vijayanagara king with the layout of the city was not, therefore, a mere synchronic fact of the Vijayanagara world but rather the result of a collaborative project on the part of both royal and Śrīvaiṣṇava agents. If Fritz, Michell and Rao's analysis of axial systems is accurate, Śrīvaiṣṇavas were crucially involved in the conceptualization of kingship at Vijayanagara.

We must be wary of any effort to treat Rāma worship wholly from the perspective of kingship without consideration of the agency of the actual participants in these practices, the composers and redactors of texts, the liturgists, those responsible for establishing and worshipping Rāma icons. This neglect seems to presuppose some version of legitimation theory – naturalizing relationships of domination and subordination through the use of mystifying symbols and practices, as is apparent in the reliance of Fritz, Michell and Rao on Kulke's (1980) sequential model for royal empowerment. Pollock has developed an extremely nuanced critique of legitimation theory in the context of South Asian systems of culture and power.[27] Legitimation theory does not explain why these signifying practices perdure, nor does it provide a plausible account for the way real historical agents think and act. We need to focus on the complex partnership between royal and religious agents, the role of the religious orders as a constitutive component of imperium.

4.3 From devotional poetry to liturgy

The early history of literary sources integrating the Rāma story into south Indian temples bears out the hypothesis that causal factors apart from the demonizing of Muslims were responsible for the rise of the Rāma cult. This process began in the ninth century with Kulacēkarāḻvār's *Perumāḷ Tirumoḻi*.

The first step in drawing the *Rāmāyaṇa* into the institution of the temple was to identify the figure of Rāma with the worship of Viṣṇu in existing temples. The earliest evidence for this practice is in the poetry of the Āḻvārs, especially Tirumaṅkaiyāḻvār, Nammāḻvār, Periyāḻvār, Āṇṭāḷ and Kulacēkarāḻvār, in both individual verses and entire songs (stanzas or decads). Notable features of the Āḻvār poems on Rāma include: (1) evidence for a separate Tamil oral tradition of Rāma stories; (2) the voicing of parental and erotic love directed through specific characters from the epic; and, most significantly, (3) the superimposition of scenes from the *Rāmāyaṇa* onto Vaiṣṇava pilgrimage sites. In her excellent summary of this material, Narayanan identifies four stories referred to in the Āḻvār poetry which find no precedent in Vālmīki's *Rāmāyaṇa*: (1) Viṣṇu lies as a baby on Brahmā's lap and warns him not to grant Rāvaṇa's boon (cited in Poykaiyāḻvār, Pēyāḻvār and Tirumāḻicaiyāḻvār, the earliest Āḻvārs); (2) Rāma touches a squirrel who assists in building the bridge to Laṅkā, imprinting the three marks visible on all squirrels today; (3) Sītā binds Rāma inside the house with a garland of jasmine flowers; and (4) Rāma shares a meal with Hanumān. Note that all of these incidents involve Viṣṇu's proximity to and intervention in the world (his antipathy towards Rāvaṇa, affection for the squirrel, intimacy with Sītā and accessibility to Hanumān). The fact that these stories are so apposite to a *bhakti* sensibility raises the possibility of an early Tamil Vaiṣṇava substratum of Rāma legends.

In a more direct precedent for the later uses of the epic by Śrīvaiṣṇavas, some of the Āḻvār poets refer to what I have described as the most powerful association between the *Rāmāyaṇa* and Śrīvaiṣṇava iconic mythology: identifying the image of Raṅganātha at Śrīraṅgam as Rāma's gift of a family heirloom (*kuladhana*) to Vibhīṣaṇa as described in the last chapter of the Yuddhakāṇḍa. Periyāḻvār and Toṇṭaraṭippoṭi make explicit mention of this connection. In the *Periyāḻvār Tirumoḻi*, Periyāḻvār says that in Śrīraṅgam the reclining Viṣṇu 'directs his flower-like eyes towards the fortified city of Laṅkā, for the sake of Vibhīṣaṇa.' Similarly, in the *Tirupaḷḷiyeḻucci*, Toṇṭaraṭippoṭi refers to the lord at Śrīraṅgam as 'the king of Ayodhyā,' who 'with his bow, ruined the whole clan of people at Laṅkā.'[28]

I would like to focus in more detail on a few verses from Kulacēkarāḻvār's *Perumāḷ Tirumoḻi* (and the fourteenth-century commentary of Periyavāccāṉ Piḷḷai), whose novelty is difficult to overestimate. Kulacēkara, a ninth-century Cēra king who claimed (hyperbolically) suzerainty over the Pāṇṭiya and Cōḻa regions, for the first time connected the *Rāmāyaṇa* with a contemporary temple site, the Govindarāja shrine at the Śaiva centre of Cidambaram (reconfigured as Citrakūṭa, the mountain where Rāma and Sītā spent their forest exile). Kulacēkara's approach provides an early precedent for the veneration of Rāma in generic Vaiṣṇava temples. We must remember that the construction of temples dedicated specifically to Rāma represents the culmination of developments over several hundred years and that the radical element of the early reception of the *Rāmāyaṇa* in the Śrīvaiṣṇava community was precisely the identification, visually and, for Śrīvaiṣṇavas, ontologically, of Rāma with the universal iconic imagery of Viṣṇu. Throughout the period under consideration, the oral Maṇipravāla discourse and other vernacular forms associated with the *Rāmāyaṇa* occurred in these generic Vaiṣṇava temples and not in Rāma temples.

In the first half of each verse of the tenth decad of the tenth section of the *Perumāḷ Tirumoḻi*, Kulacēkara recounts events from the epic only to assert in the subsequent half that the very Rāma who performed these acts stands before him at Cidambaram.[29] In the first half of 10.1, Kulacēkara identifies Rāma as 'the hero who redeemed the whole celestial world' (*viṇ muḻutum uyakkoṇṭa vīraṉ*), a phrase recast by Periyavāccāṉ Piḷḷai as a reference to Rāma's fulfilling the god's request. In the second half, he compares Rāma with the image of Govindarāja: for Rāma bears the distinctive lotus-eyes of Viṣṇu (*seṅkaṇ eduṅkarumukilai*; Skt *puṇḍarīkākṣa*) and is dark like a big black cloud that has drunk the water of the ocean, leaving behind only sand. Periyavāccāṉ Piḷḷai connects the presence of Rāma with a soteriological objective: he appears in Citrakūṭa/Cidambaram so that those who missed experiencing him in his previous *avatāra* can experience him now. Here we have an institutional parallel to the mapping of the philosophical conception of *avatāra* onto Rāma, since the sensory experience of Rāma facilitated by the Govindarāja image fulfils Viṣṇu's incarnation. And as with all the verses, the lingering last image is a statement of the Āḻvār's own devotional experience: 'When will I see him to the full satisfaction of my eyes?' (*eṉṟukolō kaṇkaḷirak kāṇu nāḷē*). Kulacēkara neatly constructs an imaginative act of worshipping Rāma in a sequence of images, first through the identification of Rāma with the Govindarāja icon and then with allusions to the veneration of that icon by himself and other devotees.

A similar structuring of half-verses can be seen in 10.3 and 10.4. In the first half of 10.3, Kulacēkara ties together Rāma's heroic acts of breaking Śiva's bow (at Sītā's *svayaṃvara*) and winning Viṣṇu's bow (from Paraśurāma), referring to him as '*vīraṉ taṉṉai*' – the great hero. In the second half, he describes the high walls of Cidambaram and his desire to 'worship at the feet of those who worship at his feet.' The first half of 10.4 lists pivotal scenes from the Ayodhyā Kāṇḍa such as Kaikeyī's exile of Rāma and Bharata's receipt of Rāma's sandals; it ends with Rāma approaching the Citrakūṭa Mountain, which provides Kulacēkara with a transition to the second half about Citrakūṭa/Cidambaram. Finally, Kulacēkara says suggestively that those residing in this pilgrimage site, satiating their eyes with a vision of the lord, surpass those eternally in the divine realm (the *nityasūris*), since the latter stray from his presence through their engagement in works. This last statement anticipates the strong Śrīvaiṣṇava view of the icon as an *arcāvatāra* – an actual descent of the lord.

Kampaṉ's *Irāmāvatāram*, whose theological vision contrasts in important ways with that of the Śrīvaiṣṇavas, as discussed in the first chapter, prefigures cultic worship of Rāma in as distinctive a way as does Kulacēkara's *Perumāḷ Tirumoḻi*. As Shulman has argued, the ritualized devotional quality of the narration is related to a fundamental difference in Rama's divinity for Kampaṉ in comparison to Vālmīki: in Vālmīki's *Rāmāyaṇa*, Rāma is a man-god who remains unaware of his divinity except at key moments of recognition, but in Kampaṉ's *Irāmāvatāram* Rāma is god throughout, as is clear to the poet, the audience, many of the characters and (presumably) the hero himself. Shulman has also shown how this difference results in some of the subtlety and texture of Kampaṉ's poem, with the identification of the omniscient god with Rāma's human and sometimes morally ambiguous actions giving rise to irony and somewhat uncomfortable theological implications. If Rāma is God while lamenting after receiving Sītā's jewellery and garments from Sugrīva, the shame he experiences can be understood as God's newfound awareness of the pain and inadequacy of human existence.[30] If he is God while unfairly killing Vālin, the action engenders an implicit, distinctively Tamil theodicy: God is *both* the order and the chaos of the universe.[31] And if he is God while rejecting Sītā after the war, the devastating alienation between the characters is a sign of God's relationship with the world.[32]

This theological vision also paves the way for a worshipful attitude towards Rāma as deity. As discussed by Shulman, the fusion of god and man in the *Irāmāvatāram* involves a reverse movement from the anamnesis that is pivotal to the Vālmīki *Rāmāyaṇa*: Rāma in the Sanskrit epic gains an awareness, as a man, of his identity as a god, but Rāma in the Tamil poem, as god, gains a converse understanding of human emotions and frailties. This gracious condescension parallels the theology of the presence of the lord in icons according to the Śrīvaiṣṇava concept of the *arcāvatāra*, where the infinite is similarly delimited in finite form.[33] The iconic dimensions of the *Irāmāvatāram* are most evident in Kampaṉ's frequent use of clichéd metaphors, removing the action from mundane linear temporality to a mythic context outside of time and yet also oriented to the present. These clichés craft an imagistic, ritualized iconography of the deity.

We can get a sense of the dynamics involved by reviewing just one of the examples examined by Shulman:

> *karu mukil tāmaraik kāṭu pūttu nīṭu*
> *iru sūṭar iru puṟattu ēnti ēṭu aviḻ*
> *tiruvoḍum poliya ōr sempon kuṉṟiṉ mēl*
> *varuva pōl kaluḻan mēl vantu tōṉṟiṉāṉ*
>
> A dark cloud burst out in lotuses
> the two lights of heaven shining far on either side
> over a hill of gold:
> thus came the god who grants the highest way to those of true knowledge,
> upon Garuḍa,
> with lotus-borne Śrī shining by his side.[34]

The simile in the colour contrasts between light and dark involves a comparison that is literalized with the appearance of the goddess Śrī in the second verse. The images evoke the lord's iconic form, from the comparison of Viṣṇu's colour to a dark cloud to the lotus associations with his hands, feet and eyes. Yet the narrative context of the preceding verse, 190, draws this stock imagery into relation with the familiar epic plot. In that verse, Rāvaṇa is said to be without Śrī (auspiciousness), and Sītā's identity with the goddess Śrī for Kampaṉ makes the statement a not-so-subtle allusion to Rāvaṇa's abduction of Sītā and Rama's efforts to be reunited with her.[35] Kampaṉ seems to be accomplishing an identification between the epic story and the iconography of Viṣṇu similar to that of Kulacēkarāḻvār. The theological poetics is oriented towards the audience's emotional response to the god's presence in the world (and withdrawal), making the act of reading an approximation of the worship of the deity.

As with Kampaṉ, a generic Vaiṣṇava liturgical connection with the epic narrative is evident in some important works of Śrīvaiṣṇava devotional poetry, for example, Vedānta Deśika's Sanskrit praise-poem, the *Mahāvīravaibhava.* Some perspective on this work may be gained by framing the *Mahāvīravaibhava* in terms of the broader context of transformations in Sanskrit praise poetry (*stotrakāvya*) in the Tamil milieu from the tenth century. Sustained composition of lyrical *stotras* marks the influence of Tamil devotional genres, as evident in the works of Śrīvaiṣṇavas like Yāmuna, Kūreśa and Parāśara as well as in the *Bhāgavata Purāṇa*; as Friedhelm Hardy has put it regarding the direction of influence between the *Bhāgavata Purāṇa* and Āḻvār poetry, 'the BhP uses the Āḻvārs and not vice versa.'[36]

This transformation of the *stotra* from lists of philosophical epithets to poetic descriptions of icons also involved a revaluation of *stotra* as a form of liturgical utterance or *mantra* in Pāñcarātra Āgamic literature.[37] Interestingly, the *stotras* that occur as part of the *Irāmāvatāram* more closely resemble the older form of Sanskrit *stotra* and are not deeply integrated into the flow of the narrative. The *Mahāvīravaibhava*, on the other hand, incorporates some elements of the intense emotion of Tamil devotional poetry and is marked liturgically by its rhythmic structure resembling mantras and prose-poem (*gadya*) form, recalling the central collection of three prose-poems (*Gadya Traya*) attributed to Rāmānuja. The *Gadya Traya* is widely performed in temples. The liturgical context for *stotrakāvya*, especially of the type adapted from Tamil devotional poetry, makes the recitation of the poem an illocutionary act of prayer. We might note in this context a parallel liturgical use of the Vālmīki *Rāmāyaṇa* itself, though the practices involved are of uncertain provenance. Of interest are the Śrīvaiṣṇava daily recitation (*pārāyaṇa*) of *Rāmāyaṇa* verses and the recitation of a 'Gāyatrī *Rāmāyaṇa*,' discussed in Chapter 3.

The direct Tamil precedent for the *Mahāvīravaibhava* is the genre of *pāṭān tiṇai*, the Tamil panegyric, a genre in the Tamil Caṅkam corpus appropriated by Tamil Vaiṣṇava poets. Although *akam* poetry (poetry of love) more strongly informs Tamil representations of the relationship between soul and god, it is the heroic tone of *puṟam* poetry (poetry of war) that is relevant for understanding this particular model of devotion. *Pāṭān tiṇai*, which is included among the seven subdivisions of *puṟam* poetry in the *Tolkāppiyam*, is the basis for Vaiṣṇava devotional poetry from the earliest examples in the *Paripāṭal* to the poetry of the Āḻvārs, including portions of the *Tiruvāymoḻi*. Ramanujan has traced the correspondences between classical Tamil and *bhakti* panegyrics, noting that 'themes such as praise of a hero's (god's) fame, praise of a victorious hero (god), and praise of a king (god) for providing shelter and security fall into this category.'[38] The hyperbolic praise of *pāṭān tiṇai* conduces to the construction of respectful devotion in the *Mahāvīravabhava*, which differs from the erotic mood of Kṛṣṇa *bhakti*.

The design of the *Mahāvīravaibhava* is as a set of descriptive epithets to Rāma, each recounting a separate episode from the epic; the overall effect is to render every dimension of the *Rāmāyaṇa* narrative into a chronicle of Rāma's heroic exploits, reprocessed through a devotional prism as a prayer. The poem is as a single, extended sentence comprised of vocatives culminating in a final indeclinable ('I bow down to you, again I bow down to you,' *namas te punas te namaḥ*). Each of the vocatives narates a major episode from the epic. An example of the way the poem repeatedly draws attention towards the figure of Rāma is the sole verse describing the acts of Hanumān in the Sundara Kāṇḍa:

> *apārapārāvāraparikhāparivṛtaparapuraparisṛtadavadahanajavanapavana bhavakapivarapariṣvaṅgabhāvitasarvasvadāna*
>
> You made the ultimate gift of an embrace to the best of monkeys, the agile son of the wind, who had spread a forest fire through the great city surrounded by the impassable moat of the ocean.[39]

Rāma, through his embrace of Hanumān, is at the head of the compound and the semantic focus, though it is Hanumān's acts that are being described. Similar is the description of Śatrughna's killing of Lavaṇāsura, rendered subsidiary to Śatrughna's own service to Rāma – 'served by Śatrughna who punished Madhusuta' (*śāsitamadhusutaśatrughnasevita*).[40]

The choice of actual events represented and the length of treatment conduce to the overall heroic mood. Notice for instance the paired descriptions of the breaking of Śiva's bow ('your intoxicated club-arms were powerful enough to break the great bow of Śiva,' *khaṇḍaparaśukodaṇḍaprakāṇḍakhaṇḍanaśauṇḍabhujadaṇḍa*) and acquisition of Viṣṇu's bow ('you showed your supremacy in taking back your own bow,' *nijadhanurākarṣaṇaprakāśaṇapārameṣṭhya*).[41] These images are matched by phrases such as 'one of unimpeded furious deeds' (*anapāyasāhasa*), 'hero' (*vīra*), 'one whose enemies are as non-existent as a flower in the sky' (*khapuṣpitaripupakṣa*), 'lion among the Rāghavas' (*rāghavasiṃha*), etc., and also by the lengthy treatment of the war (stanzas fifty-five to sixty-nine) and the entire Yuddha Kāṇḍa (thirty-one out of ninety-six stanzas or almost one-third of the poem).[42] Typical is the treatment of the killing of Vālin, which relates the heroes, Rāvaṇa, Vālin and Rāma in a hierarchy absent any consideration of the ethical entailments foregrounded by Kampaṉ:

> *vipulabhujaśailamūlanibiḍanipīḍitarāvaṇaraṇaraṇakajanakacaturudadhiviharaṇacaturakapikulapatihṛdayaviśālaśilātaladāraṇadāruṇaśilīmukha*
>
> Your fierce arrow rent the giant, rock-like heart of the king of the monkeys, who was skilled at wandering the four oceans and who once made Rāvaṇa anxious by tightly squeezing his vast, mountain-like arm.[43]

Despite the elements reminiscent of the panegyric style of *pāṭāṇ tiṇai*, the poem is an ornate Sanskrit *kāvya*, replete with elaborate compounding and the frequent use of the sound figure of phonemic repetition (*anuprāsa*), which contributes to its rhythmic, recitational quality. An excellent example of such *anuprāsa* is the seventh stanza describing Rāma's birth:

> *kosalasutākumārabhāvakañcukitakāraṇākāra*
>
> Since the whole universe comes into existence depending on you, you are the ultimate cause. Yet hiding this fact from everyone, you were born as a son to Kausalyā just like any other child.[44]

The repetition of initial 'k' sounds is straightforward alliteration, but more complex forms of *anuprāsa* occur in other stanzas, for example 14 and 44. Note the repetition of whole syllables in each of these verses (*locana* in 14 and *dakṣa* in 44):

> *maithilanagarasulocanālocanacakoracandra*
>
> You were like a moon to the partridge-eyes of the beautiful-eyed women of Maithila.[45]
>
> *dṛḍhaghaṭitakailāsakoṭivikaṭadundubhikaṅkālakūṭadūravikṣepa-dakṣadakṣiṇetarapādāṅguṣṭhadaracalanaviśvastasuhṛdāśaya*
>
> He reassured the heart of his friend by moving his little left toe slightly, which was capable of casting away the pile of bones of Duṇḍubhi. Those bones were very hard and as massive as Kailāsa.[46]

These and other rhetorical effects of the poem make it, like other examples of *stotrakāvya* from this period, both an aesthetic and a ritual object, and in this sense the poem redirects the receptive history of Sanskrit Rāma *kāvya* no less than the *Haṃsasandeśa* or the *Pādukāsahasra*.

The *Mahāvīravaibhava* makes an occasional nod to incidents in the epic that are especially favoured by Śrīvaiṣṇavas, but it is otherwise cast in a universal Vaiṣṇava mould. The poem does include brief references to the *kākāsura* incidents (26–27) and Vibhīṣaṇa's surrender (48–49). However, in this poem Rāma's salvific relationship with the world does not take on overtly Śrīvaiṣṇava theological associations (typical, for example, is the generic description of Rāma as *bhavatapanatāpitabhaktajanabhadrārāma*, 'the auspicious relief to devotees oppressed by the burning of transmigration.'[47] In both its rendering of events and basic theology, the *Mahāvīravaibhava* presents an intermediate vision between the deep interpretive engagement with the epic in Maṇipravāla sources and the image of ideal kingship that would later be enacted in the Mahānavamī festival at Vijayanagara. The poem makes the connection with divine kingship explicit towards the very end, upon Rāma's return to Ayodhyā:

> *hāṭakagirikaṭakalaḍahapādapīṭhanikaṭataṭapariluṭhitanikhilanṛpatikirīṭa-koṭivividhamaṇigaṇakiraṇanikaranirājitacaraṇarājīva*

Your lotus feet were lustrated with the mass of rays from the collection of variegated jewels in all the crowns of the kings who were defeated. They bowed down near your footstool, which was as beautiful as the arm-bracelet of Mount Meru.

divyabhaumāyodhyādhidaivata

You who are the presiding deity of the divine and earthly sites of Ayodhyā.

pitṛvadhakupitaparaśudharamunivihitanṛpahananakadanapūrvakāla prabhavaśataguṇapratiṣṭāpitadhārmikarājavaṃśa

You established a *dhārmika* royal line possessing a hundred times the virtues manifest in the time before the killing of kings by Paraśurāma, who was angry at the murder of his father.[48]

Here we can see the two conceptions of divinity described in the first chapter – Rāma as divine king and Rāma as the embodiment of Śrīvaiṣṇava conceptions of the godhead – collapsed together. There is some evidence that this distinctively Vaiṣṇava (Śrīvaiṣṇava-inflected) theological conception of divine kingship eventually became a model for Vijayanagara kings, seen for example in the homology between the appearance of Kṛṣṇadevarāya and his wives, on the one hand, and Veṅkaṭeśvara and Bhū and Lakṣmī, on the other, in the famous life-sized portrait sculptures of the Kṛṣṇadevarāya at Tirupati.

4.4 Rāvaṇa and Vibhīṣaṇa

If we return to the vast corpus of material examined so far in this book, the content of the devotional engagement with the epic appears even less focused on the mythopoetics of othering. This is the richest and deepest source for reconstructing Rāma *bhakti* as an antecedent for Rāma worship in relation to what took place at the Vijayanagara capital, in part because Govindarāja and others wrote at the Ahobila Maṭha, an institution heavily patronized by Vijayanagara kings during the exact time in the mid-fifteenth to sixteenth centuries when the Rāma temples were being constructed. Establishing a connection between Śrīvaiṣṇava devotionalism and the Rāma temples at Vijayanagara allows us to look at the political use of the epic in a new light. None of the Śrīvaiṣṇava Maṇipravāla or Sanskrit commentaries speak of Muslims.

We can observe the marked difference between the thematics of these commentaries and the inscriptions and historical narratives from the northwest such as the *Pṛthvīrājavijaya* corpus, which do demonize Muslims, by returning to the most significant encounter with a demon, and the most politically and theologically charged event in the epic for Śrīvaiṣṇavas: Vibhīṣaṇa's surrender. Śrīvaiṣṇava interpretations cleave to the central dynamic of the epic narrative, valorizing Rama's defeat of Rāvaṇa (evident in their configuration of the benediction in the *śleṣa* reading of *mā niṣāda* around this event). But the emphasis of Śrīvaiṣṇavas on the counter-narrative implicit in their reading of Vibhīṣaṇa's surrender indicates that the eventual killing of Rāvaṇa is not really of most significance to them. Recall how after rebutting the sceptical monkeys, Rāma asks Sugrīva to bring forward whoever is asking for protection, whether he be Vibhīṣaṇa 'or Rāvaṇa himself' (*yadi vā rāvaṇaḥ svayam*). As is evident in Govindarāja's commentary on the verse', the demons – Vibhīṣaṇa and even Rāvaṇa – are, according to the Śrīvaiṣṇava reading, the recipients of theological grace, rather than the object of othering:

> *ānayainaṃ hariṣreṣṭha dattam asyābhayaṃ mayā/*
> *vibhīṣaṇo vā sugrīva yadi vā rāvaṇaḥ svayam//*
>
> Bring him forward, O best of monkeys,
> after assuring him of my protection,
> whether he be Vibhīṣaṇa or Rāvaṇa himself, Sugrīva.
>
> 'Whether he be Vibhīṣaṇa' implies that since Vibhīṣaṇa is righteous, accepting him is not anything special. Accepting unrighteous Rāvaṇa would really be special. If we accept Vibhīṣaṇa and his attendants, we are protecting just four people. But if we accept Rāvaṇa, we would be able to protect all of Laṅkā, and that would be fabulous. Or leave aside the doubt you have because of Vibhīṣaṇa's close connection with Rāvaṇa. Let Rāvaṇa himself come, even if he doesn't bring Sītā with him. Or even if this person is not Vibhīṣaṇa but actually Rāvaṇa himself in another form, pretending to be Vibhīṣaṇa, still I will protect him. Don't come again just to tell me: 'This is Rāvaṇa, not Vibhīṣaṇa.' Just bring him.[49]

Govindarāja implies that Rāma seems to be favouring the possibility that the demon at hand is Rāvaṇa and not Vibhīṣaṇa, since he secretly desires to offer protection to Rāvaṇa.

This perspective on Rāvaṇa also occurs elsewhere in Govindarāja's commentary, where he elaborates what he takes to be the theological implications of other signs that Rāma's grace is specially inclined in favour of Rāvaṇa. For example, when Aṅgada is sent as a messenger to Rāvaṇa, Rāma conveys the message that if Rāvaṇa does not surrender he will rid the world of demons. According to Govindarāja, what this means is that Rāma really wants to forgive Rāvaṇa, so long as he *does* surrender.

> *arākṣasam imaṃ lokaṃ kartāsmi niśitaiḥ śaraiḥ/*
> *na cec charaṇam abheṣi mām upādāya maithilīm//*
>
> I will rid this world of demons
> with my sharp arrows
> if you don't return Sītā and surrender.
>
> If you don't return Sītā and surrender, I will rid the world of demons. But if you do surrender to me, I will forgive you. 'If you don't return Sītā,' means that just as someone who steals gold cannot receive absolution unless they return the gold, so it is for you if you don't return Sītā. But, Rāvaṇa, the point is, if you surrender I'll send Vibhīṣaṇa to be king of Kosala.[50]

Govindarāja transforms what appears to be a belligerent challenge to Rāvaṇa into the Śrīvaiṣṇavas' favoured imagined scenario of Rāma granting Rāvaṇa protection. Later, when Rāma does not kill Rāvaṇa when he is exhausted in the battlefield but gives him another chance to return after he has rested, Govindarāja again sees a theological implication:

> *kṛtaṃ tvayā karma mahat subhīmaṃ hatapravīraś ca kṛtas tvayāham/*
> *tasmāt pariṣrānta iva vyavasya na tvāṃ śarair mṛtyuvaśaṃ nayāmi//*
>
> You have done great and terrifying acts
> and you have destroyed many of my warriors.
> Therefore, seeing that you seem exhausted,
> I will not use my arrows
> and bring you under the power of death.[51]

According to Govindarāja, the lord's generosity (*audārya*) is on display here, for his protection is conferred on Rāvaṇa though the latter does nothing at all – in fact dropping his bow and relinquishing effort altogether (thereby submitting to the will of the lord) (*ābhyāṃ ślokābhyāṃ bhagavadrakṣaṇe nimittaṃ svaprayatnanivṛttir eva ity uktam*). This is a clear Teṅkalai position regarding God's unconditional grace. Govindarāja often incorporates such Teṅkalai positions indiscriminately from Maṇipravāla sources, though the commentary as a whole cannot be pinned down to either a Teṅkalai or Vaḍakalai affiliation. Vedānta Deśika's *Mahāvīravaibhava* also devotes a stanza (58) to this event.

If we factor in the trajectory of Śrīvaiṣṇava engagement with the *Rāmāyaṇa*, it appears that the Rāma cult involved the confluence of a number of complementary circumstances and agendas, including this heightened conception of the divinity of Rāma and the integration of the Rāmāyaṇa story into Śrīvaiṣṇava temples, the proximity to imperial power of Śrīvaiṣṇavas in the fifteenth and sixteenth centuries, the shift towards temple donation as the primary form of royal gift-giving in the post-Cōḻa era, the identification of historical kings with Rāma, and the pre-Vijayanagara mythic associations of the site.

4.5 Islamicization and Persian culture in the Deccan

It is important to frame our understanding of the relationship between Vijayanagara and the expansion of the Delhi Sultanate and successor sultanate states in the Deccan in light of the recent scholarship of Philip Wagoner and Richard Eaton on the 'Islamicization' of Hindu culture at Vijayanagara, which casts doubt on nationalist characterizations of the Vijayanagara state's resistance to Islamic rule. Wagoner defines Islamicization as the involvement of indigenous elites in the universal political culture of Islamic empires, as opposed to conversion or membership in a community of faith understood as Islamization.[52] Islamicization was limited in impact, leaving many aspects of indigenous culture intact.

Wagoner has focused on a wide range of Vijayanagara documentary sources and material culture, including inscriptions, historiographic legends, courtly dress, architecture, administrative apparatus and military technology. Perhaps the most significant evidence is the use of the phrase 'Sultan among Hindu Kings' (*hindūrāyasuratrāṇa*) from the time of Bukka I (r. 1344–1377) on through the changes in dynasties throughout the entire period of Vijayanagara rule. The occasional use of the Telugu word for sultan (*suratāḷu*) without the modifier 'of Hindu kings' (*hindūrāya*) in these inscriptions indicates the importance of the Vijayanagara ruler presenting himself as belonging to the more universal political regime of Islamicate empires and being thereby differentiated from other local South Indian kings.[53] The evidence from inscriptions is corroborated by a series of legendary accounts in the sixteenth century of the founding of the empire – the *Rājakālanirṇaya, Vidyāraṇyakālajñāna, Vidyāraṇyavṛttānta,* and *Vidyāraṇyaśaka.* These accounts centre on the capture and release of the brothers, Harihara and Bukka, by an unnamed sultan of Delhi during the latter's southern conquest. Modern Indian historians have used the story to suggest that the brothers first converted to Islam and then re-converted to Hinduism before their founding of the empire, but as Wagoner has shown there is no reference to conversion in the Sanskrit narrative or in the stray references to the founding of the empire in contemporary Persian sources. Wagoner's careful reading of the Sanskrit narratives and other similar narratives in Telugu and Kannada shows that, on the contrary, the trope of abduction enhances the status of Harihara and Bukka and casts Vijayanagara as a successor state to the sultanate.[54]

The ideological self-understanding of Vijayanagara kingship is mirrored by the large-scale adaptation of a wide range of Persianate cultural and material practices. Paintings and accounts by foreign travellers suggest that the long tunic, *kabāyi*, and conical hat, *kuḷḷāyi*, worn by figures in the Vijayanagara court had their respective sources in styles of dress widely prevalent in Islamicate polities: the *qabā'* tunic and *kulāh* hat. According to Wagoner, the *kabāyi* and *kuḷḷāyi* were worn exclusively in the performative area of the royal centre at the Vijayanagara capital and not in the inner apartments or sacred centre, with these two centres corresponding to the ancient Dravidian division between *puram* and *akam* as, respectively, public and domestic spaces.[55] There is no evidence prior to Vijayanagara for this selective adaptation of Islamicate styles of dress. The exclusively courtly context dovetails with other examples of 'cultural cross-dressing' in medieval South Asia, studied by Finbarr Flood, where assuming the dress of cultural neighbours functioned both horizontally in connecting transregional elites and vertically in differentiating those who engaged in such self-fashioning from those who did not.[56] Flood's analysis suggests that cultural cross-dressing in South Asia was not driven by the religious or even ethnic associations of dress, but out of a sense of the attractiveness of displays of authority. Flood also argues for a constitutive relationship between dress and identity, with imitation enabling one to cross boundaries (or 'pass'). The political dimensions of cultural cross-dressing suggest that vectors of difference between Muslims and Hindus were likely not as significant historically as those between elites and non-elites in both cosmopolitan and regional polities.

Perhaps the most visible lasting remnants of Islamicate influence at Vijayanagara are in the realm of architecture, including the use of plaster-coated masonry, the structuring of the citadel off to the side (rather than at the centre) of the city, the construction of a north-facing throne hall, and the carving of figures as sculptural reliefs on the Mahānavamī Dibba itself.[57] The fact that this influence did not extend to temples, which early in Vijayanagara conformed to norms proper to the Deccan and later on reflected the influence of Tamil styles, suggests another (not necessarily parallel to the public versus domestic) restriction of Islamicization to political and administrative buildings rather than religious and other cultural institutions. The architectural evidence suggests self-conscious imitation at Vijayanagara of Persianate courts at Sultānpūr, Tughluqābād and Samarqand. But as Catherine Asher has argued, it is also likely in some cases that specific architectural features had such a deep history in South Asia, occurring in such a wide variety of structures, that they were no longer recognized as either Islamicate or indigenous, along the lines of linguistic borrowing.[58]

In the case of the incorporation of Islamicate technologies of military and revenue administration, there was a clear functional dimension as well as an intensity of interaction requiring cooperation between agents and a shared or translatable linguistic medium. The most dramatic impact in military technology was seen in cavalry warfare equipment, especially the use of a new type of saddle. It appears that Devarāya II (1422–1446) was a major innovator in this regard, as there is evidence of his integration of large numbers of 'Turkish' (likely Deccani Muslims or Westerners from beyond the Arabian Sea) mounted troops into the Vijayanagara army. In terms of revenue administration, inscriptions and other sources reveal that the *nāyaka* system, so distinctive of Vijayanagara, was a direct adaptation of the *iqṭā*ʾ as an Islamicate form of apanage.[59] On the other hand, Flood has argued that the *iqṭā*ʾ in turn may have developed in north-west India as an adaptation of the existing South Asian practice of incorporating subordinate chiefs as *sāmantas*. According to Flood, it is possible that 'the emergence of hybrid modes of governance was facilitated by homologies in the exercise and devolution and authority in both domains.'[60]

Specific cases of the translation of forms of life at Vijayanagara indicate that such convergences aided in the development of transcultural identities and practices. One such example is the 1439 'Dharmaśāle' mosque of Aḥmad Khān, which has been studied in detail by Wagoner.[61] Several aspects of this mosque are distinctive: (1) the mosque is described in its founding inscription as a *dharmaśāle*, a Sanskritic term for a religious institution that is not necessarily a place of worship; (2) the language of that inscription is Kannada, rather than Persian or Arabic; (3) the inscription mentions transfer of merit from the construction of the mosque to the Vijayanagara king, Devarāya II; (4) the architectural form includes the heavy presence of Indic stylistic figures associated with the *maṇḍapa* (pillared hall) rather than the arches and domes of other South Asian mosques. Despite the resemblance of the building to non-Islamic cultural institutions at Vijayanagara, some key structural features were common to both mosques and temples, including rectangular halls of three-by-five bays and the existence of a pillared façade across one side. The presence of such homologous cultural elements and modes of translatability may have aided in the mobility of ideas and people in the Deccan between Vijayanagara to the south and the sultanates to the north.

Wagoner and Eaton have charted lived histories of individuals who moved back and forth between Vijayanagara and the sultanates in the sixteenth century, during the height of Śrīvaiṣṇava influence at Vijayanagara when, as discussed in this chapter, some of the key Rāma temples were built in the capital. These histories cast light especially on the era of Rāmarāya, the dominant figure in sixteenth-century Vijayanagara who traversed roles from general to regent under Sadāśivarāya to de facto ruler of the kingdom. Two of the figures are referred to respectively in Persian sources as Rāmarāya's adopted 'brother' and 'son': 'Ain al-Mulk Gīlāni and 'Ali 'Ādil Shāh. 'Ain al-Mulk Gīlāni figures in the Persian *Tārīkh-i Firishta* and Telugu *Rāyavācakamu*, as well as in Sanskrit inscriptions as the donor of Brahmin settlements dedicated to Śaiva or Vaiṣṇava village deities. It is generally presumed that 'Ain al-Mulk Gīlāni was Muslim based on his name, but as Wagoner has shown none of the sources focuses on his religious practices or beliefs, outside his endowment of the Brahmin settlements. His career includes periods of service to both the Bijāpur Sultanate and Vijayanagara, with the passage between these kingdoms apparently being seamless. According to the *Tārīkh-i Firishta*, Rāmarāya's relationship with 'Ain al-Mulk Gīlāni was so close that Rāmarāya referred to him as his brother.[62] Another such figure who formed a close bond with Rāmarāya was 'Ali 'Ādil Shāh, the Bijāpur sultan. In forming an alliance, the two exchanged robes and feasted, with Rāmarāya's wife calling the sultan her son.[63] Finally, there is the career of Rāmarāya himself. Rāmarāya was a Telugu warlord who hailed from deep in the Tamil region, and he was first the holder of an *iqṭā* under the Golkonda sultan Qulī Quṭb ul-Mulk before arriving at Vijayanagara. Yet another dimension of elite mobility is indicated by the several cases of marriage sealing alliances between Vijayanagara and the neighbouring sultanates. One such example involved, significantly, the marriage of the Bahmanī sultan Firoz Shāh to the daughter of Devarāya I – the emperor who commissioned the construction of the Rāmacandra temple in the Vijayanagara capital in 1407.

Wagoner has argued that the ease with which these figures moved between Vijayanagara and the Deccan sultanates points to the military–political class as 'a single transcultural social formation' transcending boundaries between Muslim and Hindu.[64] The political and cultural significance of this class vitiates the notion of mutually opposed Islamicate and Indic spheres of culture and power in the Deccan. While this elite culture resulted through a long period of interaction between indigenous military elites and the Perso-Turkic elite that migrated to the Deccan with the southern conquests of the Delhi Sultanate, the continued existence of significant linguistic and cultural differences meant that elites needed to be proficient in a kind of code-switching between cultural registers. It is likely that the homologies discussed above (e.g. in architecture and the revenue system) enabled such patterns of mobility.

Twentieth-century nationalist and colonial historians have focused attention especially on the Battle of Tālikoṭa (1565), represented as the result of the collaboration of the sultanates (Aḥmadnagar, Bijāpur, Golkonda and Bīdar, with Berār abstaining) in an effort to do away with the last 'Hindu' empire in the south. Much has been made of the ravaging of the capital in the aftermath of the battle, as described in Persian sources. However, as Eaton has persuasively shown, this account of the causes and scale of the battle is problematic on several grounds.[65]

In addition to the evidence cited so far regarding relationships between Vijayanagara and the sultanates, the specific events leading up to the Battle of Tālikoṭa, when examined carefully, paint a far different picture than emerges from the broad brushstrokes of presumed Hindu–Muslim conflict. The crucial instigating factor was Rāmarāya's obsessive fascination with the former Cālukya capital of Kalyāṇa. Unlike his predecessors, Rāmarāya sought to identify his own rule with that of the defunct Cālukya dynasty that had also ruled much of the Deccan. The capital at Kalyāṇa became an emblem of the Cālukya past. Eaton suggests that reasons for Rāmarāya's obsession might include the strategic location of Kalyāṇa at the centre of the Deccan plateau, making it an ideal centre for imperial rule transcending regional linguistic zones. Another possible reason was the availability of memories of previous Cōḻa attacks on Kalyāṇa, with which Rāmarāya could identify himself as an upstart general originally hailing from the core Cōḻa region. The path from Kalyāṇa to Tālikoṭa was paved by a series of alliances Rāmarāya forged with various sultanates. Kalyāṇa was never directly under the rule of Vijayanagara. As Eaton has demonstrated, shifts in alliance and efforts to incite the sultanates in battle with each other were motivated by a desire on the part of Rāmarāya to be constantly associated with the sultanate that controlled Kalyāṇa. After he humiliated the ruler of Aḥmadnagar, Husain Nizām Shāh, and plundered and arrogated districts in Golkonda upon conquering Kalyāṇa for the last time, the sultanates united to attack Vijayanagara, antagonized by Rāmarāya's actions. As Eaton points out, there is no evidence of any religious motivation in these events, including the Battle of Tālikoṭa itself.

The Cālukya revival was an ongoing project of Rāmarāya and the Aravīḍu dynasty he established, as is evident from epigraphic, archaeological and literary evidence studied by Wagoner.[66] The reuse of Cālukya antique styles and material remnants was common in sixteenth-century Vijayanagara buildings. The Cālukyas had remained alive in Vijayanagara cultural memory through the popularity of Bilhaṇa's *Vikramāṅkadevacarita*, which depicted the life of the Cālukya emperor Vikramāditya VI (r. 1076–1126), and provided the model for the genre of biographical or *carita* poetry in Sanskrit that became especially popular during this period. Kalyāṇa also figures prominently in an entirely different set of literary sources, Kannada and Telugu hagiographies from the Vīraśaiva tradition. Finally, a series of inscriptions in Telugu and Kannada directly traced the Aravīḍu dynasty genealogically back to the Cālukyas instead of earlier dynasties at Vijayanagara. Interestingly, the Cālukyan revival in architecture also occurred during the 'Ādil Shāhi dynasty in Bijāpur in the sixteenth century, yet another sign of the weakness of Persianate and Indic boundaries in the medieval Deccan.

Careful examination of the aftermath of Tālikoṭa may also challenge the presumption of anti-Hindu Islamic iconoclasm. As Eaton's work has shown, temple desecration in South Asia, both prior to and during the expansion of Indo-Muslim states, paradigmatically involved the looting or destruction of the state deity (*rāṣṭradevatā*) as a symbol of the abrogation of the power of the defeated ruler in the aftermath of a conquest.[67] Even though there was damage to the Vaiṣṇava Viṭṭhala temple, which from the time of the Tuḷuva and Saṅgama dynasties had replaced the Virūpākṣa temple as the de facto state sanctuary, other smaller shrines around the city were also affected. The desecration did not result in the actual razing of temples but selective mutilation of icons in shrines that were, as it turns out, almost exclusively Vaiṣṇava and not Śaiva. Not only was the Virūpākṣa untouched, but a comparison of side-by-side Śaiva and Vaiṣṇava temples demonstrates a number of cases where only the Vaiṣṇava temple was damaged (e.g. the Śaiva Giant Liṅga and Vaiṣṇava Lakṣmīnarasiṃha temples; the Śaiva Mudu Vīraṇṇa and Vaiṣṇava Tiruveṅgalanātha temples).[68] What seems to be the most likely explanation for this discrepancy is that it was actually Śaivas at Vijayanagara who were responsible for the desecration of temples.

The actions of Śaivas may very well have been a reaction to the dramatic loss of patronage to Śaiva institutions that occurred during the Aravīḍu dynasty from the time of Rāmarāya. I have focused in detail on the significance in the shift in religious affiliation from the Śaiva Saṅgama dynasty to the Vaiṣṇava Sāḷuva, Tuḷuva and Aravīḍu dynasties, but all rulers prior to the Aravīḍu dynasty extended material support widely to Śaivas, Vaiṣṇavas, Muslims and Jains (though conflict did arise, as recorded for instance in the famous Jaina-Śrīvaiṣṇava accord of Bukka I in 1368).[69] This practice of diverse patronage was abandoned by Sadāśivarāya (r. 1542–1570), the last, lame-duck Tuḷuva emperor, and Rāmarāya, who was the regent under Sadāśivarāya and de facto ruler of Vijayanagara for much of the sixteenth century. Now for the first time, Vijayanagara rulers almost exclusively commissioned the construction of Vaiṣṇava temples, and these did not even include Śaiva reliefs on walls as in the past at Vijayanagara.[70] Aravīḍu rulers expanded these policies after the fall of Vijayanagara in 1565: after Tirumala (r. 1570–1572), implemented the 'three swami pagoda coin' (representing Veṅkaṭeśvara and his two wives), Veṅkaṭa II finally formally replaced Virūpākṣa (a form of Siva) with Viṭṭhala (a form of Viṣṇu) as the Vijayanagara ensign. A critical role in this process was played by two of the later Tātācāryas, Pañcamatabhañjana Tātācārya and his son, Lakṣmīkumāra Tātācārya, who served as *rājagurus* for Sadāśivarāya and the Aravīḍu kings.

Corroboration that Śaivas were involved in the post-Tālikoṭa destruction comes from literary sources such as the Kannada Vīraśaiva prophetic text, the *Jaṅgama Kālajñāna*, which retrospectively characterizes the defeat at Tālikoṭa as punishment on the part of Virūpākṣa for his abandonment at Vijayanagara, as well as the evidence of several other cases of conflict between Śaivas and Vaiṣṇavas, especially after the fall of the capital. Outside of the Vijayanagara capital, conflict occurred primarily in the core Cōḻa sector of the Tamil region, after Vijayanagara rulers shifted first to Penukoṇḍa and then Candragiri in the south. Specific cases include Mādhva incursions onto Śaiva temples, as well as conflicts precipitated by Vijayanagara agents or their subsidiaries, such as the reaction of Śaiva priests to the re-installation of the Govindarāja icon in the Śaiva centre of Cidambaram (as described, venerated by Kulacēkarāḻvār), resulting in suicides and the killing of Śaivas by agents of Kṛṣṇappa Nāyaka of Gingee.[71] Another case involves radical alterations and the removal of relief sculptures at Mahābalipuram, likely by agents of Vijayanagara, aimed at denuding several cave temples of their composite character and rendering them exclusively Vaiṣṇava.[72] It is important to distinguish the gradual state boundaries of the Vijayanagara Empire from the relationship between territory and ethnic conflict that often exists in modern times, and to keep in mind the limits of the administrative apparatus of the Vijayanagara state, especially with regard to the Tamil region. But it would appear that the actions of royal agents of Vijayanagara, or of Nāyakas closely associated with Vijayanagara, led to a series of specific incidents after Tālikoṭa.

Some conclusions may be drawn from the spread of Persian culture at Vijayanagara and the intensified Śaiva-Vaiṣṇava conflict in the sixteenth century with regard to our understanding of the development of the Rāma cult at Vijayanagara. First, homologies between systems of culture and power, ideological and personal connections, and the influence of Islamicate cultural forms throughout the Deccan make it unlikely that Rāma cultic worship at Vijayanagara was related to a reaction to Indo-Islamic power. As discussed in this chapter, Śrīvaiṣṇava usage of the epic must also be brought into the equation in ascribing royal motives, given the influence of Śrīvaiṣṇavas at the Vijayanagara court in the fifteenth and sixteenth centuries and their role in promulgating the *Rāmāyaṇa* and in constructing major Rāma temples. Second, the later Śaiva-Vaiṣṇava conflict, though predicated on specific developments before and after the collapse of the empire, tell us that it is unlikely that the shift in Śaiva to Vaiṣṇava affiliation of dynasties met with no opposition and that the Śrīvaiṣṇava takeover or reinvigoration of the Rāma cult was uncontroversial. Such a backdrop may very well be behind the intense debate between Appayya Dīkṣita and Govindarāja on the Śaiva or Vaiṣṇava nature of the *Rāmāyaṇa*'s poetic message.[73] Both Govindarāja and Appayya Dīkṣita wrote during this last period dominated by the figure of Rāmarāya. The question arises: were Appayya's seemingly idiosyncratic Śaiva perspective on the *Rāmāyaṇa*, as expressed in his *Rāmāyaṇatātparyanirṇaya*, related to an effort to stake a claim on the Rāma cult, which had earlier been compatible with the Śaiva Virūpākṣa cult at Vijayanagara? It seems plausible that the two projects of *Rāmāyaṇa* commentary and royally sponsored veneration of the figure of Rāma were indeed connected.

Conclusion

I began this book with a reference to the contemporary status of the Vālmīki *Rāmāyaṇa* as a foundational religious text. The epic's religious dimension has been at the heart of a number of public controversies in India in recent years, such as the well-publicized series of court disputes in 2007 related to the land mass known as Rāma Setu or Adam's bridge. The Sethusamudram Shipping Canal Project sought (and still seeks) to build a channel between the southern coast of Tamil Nadu and Sri Lanka, which would involve digging up the Rama Setu, traditionally considered to be the bridge built by Rāma to cross over to Laṅkā, as described in the Yuddha Kāṇḍa. Hindu nationalists mobilized opposition to an affidavit submitted by the ruling Congress government.

Consider the language used by both the government and the opposition in this case. The September 2007 government affidavit states:

> The Valmiki Ramayana, the Ramcharitmanas by Tulsidas and other mythological texts, which admittedly form an ancient part of Indian literature, cannot be said to be historical records to incontrovertibly prove the existence of the characters or the occurrence of the events depicted therein.[1]

Here reference to the Vālmīki *Rāmāyaṇa* is framed with regard to its status as valid documentary evidence for identifying the landmass. In the debate that ensued, the challenge of this epistemological standard of historical truth, and the rejection of the facticity of the *Rāmayaṇa*'s account of events, were construed as an affront to religion. In a letter to the prime minister, the leader of the opposition argued that the 'Ramayana is not only a religious epic but also a national heritage and part of the culture of this country.'[2] Responding to public protests, the government withdrew its affidavit, citing 'religious sensibilities, including the unique ancient and holy text of Ramayana.'[3] What was not the subject of debate was how the *Rāmāyaṇa* came to be regarded as a text worthy of the state's neutrality with regard to religion.

There is a growing body of critical scholarship on modern uses of the Rāma story in relation to new forms of devotionalism and the historical emergence of political Hinduism. Recent scholarship has explored the role postcolonial forms of media, especially the Doordarshan Ramanand Sagar serial and the mobilizing medium of television, have played in heightening a generic emotional response to the epic.[4] Among other dimensions of modernity, any understanding of the modern significance of the *Rāmāyaṇa* must take into account the way religious identities were constructed by processes of enumeration and new translocal frames of belonging set into motion by the institutions of the colonial administration in India, as well as the complex partnership between colonial authorities and Sanskrit pandits in the selective ascription of centrality to ancient texts like the Vālmīki *Rāmāyaṇa*.

This book extends this inquiry and pushes back the historical genealogy to the centuries before colonial rule in South Asia. It augments the work of textual scholars who have emphasized not only the fluidity of the Rāma story as a living genre of retelling, but also the contestation and questioning involved in the elaboration, contraction, elision or alteration of episodes and the modification of the skeletal structure holding the narrative together.

Our study of commentaries and poetic retellings based on the Vālmīki *Rāmāyaṇa* in Sanskrit has highlighted the challenge posed by one interpretive community to another in an effort to transform the receptive history of the epic through the translation of vernacular devotional exegetical modes into Sanskrit and the radical alteration of categories of Sanskrit poetics. The distance between the theological poetics of late-medieval intellectuals and the text itself – the alterity of the past – is perhaps most evident in the figure of Rāma, who travels through interpretation from being the ideal divine king who must be reminded that he is an embodiment of divinity to being the omniscient and salvific godhead encapsulating scholastic definitions of the divine nature. That this hermeneutic encounter was characterized by rupture is evident most dramatically in the effort to read the most famous verse of the epic doubly, as a *śleṣa*. Similar transformations of the epic paradigm occurred in other devotional Rāma traditions throughout the subcontinent. What we see in the parallel project of the political use of the epic and the inauguration of a royal Rāma cult in sixteenth-century Vijayanagara is that, in the precolonial period, the othering of Muslims does not appear to have been a factor in the development of Rāma devotional and liturgical traditions, despite the fact that the epic provided conceptual resources for such a usage, with narratives of othering occurring in other regions and in literary and inscriptional genres. The earliest history of Rāma theology and Rāma cultic worship, at least in the south, is therefore congruent with much recent scholarship attesting to the weakness of the categories of Hindu and Muslim as forms of collective identification in premodern South Asia.

Notes

1 Two conceptions of divinity

1 Six volumes of the Princeton series have been published to date: Goldman 1984, Pollock 1986, Pollock 1991, Lefeber 1994, Goldman and Sutherland Goldman 1996, and Goldman, Sutherland Goldman, and van Nooten 2009. On multiple *Rāmāyaṇas*, see, for examples, the edited volumes of Raghavan, 1980, Thiel-Horstmann 1991, Richman 1991, Richman 2001, Bose, 2004.

2 Readers interested in the broader comparative dynamics of *Rāmāyaṇa* commentary beyond the history of commentaries produced by Śrīvaiṣnavas should consult the several essays devoted to this topic in the Princeton translation series: Goldman 1984: 114–117, Lefeber 1994: 17–28, Goldman and Sutherland Goldman 1996: 91–93 and Goldman, Sutherland Goldman, and van Nooten 2009: 99–107. The translators have also included notes from several commentaries in their verse-by-verse annotations; especially useful and of particular interest are the copious notes for the Yuddha Kāṇḍa (Goldman, Sutherland Goldman, and van Nooten 2009: 495–1552). Other sources which discuss *Rāmāyaṇa* commentaries include Krishnamachariar 1906, Raghavan 1940–42, Shastri 1942, Aiyangar 1942, Bhatt 1964 and Goldman 1992, 2005, 2006. Those treating the interpretation of the *Rāmāyaṇa* in Tamil and Maṇipravāla sources are Mumme 1991 and Narayanan 1994a. For further discussion specifically on commentaries on the *Tiruvāymoḻi* see Clooney 1996: 213–227 and Raman 2007: 98–126.

3 Jacobi 1893. For a sophisticated, more recent analysis of the history of *Rāmāyaṇa* accretion, see Brockington 1984.

4 Pollock 1991: 15–55.

5 I draw this characterization of ancient Indian conceptions of divine kingship from Inden 1985.

6 Shulman 1991.

7 Carman 1974: 77–87.

8 *Bhagavad Gītā* with Eleven Commentaries 4.8.

9 *Bhagavad Gītā* with Eleven Commentaries 4.8: sādhava uktalakṣaṇadharmaśīlā vaiṣṇavāgresarā matsamāśrayaṇe pravṛttā mannāmakarmasvarūpāṇām avāṅmanasagocaratayā maddarśanād vinā svātmadhāraṇapoṣaṇādikam alabhamānāḥ kṣaṇamātrakālam api kalpasahasraṃ manvānāḥ praśithilasarvagātrā bhaveyur iti matsvarūpaceṣṭitāvalokanālāpādidānena teṣāṃ paritrāṇāya tadviparītānāṃ vināśāya ca kṣīṇasya vaidikasya dharmasya madārādhanarūpasyārādhyasvarūpadarśanena sthāpanāya ca devamanuṣyādirūpeṇa yuge yuge sambhavāmi. All translations in this book are mine unless otherwise noted.

10 *Vālmīki Rāmāyaṇa* with the Commentaries of Govindarāja, Maheśvaratīrtha and Rāmānuja, general introduction: śriyaḥ patir avāptasamastakāmaḥ samastakalyāṇaguṇātmakaḥ sarveśvaraḥ 'vaikuṇṭhe tu pare loke śriyā sārdhaṃ

jagatpatiḥ/ āste viṣṇur acintyātmā bhaktair bhāgavataiḥ saha//' ityuktarītyā śrīvaikuṇṭhākhye divyaloke śrīmahāmaṇimaṇḍape śrībhūminīlābhiḥ saha ratnasiṃhāsanam adhyāsīno nityair muktaiś ca nirantaraparicaryamāṇacaraṇanalino 'pi tadvad eva svacaraṇayugalaparicaraṇārhān api taddhīnān pralaye prakṛtivilīnān madhūcchiṣṭamagnahemakaṇasadṛkṣān kṣīṇajñānān jīvān avalokya 'evam saṃsṛticakrasthe bhrāmyamāṇe svakarmabhiḥ/ jīve duḥkhākule viṣṇoḥ kṛpā kāpy upajāyate//' ityuktarītyā dayamānamanāḥ 'vicitrā dehasaṃpattir īśvarāya niveditum/ pūrvam eva kṛtā brahman hastapādādisaṃyutā//' ityuktaprakāreṇa mahadādisṛṣṭikrameṇa teṣām svacaraṇakamalasamāśrayaṇocitāni karaṇakalevarāṇi dattvā nadītaraṇāya dattaiḥ plavair nadīrayānusāreṇa sāgaram avagāhamāneṣv iva teṣu tair viṣayāntarapravaṇeṣu teṣāṃ sadasadvivecanāya 'śāsanāc chāstram' ityuktarītyā svaśāsanarūpaṃ vedākhyaṃ śāstraṃ pravartyāpi tasmin apratipattivipratipattyanyathā pratipattibhis tair anādṛte svaśāsanātilaṅghinaṃ janapadaṃ svayam eva sādhayitum abhiyiyāsur iva vasudhādhipatiḥ svācāramukhena tān śikṣayituṃ rāmādirūpeṇa caturdhāvatitīrṣur antarāmaragaṇaiḥ sadruhiṇair abhyarthitaḥ svārādhakasya daśarathasya manoratham api pūrayituṃ caturdhāvatatāra.

11 *Taittirīya Upaniṣad* 3.3.1.

12 *Vālmīki Rāmāyaṇa* with the Commentaries of Govindarāja, Maheśvaratīrtha and Rāmānuja 1.5.1 (1.5.1): śrīviṣṇoḥ prathame kāṇḍe jagajjananahetutā. dvitīye sthitihetutvaṃ tṛtīye mokṣadāyitā. caturthe guṇasampattiḥ pañcame sarvahantṛtā. ṣaṣṭe vedāntavedyatvaṃ saptame sraṣṭṛhetutā. evaṃ viṣṇuḥ paraṃ tattvaṃ rāmātmeti suniścitam. I have enumerated all *Rāmāyaṇa* verses according to the specific southern recension commented on by Govindarāja and other Śrīvaiṣṇavas, as it appears in the Nag publishers reprint of the Venkatesvara Steam Press edition. I have also included the verse number listed in the critical edition in parentheses.

13 Pollock 2006: 77.

14 See Altekar 1987, Cone and Gombrich 1977 and Collins 2003. For a summary of relationships between the Vālmīki *Rāmāyaṇa* and other early versions of the Rāma story, including the *Daśaratha Jātaka* and the *Rāmopakhyāna*, see Goldman 1984: 14–59.

15 See Bulcke 1962, Hess and Schechner 1977, Whaling 1980, Doniger 1986, 1999, van der Veer 1988, Slaje 1990, 1994, Lutgendorf 1991.

16 Behl 2007.

17 Burghart 1978.

18 See Shulman 1978, 1979, 1987, 1991, Ramanujan 1991, Blackburn 1996.

19 I have consulted two *grantha* manuscripts of the *Vivekatilaka*, R 3409 at the Government Oriental Manuscripts Library and 9386 at the Sarasvati Mahal Library.

20 Raghavan 1940–42: 1–8.

21 Virtually nothing is known about the actual author and the text's provenance. Shastri (1942: 413) cites 1400 as a possible date, which is corroborated by other editors of the critical edition, but not much evidence for this claim is provided. Shastri also identifies this Rāmānuja as the Kaṇṭāṭai Rāmānuja Ayyaṇkār who was the *rājaguru* for the Vijayanagara king Sāluva Narasiṃha, but Kaṇṭāṭai Rāmānuja Ayyaṇkār lived in the sixteenth century. A more plausible explanation is that the *Rāmānujīya* is an eponymous work titled for the school of the *Rāmānujīyas*, i.e. the Śrīvaiṣṇavas.

22 Krishnamachariar 1906: 24. Goldman, Sutherland Goldman, and van Nooten 2009: 105–106, 1227, 1363.

23 Shastri 1942.

24 Aiyangar 1942: 40–41.

2 Translating pearls into coral

1 As discussed by Freeman 1998, the Sanskrit *Līlātilaka* from fourteenth-century Kerala identifies *maṇi* as the vernacular and *pravāla* as Sanskrit, although *maṇi* is here ruby

and not pearl. Such a directionality is also suggested by the phrasing of two unidentified Tamil verses cited in Raman 2007: 199.

1) teṉmoḻiyum āriyamum cērnta maṇipavaḷa
meṉmoḻiyiṉṟaṉmaiy iyampaṟkut – toṉmaiy
irumoḻiyiṉāraṇamum ēttumeḻil emmāṉ
ṟirumakaḷkoṉṟāḷai neñcē cēr
2) muttukaḷālum iha naṟpavaḻaṅkaḷālum
ottuk kalanta tamiḻāl abhisaṃskṛtena
ettikkilum bhavaduhārala devabaddhā
buddhikum madkṛtriyam kṛtināṃ vibhūṣā

2 *Āṟāyirappaṭi Guruparamparāprabhāva* of Piṉpaḻakiya Perumāḷ Cīyar 373, 391. See Narayanan 1994b: 105–106.
3 Hardy 1998: 104.
4 Narayanan 1994b: 124–125.
5 *Vālmīki Rāmāyaṇa* with the Commentaries of Govindarāja, Maheśvaratīrtha and Rāmānuja 1.48 (1.47).
6 Raghavan 1958: 337; Hiltebeitel 1988: 14.
7 Bonazzoli 1983.
8 Gurumurthy 1994: 5, 14.
9 *Śrīvacanabhūṣaṇa* of Piḷḷai Lokācārya with the Commentary of Maṇavāḷamāmuni 142–144. See Mumme 1991: 205–206.
10 *Tiruvāymoḻi* of Nammāḻvār with the Commentary of Vaṭakkutiruvītip Piḷḷai, introduction.
11 *Abhayapradānasāra* of Vedānta Deśika 5.2.1–5.2.2.
12 *Nāṭya Śāstra* with the Commentary of Abhinavagupta 32.389.
13 Pollock 2006: 323.
14 Monius 2000.
15 Raja 1994–1997: 64–67.
16 Freeman 1998: 38–39.
17 I draw this idea of voice from Monius's (2000) discussion of the way the *Vīracōḻiyam* develops a Buddhist approach to the multiple literary registers of the medieval Tamil region. Such a characterization seems even more apposite in the Śrīvaiṣṇava case, where the connection between religious identity and language use was absolute.
18 Venkatachari 1994–1997: 95–96.
19 Fergusen 1994: 20.
20 *Meghadūta of Kālidāsa* with the Commentary of Dakṣiṇāvartanātha.
21 *Meghadūta of Kālidāsa* 2.31.
22 *Vālmīki Rāmāyaṇa* with the Commentaries of Govindarāja, Maheśvaratīrtha and Rāmānuja 5.34.21 (5.32.20).
23 *Meghadūta* of Kālidāsa 2.32.
24 *Vālmīki Rāmāyaṇa* with the Commentaries of Govindarāja, Maheśvaratīrtha and Rāmānuja 5.20.8 (5.18.8).
25 *Meghadūta* of Kālidāsa 2.35. *Vālmīki Rāmāyaṇa* with the Commentaries of Govindarāja, Maheśvaratīrtha and Rāmānuja 5.27.49 (5.25.35).
26 *Meghadūta* of Kālidāsa 2.47.
27 *Vālmīki Rāmāyaṇa* with the Commentaries of Govindarāja, Maheśvaratīrtha and Rāmānuja 6.6.6 (6.5.6).
28 For an extensive list of Sanskrit messenger poems, see Sastri 1963.
29 Ramanujan 1989: 189.
30 *Haṃsasandeśa* of Vedānta Deśika 2.2.
31 *Vālmīki Rāmāyaṇa* with the Commentaries of Govindarāja, Maheśvaratīrtha and Rāmānuja 5.22.20 (5.20.20).

32 *Vālmīki Rāmāyaṇa* with the Commentaries of Govindarāja, Maheśvaratīrtha and Rāmānuja 5.55.29 (5.53.23).
33 *Haṃsasandeśa* of Vedānta Deśika 2.7.
34 *Vālmīki Rāmāyaṇa* with the Commentaries of Govindarāja, Maheśvaratīrtha and Rāmānuja 1.15.10 (1.14.10).
35 *Vālmīki Rāmāyaṇa* with the Commentaries of Govindarāja, Maheśvaratīrtha and Rāmānuja 5.37.2 (5.35.2).
36 *Vālmīki Rāmāyaṇa* with the Commentaries of Govindarāja, Maheśvaratīrtha and Rāmānuja 5.33.11. *Haṃsasandeśa* of Vedānta Deśika 2.23.
37 *Vālmīki Rāmāyaṇa* with the Commentaries of Govindarāja, Maheśvaratīrtha and Rāmānuja 5.37.4 (5.35.4).
38 *Meghadūta of Kālidāsa* 1.11.
39 *Haṃsasandeśa* of Vedānta Deśika 1.13.
40 Bronner and Shulman 2006: 13.
41 These correspondences are laid out in *Saṅkalpasūryodaya* of Vedānta Deśika 1.71.
42 Cutler 1987: 93–110.
43 *Haṃsasandeśa* of Vedānta Deśika 2.40.
44 *Haṃsasandeśa* of Vedānta Deśika 2.22.
45 *Haṃsasandeśa* of Vedānta Deśika 1.1.
46 *Haṃsasandeśa* of Vedānta Deśika 1.54.
47 *Muṇḍaka Upaniṣad* 2.2.4.
48 Blackburn and Flueckiger 1989: 1–11.
49 *Pādukāsahasra* of Vedānta Deśika 4.8.
50 *Pādukāsahasra* of Vedānta Deśika 4.10.
51 Bronner and Shulman 2006: 12.
52 Bronner and Shulman 2006: 7–12.
53 Ludden 2002.
54 See Champakalakshmi 1994. For an alternative perspective, see Orr 2007.
55 See Shulman 1980.
56 For lists and descriptions of the divine places see Gopalan 1972 and Young 1980.
57 *Haṃsasandeśa* of Vedānta Deśika 1.9.
58 *Haṃsasandeśa* of Vedānta Deśika 1.18.
59 Aiyangar 1941: 2.
60 *Haṃsasandeśa* of Vedānta Deśika 1.21.
61 *Haṃsasandeśa* of Vedānta Deśika 1.22.
62 *Haṃsasandeśa* of Vedānta Deśika 1.26.
63 *Haṃsasandeśa* of Vedānta Deśika 1.33.
64 *Haṃsasandeśa* of Vedānta Deśika 1.45.
65 *Haṃsasandeśa* of Vedānta Deśika 1.46.
66 Bronner and Shulman 2006: 22.
67 Ramanujan 1989: 189.
68 Ramanujan 1989: 189.
69 Ramanujan 1991: 45.
70 Ramanujan 1991: 46.
71 Genette 1992, 1997.
72 Jauss 1982: 23.
73 I am indebted to Bronner's forthcoming article on Vāmana Bhaṭṭa Bāṇa's *Haṃsasandeśa* for much of what follows regarding this work and other *Haṃsasandeśas*.
74 See Bronner forthcoming.
75 Bauman 1977: 9.
76 Schegloff 1982.
77 Lutgendorf 1991: 22.
78 Bauman 1977: 18.

79 Narayanan 1994b: 109. See also Groesbeck 1999.

80 Kirshenblatt-Gimblett 1975.

81 Goldman 2005, 2006.

82 *Taniślokam* of Periyavāccāṉ Piḷḷai 1–26. See Goldman and Sutherland Goldman 1996: 406–407 for a summary of the many interpretations of this verse.

83 *Vālmīki Rāmāyaṇa* with the commentaries of Govindarāja, Maheśvaratīrtha and Rāmanuja 1.5.1 (1.5.1):

rāmatvenāvatīrṇo viṣṇur eva vedāntavedyaṃ parabrahmety ucyate. 'upakramopasaṃhārāv abhyāso 'pūrvatāphalam/ arthavādopapattī ca liṅgaṃ tātparyanirṇaye//' ityuktaṣaḍvidhatātparyaliṅgasambhavāt. tathāhi upakrame tāvat 'ko nvasmin' ityādinā vedāntoditasakalaguṇasampannaḥ kiṃ viṣṇur utānyo brahmādiṣv anyatama iti vālmīkinā pṛṣṭe 'ikṣvākuvaṃśaprabhavo rāmaḥ' ityādinā rāmatvenāvatīrṇo viṣṇur eveti nāradenoktam. upasaṃhāre ca caturmukhaḥ prāha 'tavāhaṃ pūrvake bhāve putraḥ parapurañjaya/ saṅkṣipya ca purā lokān māyayā svayam eva hi// mahārṇave śayāno 'psu māṃ tvaṃ pūrvam ajījanaḥ/ padme divye 'rkasaṅkāśe nābhyām utpādya mām api// prājāpatyaṃ tvayā karma mayi sarvaṃ niveśitam//' iyādinā sarva-jagatkāraṇaprajāpatijanakatvena sakalajagatkāraṇaṃ brahma viṣnur evety uktam. abhyāsaś ca tasyaiva dṛśyate. bālakāṇḍe 'etasmin antare viṣṇur upayāto mahādyutiḥ/ śaṅkhacakragadāpāṇiḥ pītavāsā jagatpatiḥ//' iti jagatkāraṇatvam uktam. tata uttaratra devāḥ 'tvaṃ gatiḥ paramā deva sarveṣāṃ naḥ paraṇtapa/' ity āhuḥ, tena paratvāsādhāraṇaṃ sarvaśaraṇyatvam uktam. tata uttarata 'tato devarṣigandharvāḥ sarudrāḥ sāpsarogaṇāḥ/ stutibhir divyarūpābhis tuṣṭuvur madhusūdanam//' iti sarvastu-tyatvam uktam. tato viśvāmitraḥ 'ahaṃ vedmi mahātmānaṃ rāmaṃ satyaparākramam/ vasiṣṭho 'pi mahātejā ye ceme tapasi sthitāḥ' iti. 'vedāham etaṃ puruṣaṃ mahāntam/ tam etaṃ vedānuvacanena brāhmaṇā vividiṣanti yajñena dānena tapasānāśakena' ityuktarītyā mahāpuruṣatvaṃ tapobalaṃ vinā tasya durjñeyatvaṃ cāha. sītāvivāhe vasiṣtho 'pi 'avyaktaprabhavo brahmā śāśvato nitya avyayaḥ/ tasmān marīciḥ saṃjajñe marīceḥ kāśyapaḥ sutaḥ//' iti sarvamūlakāraṇatvaṃ prācīkaśat. paraśurāmo 'pi 'adhikam menire viṣṇuṃ devāḥ sarṣigaṇās tadā' iti sarvādhikatvaṃ nidarśitavān. ayodhyākāṇḍe 'sa hi devair udīrṇasya rāvaṇasya vadhārthibhiḥ/ arthito mānuṣe loke jajñe viṣṇuḥ sanātanaḥ//' iti sanātanatvam uktam. uttaratra 'ākāśaprabhavo brahmā śāśvato nitya avyayaḥ' ity ākāśaśabdena svayaṃprakāśatvaṃ vyāpakatvaṃ cāha. āraṇyakāṇḍe mārīcena 'aprameyaṃ hi tattejo yasya sā janakātmajā' iti paricchedātītamahimattvam uktam. kiṣkindhākāṇḍe tārāvacanam 'tvam aprameyaś ca durāsadaś ca jitendriyaś cottamadhārmikaś ca/ akṣayyakīrtiś ca vicakṣaṇaś ca kṣitikṣamāvān kṣatajopamākṣaḥ// nivāsavṛkṣaḥ sādhunām āpannānāṃ parāgatiḥ/ ārtānāṃ saṃśrayaiś caiva yaśasaś caikabhājanam// jñānavijñānasaṃpanno nideśe nirataḥ pituḥ/ dhātūnām iva śailendro guṇānām ākaro mahān//' iti. anena ca jñānānand ādisamastakalyāṇaguṇākaratvam uktam. sundarakāṇḍe 'brahmā svayambhūś caturānano vā rudras trinetras tripurāntako vā/ indro mahendraḥ suranāyako vā trātruṃ na śaktā yudhi rāmavadhyam//' iti sarvasaṃhartṛtvaṃ dyotitam. uttaratra 'kiṃ vaiṣṇavaṃ vā kapirūpam etya rakṣovināśāya paraṃ sutejaḥ/ anantam avyaktam acintyarūpaṃ svamāyayā sāṃpratam āgataṃ vā//' dvitīyo vākāro 'vadhāraṇārthaḥ. anenānantarūpatvam uktam. yuddhakāṇḍe viṣnur eva kathaṃ jagatkāraṇam? anyeṣām api 'hiraṇyagarbhas samavartatāgre' 'yadā tamas tan na divā na rātrir na san na cāsac chiva eva kevalaḥ' 'indro māyābhiḥ pururūpa īyate' ityādinā tattvaśravaṇād ity āśaṅkya tebhyaḥ sarvebhyaḥ śreṣṭhatvapratipādanād dhiraṇyagarbhaśivendrādiśabdāḥ sadbrahmātmaśabdavad viṣṇuparā evetyāśayenocyate 'vyaktam eṣa mahāyogī paramātmā sanātanaḥ/ anādimadhyanidhano mahataḥ paramo mahān// tamasaḥ paramo dhātā śaṅkhacakragadādharaḥ/ śrīvatsavakṣā nityaśrīr ajayyaḥ śāśvato dhruvaḥ//' iti. anena ca paramātmatvaśriyaḥpatitvādikam uktam. utaratra brahmā 'bhavañ nārāyaṇo devaḥ śrīmāñś cakrāyudho vibhuḥ /ekaśṛṅgo varāhas tvaṃ bhūtabhavyasapatnajit//' ityādi. anena tasya nārāyaṇaśabdavācyatvam uktam. apurvatā ca pramāṇāntarāprāptiḥ, na hi paratattvasya viṣṇutvaṃ pramāṇāntarād avagantuṃ śakyam. phalaṃ ca bhagavatsālokyādikam ityante suvyaktam. arthavādopapattī ca bālakāṇḍe darṣite. 'ime dve dhanuṣi śreṣṭhe' ityādinārthavādam uktvā 'jṛmbhitaṃ taddhanur dṛṣtvā śaivaṃ viṣṇur aparākramaiḥ/ adhikaṃ menire viṣṇuṃ devāḥ sarṣigaṇās tadā//' ityādinā brahmapramukhais sarṣigaṇair devair mīmāṃsāpūrvakaṃ viṣṇurudrayor madhye viṣṇor ādhikyanirṇayokter upapattir uktā. na ca vācyaṃ 'menire' iti vacanat 'mahāśūrataras tathā' iti varadānakṛtam idam ādhikyam iti. tathātve tasya roṣānupapatteḥ. 'dhanū rudrasya saṅkruddhaḥ' iti hy uktam. kiṃ cāgasyāśrame 'sa tatra brahmaṇaḥ sthānaṃ viṣṇoḥ sthānaṃ tathaiva ca. agneḥ sthānaṃ mahendrasya sthānaṃ caiva vivasvataḥ/ somasthānaṃ bhagasthānaṃ sthānaṃ kauberam eva ca//' ityādinā brahmādīnām agastyopāsyatvam uktvā rudrasya tadakathanād apūjyatvam ucyate. na cemāny agastyapūjakabrahmādisthānānīti vācyam, asambhavāt. 'atra devāḥ sagandharvās siddhāś ca paramarṣayaḥ/ agastyaṃ niyatāhāraṃ satataṃ paryupāsate//' iti vacanaṃ brahmādivyatiriktakevaladevaviṣayam/ kiṃ ca yathā gṛhasthasya gṛhe devagṛhasattve gṛhasthasyaiva pūjakatvaṃ svarasataḥ pratīyate, evam evātrāpi nāpalāpāvakāśaḥ. kiṃ ca dakṣayajñavadhe 'yasmād bhāgārthino bhāgaḥ kalpito naiva me surāḥ/ varāṅgāni mahārhāṇi dhanuṣā śātayāmi vaḥ//' iti rudrasya yajñabhāgākalpanād apūjyatvād atra tasya sthānānirdeśaḥ. nanu yadi viṣṇuḥ parā devatā kathaṃ tarhi tasya rāmatvena janma? iti cen na, 'ajāyamāno bahudhā vijāyate' ity uktarītyā lokānujighṛkṣākṛtaṃ tad iti codyānavakāśāt. mokṣapradatvaṃ ca paradevatāsādhāraṇam. atrocyate 'yā gatir yajñaśīlānām āhitāgneś ca yā gatiḥ/ aparāvartinaṃ yā ca yā ca bhūmipradāyinām// mayā tvaṃ samanujñāto gaccha lokān anuttamān/' iti. atrāparāvartitvaṃ punar āvṛttiśūnyatvam, muktir iti yāvat. 'na ca punar āvartate' iti śruteḥ. na ca raṇād apalāyanam ucyate iti vaktuṃ śakyate, tasya svataḥ siddhatvena tatphalasyānanugrāhyatvāt. tathā ca yajñādiphalāvadhibhūtāṃ muktiṃ prāpnuhi ity arthaḥ. ata eva nṛsiṃhapurāṇe, 'matkṛte nidhanaṃ yasmāt tvayā prāptaṃ dvijottama/ tasmāt tvam matprasādena viṣṇulokam avāpsyasi//' iti. evam upakramādiṣaḍvidhatātp aryaliṅgair vedāntavedyaṃ paratattvaṃ viṣṇur eveti śrīrāmāyaṇenopabṛṃhyate.

84 See Bronner 2011.

85 *Vālmīki Rāmāyaṇa* with the Commentaries of Govindarāja, Maheśvaratīrtha and Rāmanuja 1.5.1 (1.5.1): dvitīyas tu evambhūtaṃ paratattvaṃ kena prāpyata ityākāṅkṣāyāṃ tatprāptyupāyabhūtāṃ śaraṇāgatiṃ 'yo brahmāṇaṃ vidadhāti pūrvaṃ yo vai vedāṃś ca prahiṇoti tasmai/ taṃ ha devam ātmabuddhiprasādaṃ mumukṣur vai śaraṇam ahaṃ prapadye' iti śrutim upabṛṃhayan vālmīkir hy asmin rāmāyaṇe upakramaprabhṛty upasaṃhārāntam anekādhikāriphalaviśeṣādipradarśanamukhenākhila phalasādhanatayā pratipādayati. tathāhi upakrame tāvat 'etasmin antare viṣṇur upayāto mahādyutiḥ/ śaṅkhacakragadāpāṇiḥ pītavāsā jagatpatiḥ//' iti sarvaśeṣī sarveśvaro rakṣāpekṣāpratīkṣo rakṣaṇasamayo labdha iti samudbhūtaujjvalyo rakṣaṇopakaraṇaiḥ saha sannaddho 'bhyetya tasthau, tadā 'devagandharvayakṣāś ca tatas tvāṃ śaraṇaṃ gatāḥ' iti rāvaṇavadharūpaphalārthaṃ brahmarudrādidevagaṇaśaraṇāgatir uktā. tatas triśaṅkuśunaḥśephādivṛttānteṣu viśvāmitrādivyāpāraviśeṣān udīrya śaraṇāgatarakṣaṇaṃ paramo dharmaḥ samarthakāruṇikaviṣayā śaraṇāgatiḥ phalāvinābhūteti pradarśitam. tataś ca 'sa bhrātuś caraṇau gāḍham nipīḍya raghunandanaḥ/ sītām uvācātiyaśā rāghavaṃ ca mahāvratam/' iti puruṣakārapuraskaraṇapuraḥsarā śaraṇāgatiḥ kāryety udīritam/ tato bharataḥ 'śeṣye purastāc chālāyā yāvan me na prasīdati' iti rāmābhiśekaphalāya śaraṇavaraṇam akarot. atra rāvaṇavadhāya kṛtadevagaṇaprapattiphaladānāya nirgamanāt tadānīṃ rāmas svapratinidhibhūtapādukāpradānena tat saphalaṃ kṛtvā paścāt devagaṇamanorathapūraṇānantaram ātmānam abhyaṣiñcat, ato na śaraṇāgativaiphalyaṃ codyam. atha daṇḍakāraṇyavāsibhir virodhinirasanāya śaraṇāgatir anuṣṭhitā 'te vayaṃ bhavatā rakṣyā bhavadviṣayavāsinaḥ/ nagarastho vanastho vā tvaṃ no rājā janeśvara//' ityatra kosalajanapadavāsinām iva bhagavadviṣayavāsa eva śaraṇāgatiḥ. tadanantaraṃ 'sa pitrā ca parityaktaḥ surais ca samaharṣibhiḥ/ trīn lokān saṃparikramya tam eva śaraṇam gataḥ// sa taṃ nipatitaṃ bhūmau śaraṇyaḥ śaraṇāgatam. vadhārham api kākutsthaḥ kṛpayā

paryapālayat/' iti kākavṛttāntenāgrataḥ patanam eva śaraṇāgatir ity adarśi. tadanu sugrīvavṛttāntena 'kṛtāparādhasya hi te nānyat paśyāmy ahaṃ kṣamam/ anantareṇāñjaliṃ baddhvā lakṣmaṇasya prasādanāt//' iti śaraṇāgatir añjalir ūpoktā. atha sītāvacanena 'mitram aupāyikaṃ kartuṃ rāmaḥ sthānaṃ parīpsatā/ vadhaṃ cānicchatā ghoraṃ tvayāsau puruṣarṣabhaḥ// viditaḥ sa hi dharmajñaḥ śaraṇāgatavatsalaḥ/ tena maitrī bhavatu te yadi jīvitum icchasi//' ity anenānukūlyam eva śaraṇāgatir ity abodhi. upari 'so 'haṃ paruṣitas tena dāsavac cāvamānitaḥ/ tyaktvā putrāṃś ca dārāṃś ca rāghavaṃ śaraṇaṃ gataḥ' iti vibhīṣaṇaśaraṇāgatyā virodhiparityāgapūrvakatvam uktam. 'tataḥ sāgaravelāyāṃ darbhān āstīrya rāghavaḥ/ añjaliṃ prāṅmukhaḥ kṛtvā pratiśiśye mahodadheḥ// iti rāmaśaraṇāgatyā yogyasya nāyogyatānveṣṭavyā ayogyasya ca na yogyety uktam. aśucibhūtalaṇkānirgatamātra eva hi vibhīṣaṇaś śaraṇam avṛṇot. rāmaśaraṇāgateḥ phalābhāvaḥ samarthakāruṇikaviṣayatvābhāvād ity āhūḥ. uttaratra 'abhiyācāma vaidehīm etad dhi mama rocate/ rāghavād dhi bhayaṃ ghoraṃ rākṣasānām upasthitam//' iti trijaṭāvacanānumatimātreṇa hanumadbhayāt sarvāsāṃ rakṣitatvakathanād anyaviṣaye 'nyenāpi kṛtā śaraṇāgatiḥ phalavatīti nidarśitam. vibhīṣaṇaśaraṇāgatyaiva tatsacivānāṃ rakṣaṇāt śaraṇāgatasambandhino 'pi bhagavatkaṭākṣapātrabhūtā eveti niraṇāyi. evam anyatrāpi draṣṭavyam. evam upakramaprabhṛtyopasaṃhārāt pratipāditā śaraṇāgatir eva sarvaphalapradā, saiva mukter api hetur ity uktam. viśeṣas tu tatra prakaraṇena prapañcayiṣyate.

86 *Śrīvacanabhūṣaṇa* of Piḷḷai Lokācārya with the Commentary of Maṇavāḷamāmuni 23.

87 On the historical development of the theology of surrender in Maṇipravāla commentaries see Raman 2007.

88 *Vālmīki Rāmāyaṇa* with the Commentaries of Govindarāja, Maheśvaratīrtha and Rāmānuja 1.5.1 (1.5.1): upakrame devajātīyaśaraṇāgate rāmakāiṇkaryaṃ pradhānaphalam ity ucyate, apsaraḥprabhṛtiṣv avatīrya tais tadanuvartanopadeśāt. rāvaṇavadhas tu ānuṣaṅgikaḥ.

89 *Tiruvāymoḻi* of Nammāḻvār with the Commentary of Vaṭakkutiruvītip Piḷḷai, introduction.

90 *Vālmīki Rāmāyaṇa* with the Commentaries of Govindarāja, Maheśvaratīrtha and Rāmānuja 1.5.1 (1.5.1): evambhūtopāyādhikārisvarūpaṃ śeṣatvaṃ pāratantryaṃ ca. tatra śeṣatvaṃ lakṣmaṇācāreṇa prācīkaśat 'aham asyāvaro bhrātā guṇair dāsyam upāgataḥ/ kuruṣva mām anucaraṃ vaidharmyam neha vidyate// kṛtārto 'haṃ bhaviṣyāmi tava cārthaḥ prakalpate//' ityādinā. bharatamukhena pāratantryaṃ prakaṭīkṛtaṃ 'vilalāpa sabhāmadhye jagarhe ca purohitam/ rājyam cāham ca rāmasya dharmaṃ vaktum ihārhasi//' ityādinā 'sarvātmanā paryanunīyamāno yadā na saumitrir upaiti yogam/ niyujyamāno bhuvi yauvarājye tato 'bhyaṣiñcad bharataṃ mahātmā//' ityantena. śrīśatrughnavyāpāreṇa bhāgavatapāratantryaṃ prācīkaśat 'gacchatā mātulakulaṃ bharatena tadānaghaḥ/ śatrughno nityaśatrughno nītaḥ prītipuraskṛtaḥ' ityādinā.

91 *Vālmīki Rāmāyaṇa* with the Commentaries of Govindarāja, Maheśvaratīrtha and Rāmānuja 2.31.2: saḥ rāmānuvṛttirūpaprayojanāya upāyāntaraśūnyaḥ. bhrātur ity avarjanīyasambandhakathanāc charanyatvam uktam. caraṇau nipīḍya iti śaraṇāgatyuktiḥ. gāḍham ity aślathatvoktyā mahāviśvāsa uktaḥ. raghunandanaḥ lakṣmaṇaḥ. atiyaśāḥ ānukūlyasaṅkalpaprātikūlavarjanavān. ādau sītāṃ puruṣakāratvena parigṛhyovāca paścāt tatpuruṣakāreṇa mahāvratam 'na tyajeyaṃ kathaṃcana/ etad vratam mama' ity uktagurutaravratayuktam. rāghavaṃ raghurākṣasasaṃvādādiprasidd hakuladharmaśaraṇāgatarakṣaṇaṃ ca. uvāca śaraṇāgateḥ sarvaphalapradatvena svābhimataphalaṃ vijñāpayāmāsa. nipīḍyetyantena dvayasya pūrvakhaṇḍoktaśaraṇāgatir anūditā. rāghavam uvācety anenottarakhaṇḍoktaphalaprārt hanoktā. sītām uvācety ubhayatra puruṣakāraparigrahoktiḥ. This verse and the verses following describing Lakṣmaṇa's request do not appear in the critical edition. All verses that do not appear in the critical edition are cited with reference to chapter and verse numbers in the southern recension used by Govindarāja.

92 *Vālmīki Rāmāyaṇa* with the Commentaries of Govindarāja, Maheśvaratīrtha and Rāmānuja 2.31.3.

93 *Vālmīki Rāmāyaṇa* with the Commentaries of Govindarāja, Maheśvaratīrtha and Rāmānuja 2.31.4.

94 *Vālmīki Rāmāyaṇa* with the Commentaries of Govindarāja, Maheśvaratīrtha and Rāmānuja 2.31.5.

95 *Vālmīki Rāmāyaṇa* with the Commentaries of Govindarāja, Maheśvaratīrtha and Rāmānuja 2.31.5: devalokākramaṇam 'devānāṃ pūrayodhyā' ityuktaparamapadaprāptiṃ tvayā vinā na vṛṇe. tvatkaiṅkaryavinākṛtaṃ mokṣam api na vāñchāmītyarthaḥ. amaratvam 'jarāmaraṇamokṣāya' ityuktaṃ kaivalyākhyaṃ mokṣam api na vṛṇe. lokānām aiśvaryaṃ trilokādhipatitvaṃ, brahmatvam iti yāvat. mokṣam apy akāmayamāno 'haṃ kathaṃ kaivalyādikaṃ kāmayeyetibhāvaḥ. yad vā avarohakrameṇa trailokyaiśvaryādikam api na kāmaya iti. ato na tatprakarṣadoṣaḥ. devalokagamanaṃ devatvam indratvaṃ vā na kāmaya iti vākyārthas tucchaḥ.

96 *Vālmīki Rāmāyaṇa* with the Commentaries of Govindarāja, Maheśvaratīrtha and Rāmānuja 2.31.22: māṃ śeṣabhūtam. anucaraṃ śeṣatvānuguṇakaiṅkaryayuktaṃ kuruṣva. tatkaraṇam api tavaiva prayojanam ity ātmanepadāl labhyate. ihānucaratvakaraṇe vaidharmyaṃ sevyasevakadharmarāhityaṃ nāsti, tava sevyadharmaḥ paryāptaḥ svāmitvāt. mama sevakadharmaś ca pūrṇaḥ svābhāvikaśeṣatvāt. yad vā vaidharmyaṃ vaiparītyasādhakaṃ na vidyate tvadukta-hetor anyathāsiddher uktatvād ityāśayaḥ. anucarakaraṇasya kiṃ prayojanam ityapekṣāyām āha taveti. tavārthaḥ svāyāsaṃ vinā phalamūlādyāharaṇaṃ prakalpate siddhyati. ahaṃ ca kṛtārthaḥ labhatvātkaiṇkaryaphalo bhaviṣyāmi. yad vā māṃ svābhāvikaśeṣabhūtaṃ mām anucaraṃ svarūpānurūpaśeṣavṛttiyuktaṃ kuruṣva. ihāsmin jane mayi vaidharmyaṃ śeṣatvaviparyāsaḥ nāsti, anena śeṣatvasya svābhāvikatvaṃ tajjñānavataḥ phalaṃ kaiṅkaryaṃ cety uktam. kaiṅkaryākaraṇe tava kā hānir ity atrāha kṛtārtho 'ham bhaviṣyāmīti. akiñcit kurvataḥ śeṣatvānupapatter itibhāvaḥ. tac ca prāpyaṃ kaiṅkaryaṃ niṣkṛṣya darśayati tava ceti. covadhāraṇe. tavaivārthaḥ na tu mama. parārthakaiṅkaryasyaiva puruṣarthatvād itibhāvaḥ. śeṣatvādhyavasāya upāyaḥ, asvārthaśeṣikaiṅkaryam eva phalam ity upāyopeyaniṣkarṣo 'nena kṛta iti rahasyam. vaidharmyaṃ neha vidyata ityuktiḥ jyeṣthabhrātuḥ pitrusamatvāt. āvayoḥ śreyaś cāstīty āha kṛtārtha itīti kecid vyācakṣate.

97 *Taniślokam* of Periyavāccāṉ Piḷḷai 93–100.

98 *Tiruvāymoli* of Nammālvār with the Commentary of Vaṭakkutiruvītip Piḷḷai, 1.2.6, 2.3.3, 2.9.9, 3.3.0, 4.7.8, 4.8.2, 4.9.10, 5.8.7, 8.2.11, 8.3.7, 9.6.9, 9.8.2, 10.2.3, 10.6.1. See Clooney 1996: 220–227, 330.

99 *Vālmīki Rāmāyaṇa* with the Commentaries of Govindarāja, Maheśvaratīrtha and Rāmānuja 6.116.45 (6.101.36).

100 *Vālmīki Rāmāyaṇa* with the Commentaries of Govindarāja, Maheśvaratīrtha and Rāmānuja 6.116.43 (6.101.34): purā kila kaścid vyādho vyāghreṇānusṛto vṛkṣam ārūḍhaḥ, vṛkṣamūlagato vyāghro vṛkṣopari sthitam ṛkṣaṃ vanyamṛgāṇām asmākaṃ jātyā śatrur eṣaḥ, tasmād enaṃ vṛkṣāt pātaya ity abravīt. evam ukto bhallūkaḥ svavāsasthānagataṃ enaṃ na pātayiṣyāmi, tathātve dharmahāniḥ syād ity uktvā suṣvāpa. tadanantaraṃ tvāṃ rakṣiṣyāmi, suptaṃ ṛkṣaṃ pātaya iti vyāghreṇa coditaḥ san vyādhas tam ṛkṣam apātayat. sa tv abhyāsavaśena śākhānataram avalambya nāpatat. tadanu kṛtāparādham enaṃ pātaya iti punaḥ punar vyāghreṇocyamāno 'pi bhallūko bahuśaḥ kṛtāparādham apy enam tubhyaṃ na dāsyāmī ity abhidhāya rarakṣeti paurāṇikī gathā.

101 Coats 1981.

102 Mumme (1991) productively uses the category of parable to analyse the didactic use of *Rāmāyaṇa* stories in Maṇiprāvāla sources in general.

103 See Raman 2007: 138–141 for a contextualized discussion of the articulation of the goddess's compassionate tenderness (*daurlabhya*) in the following passage from the Īṭu. *Tiruvāymoli* of Nammālvār with the Commentary of Vaṭakkutiruvītip Piḷḷai 6.10.10: saṃsārattil kuṟṟamilātār yārṉ tirai nīkkik kaṭalāṭap pōmōṉ naṟkutiraiyāka bhavittirukkiṟap perumāḷ tāṉ kuṟṟavāḷar allārōṉ nāṉ kuṟṟavāṭṭiyallēṉōṉ nī tāṉ

kuṟṟavāḷaṉ allaiyōhn perumāḷ kuṟṟavāḷarāṉapaṭiyeṉṉaṉē eṉṉil tām kāṭēṟap pōntār, avar piṉṉē maṭal ūravāraip pōlē iḷaiya perumālum pōntār, tammōṭē ekāntabhogam paṇṇakkaṭavatāka ilai akalap paṭatuk koṇṭu nāṉum pōṉtēṉ, eṉṉaip pirintu pattu māsam iruntār; tām varāviṭṭāl tammatōr ampu icaṅkamāṭṭāmaiyillai iṟē ivvaḷi; ittaṉai nāḷ pirintirukka vallavarāṉa pōtē perumāḷ pakkalilēyaṉṟō kuṟṟamṉ pāratantryattukku anuguṇamāka pēcātiṟātē atu taṉṉaic coṉṉa eṉ pakkalil aṉṟō kuṟṟam. iṉi nāyakaṉ coṉna kāryam ceyta aṭiārait daṇḍikkap pārttvaṉṟu perumāḷ aruḷic ceyta kāryam ceyyap pōnta uṉṉai muṟpaṭa daṇḍittuk koṇṭaṉṟō rāvaṇaṉ coṉṉa kāryañ ceyta ivarkaḷait daṇḍippatuṉ ākaiyāl nīyallavō kuṟṟavāḷaṉ. ellāp paṭiyālum perumāḷ oru viṣayattai muṉintayaṉṟu āṟa vitukaikku nāṉ uṇṭu; nāṉum avar va i pōka vēṇṭi iruntavaṉṟaikku nīyuṇṭu eṉṟiruntēṉ; nīyum iṇṇanēyāṉa aparādhañ ceytārkkup pukavāyil uṇṭōṉ eṉkiṟāḷ. See also Abhayapradānasāra of Periyavāccāṉ Piḷḷai 538–546.

104 *Vālmīki Rāmāyaṇa* with the Commentaries of Govindarāja, Maheśvaratīrtha and Rāmānuja 6.116.45 (6.101.36): pāpānāṃ vā śubhānāṃ vā tvadabhiprāyeṇa pāpānāṃ va asmadabhiprāyeṇa śubhānāṃ vā. tad eva mamoddeśyaṃ 'doṣo yadyapi tasya syāt' itivat. malinasya hi snānam apekṣitam. tāsāṃ pāpatvād evāsmadapekṣā. kiṃ śubhānām asmābhiḥ? tatpuṇyānām eva tadrakṣakatvāt. tasmāt pāpam evāsmākam uddeśyam. nanu tarhi 'daṇḍyā daṇḍanīyāḥ nādaṇḍyāḥ' iti dharmaśāstraṃ bhavatīm āsādya bhajyetety āśaṅkya duṣṭo 'pi śaraṇāgato rakṣaṇīya iti viśeṣaśāstraṃ bhavantam āsādya kim bhañjanīyaṃ ity āha vadhārhāṇām iti. vadhārhāṇām apīty arthaḥ. saptamyarthe śaṣṭhī. plavaṅgama anabhilaṣitam evābhilaṣitavān khalu bhavān. teṣu. āryeṇa mahatā puruṣeṇa. karuṇam dayā kāryam. tiṣṭhatu puṇyaṃ pāpaṃ ca idānīm etad dayanīyadaśāṃ paśya. yad vā śubhānām iti dṛṣṭāntārtham. śubheṣu vadhārheṣu yathā karuṇaṃ kāryaṃ tathā pāpeṣu vadhārheṣv api kāryam ity arthaḥ. sāparādhādaṇḍane tiprasaṅgaḥ syād ity āśaṅkyāha na kaścin nāparādhyatīti. sarvo 'py aparādhatīty arthaḥ.

105 *Vālmīki Rāmāyaṇa* with the Commentaries of Govindarāja, Maheśvaratīrtha and Rāmānuja 3.67.9: mahābhāghaṃ mahābhāgyam. svāmyārthe tyaktaśarīratvāt.

106 *Vālmīki Rāmāyaṇa* with the Commentaries of Govindarāja, Maheśvaratīrtha and Rāmānuja 3.67.22: rāmo rurodety asyāyam abhiprāyaḥ parameśvarasya śrīrāmasya bhaktapakṣapātitvena bhatkaṃ jaṭāyuṣam āpannaṃ dṛṣṭvā paramapriyāṃ sītāṃ rāvaṇena hṛtāṃ ca śṛtvā 'vyasaneṣu manuṣyāṇāṃ bṛśaṃ bhavati duḥkhitaḥ' ityukteḥ bhaktāpadaṃ dṛṣṭvā rurodeti.

107 *Vālmīki Rāmāyaṇa* with the Commentaries of Govindarāja, Maheśvaratīrtha and Rāmānuja 3.68.29–30 (3.64.29–30). See Pollock 1991: 347–348 for a summary of the commentators' perspectives on theological issues involved with the ordering of these verses.

108 *Vālmīki Rāmāyaṇa* with the Commentaries of Govindarāja, Maheśvaratīrtha and Rāmānuja 3.68.29–30 (3.64.29–30): yā gatir ityādiślokadvayam ekānvayam. gamyata iti gatiḥ lokaḥ. yajñaśīlānāṃ yajñāḥ śīlaṃ sadvṛttaṃ yeṣāṃ te tathā, sadā yajñānuṣṭhānaparāṇāṃ gṛhasthānām ity arthaḥ. āhitāḥ paritaḥ sthāpitāḥ agnayaḥ pañcāgnayo yasya sa tathā, sarvadā tapaḥśīlasya vānaprasthasyety arthaḥ. agnyādhānasya pūrveṇaiva siddhatvāt pṛthak phalābhāvāc ca. aparāvartinām 'araṇyam iyāt tato na punar eyāt' ityuktānām sanyāsinām ity arthaḥ. raṇād apalāyitānām ityarthavarṇane jaṭāyos tādṛśatvena tatphalasya svataḥsiddhatvenānujñātavyatvābhāvāt muktānāṃ dharmaprakaraṇe uktyasambhavāt. bhūmipradāyināṃ bhūmibhogatyāgināṃ naiṣṭhikānām ity arthaḥ. tā gatīr iti yattador nityasambandhāt siddham. tā gatīḥ 'prājāpatyaṃ gṛhasthānāṃ brāhmaṃ saṃnyāsināṃ smṛtam' ityādyuktasthānāni. yad vā yajñadānatapaḥsaṃnyāsinām ity arthaḥ. teṣāṃ yā yā gatiḥ śāstravihitā tāṃ mayā saṃskṛto vraja mayā samanujñātas tu anuttamān sarvaśreṣṭhān lokān. 'atha yad ataḥ paro divo jyotir dīpyate viśvataḥ pṛṣṭheṣu sarvataḥ pṛṣṭheṣv anuttameṣūttameṣu' ityādiśrutiprasiddhān viṣṇulokān gaccha. avayavabahutvād bahuvacanam, anyathā gatiśabdena paunaruktyam ananvayaś ca, samanujñātaḥ saṃskṛtaś ceti padadvayānarthakyaṃ ca. nanu mānuṣabhāvaṃ bhāvayataḥ śrirāmasya kathaṃ muktipradānaṃ tasya paratvāsādhāraṇacihnatvād iti cet, 'satyena lokān jayati'

ityuktarītyā svārjitadharmāviśeṣeṇa svādhīnasarvalokatvāvirodhāt. kecit tu mayā saṃskṛtas tato 'nujñatas tvaṃ yajñaśīlādīnāṃ yā gatayaḥ tān lokān gaccha sarvānte māṃ vraja. 'so 'śnute sarvān kāmān saha brahmaṇā vipaścitā' ityuktarītyā muktabhogaṃ prāpnuhi, na ca nirhetukamuktipradāne 'tiprasaṅgaḥ. svakāryam uddiśya prāṇatyāgasyaiva hetutvāt. ata eva nṛsiṃhapurāṇe 'matkṛte nidhanaṃ yasmāt tvayā prāptaṃ dvijottama/ tasmān mama prasādena viṣṇulokam avāpsyasi' ity uktam. 'karmaṇaiva hi saṃsiddhim āsthitā janakādayāḥ' iti hi karmaṇo 'pi muktihetutvam uktam. 'nānyaḥ panthāḥ' iti śrutiḥ paramātmano 'nyatra sākṣānmuktihetutvaṃ niṣedhati tasyaiva prādhānyena prakṛtatvād ity āhuḥ. yad vā he gṛdhrarāja mahāsattva mayā saṃśkṛtas tvaṃ mayānujñāto bhūtvā anuttamān lokān mallokān ityarthaḥ. gaccha ānuṣaṅgikatayā yajñaśīlādinām yā yā gatayas tā api gaccha. gamyata iti gatiḥ lokaḥ. āhitāgneḥ gārhapatyāhavanīyadakṣīṇāgniratasya yā gatiḥ 'agnayo vai trayī vidyā' ity ārabhya 'tasmād agnīn paramaṃ vadanti' ity āhitāgnitvasyāpi pṛthak dharmatvaśravaṇāt. aparāvartināṃ yuddhād aparāvartamānānām. yā gatiḥ dṛṣṭāntārtham idam uktam, jaṭāyos tādṛśatvena tatphalasyedānīm adeyatvāt tiraścāṃ yajñādyadhikārābhāvena tatphalamātrasya deyatvāt. yathā 'parāvartināṃ gatiṃ prāpsyasi tathā yajñaśīlādīnāṃ lokān api brahmaprāptau vasutvādikam iva prāpnuhīty arthaḥ. asmin kalpe bhūmipradāyinām ity asya pratīyamānārthakatvam eva vraja evaṃ gaccha. yadvā mayā prathamaṃ saṃskṛtaḥ. 'atha tṛtīyena jyotiṣā saṃviśasva' ity ādimantreṇānujñāto mayā tvaṃ yajñādhikāriṇām lokān gaccha, brahmamedhasaṃskārabalena prāpnuhīty arthaḥ. idaṃ ca phalaṃ saṃskārottarakṣaṇa evānutiṣṭhatīty ucyate saṃskṛto vrajeti. gṛdhrarāja mahāsattva saṃskṛtaś ca mahāvrateti pāṭhe saṃskṛtas ca bhaveti vārthaḥ.

109 Kataka, in his commentary, mocks Govindarāja as '*Yadvābhaṭṭa*' for his propensity to multiply the number of possible interpretations. Lefeber 1994: 24.

110 *Vālmīki Rāmāyaṇa* with the Commentaries of Govindarāja, Maheśvaratīrtha, and Rāmānuja 6.17.1 (6.11.1): evam āṣṭabhiḥ sargaiḥ 'ānukūlyasya saṅkalpaḥ prātikūlyasya varjanam/ rakṣiṣyatīti viśvāso goptṛtvavaraṇaṃ tathā// ātmanikṣepakārpaṇye ṣaḍviḍhā śaraṇāgatiḥ//' ityukteṣu śaraṇāgatyaṅgeṣu prapitsor vibhīṣaṇasyānukūlyasaṅkalpaprātikūlyavarjane darśite. punaḥ punar upadeśādinā mahāviśvāso darśitaḥ. atha kārpaṇyapradarśanapūrvakaṃ śaraṇāgatisvarūpaṃ darśayitum upakramate.

111 *Abhayapradānasāra* of Vedānta Deśika: 4.3–7.

112 *Vālmīki Rāmāyaṇa* with the Commentaries of Govindarāja, Maheśvaratīrtha and Rāmānuja 6.17.15 (6.11.15): sarvalokaśaraṇyāya rāghavāya mahātmane/ nivedayata māṃ kṣipraṃ vibhīṣaṇam upasthitam.

113 *Vālmīki Rāmāyaṇa* with the Commentaries of Govindarāja, Maheśvaratīrtha and Rāmānuja 6.18.3 (6.12.3).

114 *Vālmīki Rāmāyaṇa* with the Commentaries of Govindarāja, Maheśvaratīrtha and Rāmānuja 6.18.3 (6.12.3): mitrabhāvena vāstavamitratvābhāve 'pi mitratvābhinayamātreṇāpīty arthaḥ. mitrabhāvaḥ śaraṇāgatatvam. 'rāghavaṃ śaraṇam gataḥ' 'śaraṇyam śaraṇaṃ gataḥ' iti pūrvottaratra ca tasyaiva kathanāt. anyatrāpi 'viditaḥ sa hi dharmajñaḥ śaraṇāgatavatsalaḥ' iti śaraṇāgatiśabdenopakramya 'tena maitrī bhavatu te yadi jīvitum icchasi' iti maitrīśabdena parisamāpanāt. yad vā mitraśabdaḥ svābhiprāyeṇa śaraṇāgate gauravāropād yujyate . . . yad vā mitrabhāvena mitrakriyayā. 'bhāvo līlāsvabhāvayoḥ. jantvabhiprāyaceṣṭāsu bhūtau vidvatpadārthayoḥ. kriyāyām ātmani' iti nānārtharatnamālā. mitrabhāvanayeti yāvat. ahṛdayaśaraṇoktyety arthaḥ. tad apy uktam 'śaraṇavaraṇavāg iyam yoditā na bhavati bata sāpi dhīpūrvikā' iti. śaraṇāgatabhāveneti vaktavye mitrabhāvenety uktiḥ svāśrayaṇāya katicitpadāni kurvaty api svasadṛśabuddhikāriṇo bhagavato 'bhiprāyeṇa. devyāpi śaraṇāgatim abhidadhatyā 'tena maitrī bhavatu te yadi jīvitum icchasi' ity uktam. yad vā mitrabhāvena mitratvena hetunā. 'suhṛdaṃ sarvabhūtānām' ityuktarītyā asmadīyasahajasauhārdaṃ puraskṛty ity arthaḥ. yad vā mitrabhāvena ānukūlyasaṅkalpādipūrvakam ity arthaḥ. yad vā mitāt trāyata iti mitram. īśvaropakāraṃ paricchidya tatsadṛśopakārapravṛttasya bhāvenetyarthaḥ. yad vā viśvasanīyasthalaṃ mitram 'tad mitraṃ yatra viśvāsaḥ' ity uktatvāt. viśvāsino bhāvenetyarthaḥ.

115 *Vālmīki Rāmāyaṇa* with the Commentaries of Govindarāja, Maheśvaratīrtha and Rāmānuja 6.18.3 (6.12.3): yad vā doṣo yady api tasya doṣo 'sti cet tatsambandhī khalu doṣaḥ. saḥ tasmād api ślāghyaḥ syāt. prārthanāyāṃ liṅ.

116 *Vālmīki Rāmāyaṇa* with the Commentaries of Govindarāja, Maheśvaratīrtha and Rāmānuja 6.18.3 (6.12.3): na tyajeyam āgamanamātreṇa ślāghanīye tyāgasambhāvanā kutaḥ? sambhāvanāyāṃ liṅ.

117 *Vālmīki Rāmāyaṇa* with the Commentaries of Govindarāja, Maheśvaratīrtha and Rāmānuja 6.17.1 (6.11.1): hanumadrāmavākyasya vibhīṣaṇavākyasya cānyonyavirodhaprasaṅge 'antaraṅgabahiraṅgayor antaraṅgaṃ balīyaḥ' itinyāyena vibhīṣaṇavākyasya prābalyāt. ata eva 'rājānaṃ tvām kariṣyāmi' iti bruvato rāmasya prativacanam uktvā paricaraṇamātram eva vibhīṣaṇaḥ prārthayāmāsa 'rākṣasānāṃ vadhe sāhyam laṅkāyāś ca pradharṣaṇe/ kariṣyāmi yathāprāṇaṃ pravekṣyāmi ca vāhinīm// 'iti. tasyānumatyabhāve 'pi balād rājyasvīkāra uttarakāṇḍa uktaḥ 'yāvat prajā dhariṣyanti tāvat tvaṃ vai vibhīṣaṇa/ rākṣasendra mahāvīrya laṅkāsthas tvaṃ dhariṣyasi// śāpitas tvaṃ sakhitvena kāryam te mama śāsanam/ prajāḥ saṃrakṣa dharmeṇa nottaraṃ vaktum arhasi//' iti. itham anyaprayojanatvād evāsmai rāmaḥ kuladhanaṃ śrīraṅganāthaṃ dadau.

118 *Vālmīki Rāmāyaṇa* with the Commentaries of Govindarāja, Maheśvaratīrtha and Rāmānuja 6.17.1 (6.11.1): rāmasya lakṣmaṇo vyāvartaka iti salakṣmaṇa ity uktam. yadvā puruṣakārasānnidhyam anenocyate.

119 *Yājñavalkyasmṛti* 1.7.

120 *Vālmīki Rāmāyaṇa* with the Commentaries of Govindarāja, Maheśvaratīrtha and Rāmānuja 6.18.35 (6.12.20): 'tasmād api vadhyaṃ prapannaṃ na pratiprayacchanti' ityādinā śrutiḥ, kaṇḍugāthāmukhena smṛtiḥ kapotādinā śiṣṭācāraḥ, pratipakṣanirasanapūrvakabalavadupapādanena svapriyatvaṃ cety evaṃ caturṣu pramāṇeṣu prapannarakṣaṇarūpaparamadharmaviṣayeṣu darśiteṣu samprati tatra pramāṇaṃ pañcamaṃ darśayati 'sakṛd eva' iti.

121 *Vālmīki Rāmāyaṇa* with the Commentaries of Govindarāja, Maheśvaratīrtha and Rāmānuja 6.18.27–28 (6.12.14–15).

122 *Vālmīki Rāmāyaṇa* with the Commentaries of Govindarāja, Maheśvaratīrtha and Rāmānuja 6.18.24 (6.12.11): kapotena dharmādhikāraśūnyena tiryaṅmātrena, etenāpy anuṣṭhitatve kim u vaktavyam asmākam . . . śatrūḥ kapotasya mṛgayuḥ svayaṃ bhāryāpahārī vairī, vibhīṣaṇas tv asmākaṃ na tathā. tathāpy arakṣaṇe kim asmatpauruṣeṇa? śaraṇam āgataḥ kapotādhyuṣitadrumasthalaṃ yadṛcchayā prāptaḥ. 'so 'ñjaliṃ śirasā baddhvā vākyam āha vanaspatim/ śaraṇaṃ hi gato 'smy adya devatām iha vāsinīm//' iti svāvāsavanaspatidevatāṃ pratyuktavān na tu kapotam . . . arcitaś ca lubdhakatvāt sahajaśatrutvād bhāryāpahartṛtvāc cāpanno 'py asāv ity upekṣaṇasya tadvadhopāyānveṣaṇasya ca kartavyatve prāpte 'py atithiṃ devatvena matvā śitanivāraṇāyāgnim ānīya pūjitaḥ. vayaṃ tu 'vadhyatām eṣa tīvreṇa daṇḍena sacivaiḥ saha' iti anubandhiparyantaṃ samyag arcayāmaḥ. yathānyāyaṃ yāvatkṣunnivṛtti sadmitrāgama iva samagrādareṇāntarviṣādaleśaṃ vinā ādṛtaḥ. yad vā priyavacanādibhiḥ vañcanām vinety arthaḥ. svaiś ca māṃsair nimantritaḥ. bahiḥ katicid āhārān ānīya svakīyadravyāntarāṇi katipayāni śarīraikadeśān vā dattvā nopacacāra, kintv ajñair ātmatvenābhimanyamānaiḥ prājñair apy ādyaṃ dharmasādhanam ity ādaraṇiyaiḥ śarīramāṃsaiḥ śarabhaṅga iva 'idaṃ ekam mahat tapaḥ' iti matvā vahnāvahnāya patati sma.

123 *Mahābhārata* 12.141–145. As discussed by Goldman, Goldman and Nooten 2009: 590, the story is also referred to in *Hitopadeśa* 1.41; *Pañcatantra* 3.140.141; and *Mahābhārata* 3.130.19–20; 3.131ff.

124 *Abhayapradānasāra* of Periyavāccāṉ Piḷḷai 336–414.

125 Knutson 2011.

3 Double reading

1 *Vālmīki Rāmāyaṇa* with the commentaries of Govindarāja, Maheśvaratīrtha, and Rāmanuja 1.2.15 (1.2.14).
2 See for instance, Johnston 1935–1936.
3 Raghavan 1961.
4 Pollock 1993: 262.
5 Pollock 2006: 44–45.
6 *Kāvyālaṃkāra* of Bhāmaha 1.16.
7 Gerow 1971: 25.
8 *Uttararāmacarita* of Bhavabhūti 2.5.
9 *Kāvyamīmāṃsā* of Rājaśekhara, third adhyāya.
10 Pollock 2006: 39–89.
11 Pollock 2011.
12 *Śṛṅgāraprakāśa* of Bhoja, third adhyāya.
13 *Dhvanyāloka* of Ānandavardhana with the Commentary of Abhinavagupta 1.5.
14 *Dhvanyāloka* of Ānandavardhana with the Commentary of Abhinavagupta 1.5: janita iti carvaṇāgocaratveneti śeṣaḥ.
15 *Dhvanyāloka* of Ānandavardhana with the Commentary of Abhinavagupta 1.5: krauñcasya dvandvaviyogena sahacarīhananodbhūtena sāhacaryadhvaṃsanenotthito yaḥ śokaḥ sthāyibhāvo vipralambhaśṛṅgārocitaratisthāyibhāvād anya eva.
16 *Vālmīki Rāmāyaṇa* with the Commentaries of Govindarāja, Maheśvaratīrtha and Rāmanuja 1.4.9 (1.4.8): tatra 'rāmas tu sītayā sārddham' ity ārabhya sītāpaharaṇavṛttāntaparyantena saṃbhogo darśitaḥ. tataḥpareṇa vipralambhaḥ. vikṛtācāravākyāṅgavikāraveṣair dhūtapralāpaiś ca hāsyaraso vyajyate, sa ca śūrpaṇakhādivṛttāntena sugamaḥ. iṣṭhaviyogād aniṣṭasambandhād vā karuṇaḥ, sa ca daśarathādivṛttānte. vyavasāyāviṣādāsaṃmohādibhir vīraḥ, yathā lakṣmaṇādivṛttānte. pāṭanatāḍanādibhī raudraḥ, yathā rāvaṇādivṛttānte. vikṛtakrūradarśanādibhir bhayānaka, yathā mārīcādivṛttānte. kutsitadarśanādibhir bībhatsaḥ, yathā virādhakabandhādivṛttānte. vicitraśilpavākyādibhir adbhutaḥ, yathā rāmarāvaṇayuddhādiṣu. śāntarasa śramaṇādivṛttāntādau.
17 *Vālmīki Rāmāyaṇa* with the Commentaries of Govindarāja, Maheśvaratīrtha and Rāmanuja 1.4.9 (1.4.8): atra kecit 'śoka ślokatvam āgataḥ' ityuktyāsmin prabandhe śokarasa eva prādhānyenocyate, anye tadaṅgatayety āhuḥ. anye tu vīra eva pradhānabhūtaḥ 'paulastyavadhaḥ' iti kāvyanāmakaraṇāt ity āhuḥ. vayaṃ tu brūmaḥ śṛṅgāra eva pradhānarasaḥ 'sītāyāś caritaṃ mahat' ity ukteḥ.
18 Masson 1969.
19 *Kuvalayānanda* of Appayya Dīkṣita 63.
20 *Romeo and Juliet of William Shakespeare*, 1992: 3.1.97–98.
21 *Kuvalayānanda* of Appayya Dīkṣita 64.
22 *Vālmīki Rāmāyaṇa* with the Commentaries of Govindarāja, Maheśvaratīrtha and Rāmanuja 1.2.15 (1.2.14): mā gamaḥ mā prāpnuhi. 'āśaṃsāyāṃ bhūtavac ca' iti luṅatideśāt luṅ, lṛditvād aṅ. nāyaṃ māṅ, api tu māśabda iti kāśikākāraḥ, tenāḍāgame 'pi na virodhaḥ. durghaṭavṛttikāras tu ameti padacchedaḥ. he ama he alakṣmīka iti niṣādaviśeṣaṇam. tato 'na māṅyoge' ityaḍabhāva ity āha.
23 Harold Coward and K. Kunjunni Raja include this entry on Maitreya Rakṣita: 'This Buddhist grammarian in eastern India lived between 1092 and 1122, according to Yuddhiṣṭhira Mīmāṃsāka, who thinks he may have been a Bengali. In addition to works on Buddhist Grammar, including *Dhātupradīpa, Dhurghaṭavṛtti*, and a *Tantrapradīpa* on Jinendrabuddhi's *Kāśikanyāsa* (a fragmentary manuscript, which is listed as residing at the Asiatic Society Library in Calcutta), he appears to have written a *ṭīkā* on the *Mahābhāṣya*, which has been lost.' Coward and Raja 1990: 207.
24 I draw the terms 'bitextuality' and 'resegmentation' from Bronner 2010.
25 *Kuvalayānanda* of Appayya Dīkṣita 63.

26 Bronner 2010: 13–14.
27 *Vālmīki Rāmāyaṇa* with the Commentaries of Govindarāja, Maheśvaratīrtha and Rāmanuja 1.2.15 (1.2.14): niṣīdanty asmin iti niṣādo nivāsaḥ. adhikaraṇe ghañ. mā lakṣmīḥ, tasyā niṣādo māniṣādaḥ śrīnivāsaḥ.
28 *Vālmīki Rāmāyaṇa* with the Commentaries of Govindarāja, Maheśvaratīrtha and Rāmanuja 1.2.15 (1.2.14): he śrīnivāsa tvam śāśvatīḥ samāḥ sarvakālaṃ pratiṣṭhāṃ māhātmyam agamaḥ gaccha. lakāravyatyayaḥ. yad yasmāt krauñcamithunāt rākṣasamithunād rāvaṇamandodarīrūpāt kāmena manmathena mohitaṃ sītāpahartāram ekaṃ rāvaṇam avadhīḥ, rāvaṇaṃ hatvā kṛtatrailokyatrāṇas tvaṃ yāvatkālaṃ vijayībhavety arthaḥ.
29 Bronner 2010: 195–230.
30 *Dhvanyāloka of Ānandavardhana with the Commentary of Abhinavagupta* 2.21.
31 The actual king–moon verse, however, is as Appaya Dīkṣita tells us cited by Ānandavardhana as a case of suggestion, because the two levels of meaning are respectively contextual and non-contextual.
32 *Vālmīki Rāmāyaṇa* with the Commentaries of Govindarāja, Maheśvaratīrtha and Rāmānuja 5.1.1 (5.1.1).
33 *Vālmīki Rāmāyaṇa* with the Commentaries of Govindarāja, Maheśvaratīrtha and Rāmānuja 5.1.1 (5.1.1): anena śiṣyasthānānveṣaṇaparagurusvarūpam ucyate. tataḥ mudrāpradānapūrvakabhagavadanujñālābhānantaram. śatrukarśanāḥ 'guśabdas tv andhakāraḥ syād ruśabdas tannirodhakaḥ. andhakāranirodhitvād gurur ity abhidhīyate.' ityuktarītyā ajñānanivartanaśīlo guruḥ. cārayanti ācārayanti dharmān iti cāraṇāḥ pūrvācāryāḥ tair ācarite pathi 'mahājano yena gatas sa panthāḥ' ityuktasadācāre, sthita iti śeṣaḥ. rāvayati asatpralāpān kārayatīti rāvaṇaḥ avivekaḥ, tena nītāyāḥ svavaśaṃ prāpitāyāḥ sītāyāḥ anādibhagavatparatantracetanasya. sītāśabdenāyonijatvokteḥ strīliṅgena pāratantryokteś ca 'strīprāyam itarat sarvam' iti hy uktam. padam sthānaṃ saṃsāramaṇḍalam anveṣṭum, sāttvikasaṃbhāṣaṇādicihnaṃ vā. tathoktaṃ 'viṣṇoḥ kaṭākṣaś cādveṣa ābhimukhyaṃ ca sāttvikaiḥ. saṃbhāṣaṇaṃ ṣaḍ etāni tv ācāryaprāptihetavaḥ' iti. yad vā padaṃ vyavasāyam anveṣṭuṃ kasya cetanasya bhagavadprāptāv adhyavasāya ity anveṣṭuṃ iyeṣa.
34 *Vālmīki Rāmāyaṇa* with the Commentaries of Govindarāja, Maheśvaratīrtha and Rāmānuja 5.27.61 (5.25.38).
35 *Vālmīki Rāmāyaṇa* with the Commentaries of Govindarāja, Maheśvaratīrtha and Rāmānuja 5.27.61 (5.25.38): pakṣiśabdena gamanasādhanatvāt jñānakarmaṇī ucyete. tad uktam 'ubhābhyām eva pakṣābhyām yathā khe pakṣiṇāṃ gatiḥ/ tathaiva jñānakarmabhyāṃ niyatā paramā gatiḥ//' iti. jñānakarmaṇor aṅgāṅgibhāvenātra samuccayo vivakṣitaḥ. 'brāhmaṇā vividiṣanti yajñena dānena tapasānāśakena' iti śruteḥ. anenācāryaśabdanirvacanam uktam, 'ācinoti hi śāstrārthān ācāre sthāpayaty api/ svayam ācarite yasmāt tasmād ācārya ucyate//' iti. śākhāśabdena vedaśākhā ucyate. nilayaśabdena tad ekaparatvaṃ tyāge pratyavāyaśravaṇāt ... prahṛṣṭaḥ sadā saṃtuṣṭahṛdayaḥ. anena sarvadā sevanīyatvam uktam ... kiṃ ca susvāgatāṃ vācam udīrayānaḥ. suṣṭu saṃpradāyāvicchedo yathā tathācāryaparamparayā svasmai āgatāṃ vācam aṣṭākṣarādimantrarājarūpāṃ nirhetukyaiva dayayā samūdīrayan ... punaḥ punaś codayatīva uktārthasyānuṣṭhānāya codanāṃ darśayati.
36 *Vālmīki Rāmāyaṇa* with the Commentaries of Govindarāja, Maheśvaratīrtha and Rāmānuja 1.2.15 (1.2.14): anena atra 'arthataḥ śabdato vāpi manāk kāvyārthasūcanam' ityukteḥ rāmeṇa kṛtarāvaṇavadharūpaḥ kāvyārthaḥ kāvyādāv avaśyakartavaśirvādaś ca sūcita ityavagantavyam.
37 *Pratimānāṭaka* of Bhāsa 1.1.
38 *Abhijñānaśākuntala* of Kālidāsa 1.1.
39 Leavitt forthcoming. See also Gerow 1979, 1980.
40 Shulman 2001.
41 Hudson 2001.
42 Goldman and Sutherland Goldman 1996: 3–6, 13–37.

43 *Kuvalayānanda* of Appayya Dīkṣita 73.
44 *Kuvalayānanda* of Appayya Dīkṣita 73: evaṃ nāṭakeṣu vakṣyamāṇārthasūcaneṣv api.
45 *Vālmīki Rāmāyaṇa* with the Commentaries of Govindarāja, Maheśvaratīrtha and Rāmānuja 1.2.15 (1.2.14): tathā hi mā niṣāda ityanena sītāpariṇayaparyavasāyinī bālakāṇḍakathodbodhitā. pratiṣṭhāṃ tvam agama ityanena pitṛvacanaparipālana-pratiṣṭhābhidhāyiny ayodhyākāṇḍakathāveditā. śāśvatīḥ samā ityanena ṛṣigaṇaviṣaya-pratijñānirvahaṇena rāmasya pratiṣṭhānuvṛttim abhidadhaty āraṇyakāṇḍakathā sūcitā. kṛñca gatikauṭilyālpībhāvayoḥ ity asmād dhādhoḥ 'ṛtvik' ityādinā kvinnipātanāt nalopaḥ saṃyogāntalopaś ca na bhavati. krūñceva krauñcaḥ. svārthe aṇ. tathā ca krauñcayoḥ kuṭilayos tiraścos tārāvālinor mithunād ekaṃ kāmamohitaṃ sugrīvabhāryāpahartāraṃ vālinam avadhīḥ iti kiṣkindhākāṇḍakathābhihita. krauñcau alpībhūtau kṛśāv iti yāvat. tayor anyonyavirahakleśakraśīyasoḥ sītārāmayor ekam avayavaṃ sītārūpam avadhīḥ bṛśaṃ pīḍitavān asīti sītāvirahaduḥkhātiśayavarṇanaparā sundarakāṇḍakathā bodhitā. krauñcau kuṭilau rākṣasau, tanmithunād ekaṃ kāmamohitaṃ rāvaṇam avadhīr iti yuddhakāṇḍakathā sūcitā. daṇḍakāraṇyavāsirṣipatnī-darśanābhilāṣamohitasītāpīḍābhidhānenottarakāṇḍārtho 'pi saṅkṣiptaḥ.
46 *Vālmīki Rāmāyaṇa* with the Commentaries of Govindarāja, Maheśvaratīrtha and Rāmānuja 1.2.15. (1.2.14): nanvidaṃ malayaṃ gacchato mandarapathopavarṇanam, yad ayam ātmano vailakṣaṇyaṃ param āptatvaṃ vaktum ārabhya svacaritravarṇanaṃ karoti, brahmāgamanavarapradānāder eva tadarthaṃ vaktavyatvāt. ucyate, śrūyatām avadhānena. 'arthataḥ śabdato vāpi manāk kāvyārthasūcanam' iti darśitarītyā kāvarthasūcanam iyatā granthasandarbheṇa kriyate.
47 *Vālmīki Rāmāyaṇa* with the Commentaries of Govindarāja, Maheśvaratīrtha and Rāmānuja 1.2.5. (1.2.5).
48 *Vālmīki Rāmāyaṇa* with the Commentaries of Govindarāja, Maheśvaratīrtha and Rāmānuja 1.2.15. (1.2.14): tathā hi akardamam ityādinā pāvanaṃ samudrasetusthalam ucyate.
49 *Vālmīki Rāmāyaṇa* with the Commentaries of Govindarāja, Maheśvaratīrtha and Rāmānuja 1.2.9 (1.2.9).
50 *Vālmīki Rāmāyaṇa* with the Commentaries of Govindarāja, Maheśvaratīrtha and Rāmānuja 1.2.15 (1.2.14): tasyābhyāśe ityādinā tattīre mandodaryā saha carantaṃ bhogān bhuñjānam anapāyinaṃ caturmukhavarapradānena labdhacirāyuṣkaṃ cārunisvanaṃ ramyavīṇādivinodaṃ krauñcayo rākṣasayor mithunaṃ dadarśa dharmabalenālokitavān.
51 *Vālmīki Rāmāyaṇa* with the Commentaries of Govindarāja, Maheśvaratīrtha and Rāmānuja 1.2.15 (1.2.14): tasmāt ityādinā pāpaniścayo niścitarāvaṇapāpaḥ, vairanilayo hiraṇyakaśipurāvaṇaśiśupālarūpajanmatrayānusāritvāt sahajaśātravaḥ niṣidanty atra sarvāṇi jagantīti niṣādo viṣṇuḥ. pumāṃsaṃ rāvaṇam jaghāna ity ucyate. bhāryā tu ityādinā mandodarīpralāpaḥ. dvijena pulastyavaṃśatvāt brāhmaṇena, tāmraśīrṣeṇa ratnamukuṭadhārtitvāt, patriṇā vāhanaparicchadādimatā, sahitena kumbh-akarṇendrajidādisahāyasampannena. kāruṇyaṃ jugupsā. 'jugupsā karuṇā ghṛṇā' ity amaraḥ. adharmo 'yam iti rāvaṇakṛto 'yam adharma ity etat sarvaṃ rāvaṇavadhavṛttāntam avalokya paulastyavadhābhidhānaṃ tadviṣayaprabandhaṃ niramimīteti māṇiṣādety asya rāmāyaṇārthasaṅgrahaparatvaṃ coktam.
52 *Vālmīki Rāmāyaṇa* with the Commentaries of Govindarāja, Maheśvaratīrtha and Rāmānuja 1.2.15. (1.2.14): athavā 'akardamam' ityādinā godāvarītīrtham ucyate. tattīre pañcavaṭyāṃ rāmasya sītayā saha vartanaṃ tayor ekasyāḥ sītāyā rāvaṇena durātmanā hiṃsanaṃ pīḍaṇam ity etat sarvaṃ sākṣātkṛtya vidhicodito muniḥ siṭāyāś caritam iti tadviṣayaṃ pabandham akarod ity arthaḥ. tasmin pakṣe anapāyinam ādyantaśūnyam. cāruniḥsvanaṃ sarvavedāntapravartakam. krauñcayoḥ kṛśayoḥ tapasvinoḥ sītārāmayoḥ. pāpaniścayo vairanilayo niṣādo lokahiṃsako rāvaṇaḥ sītām apajahāra sā ca ruroda. dvijena kṣatriyeṇa tāmraśirṣeṇa ratnamukuṭāruṇena patriṇā śareṇopalakṣitena sahitena lokahitapareṇa. anyat sarvaṃ samānam. mā niṣādetyādyarthaḥ śapārthena darśitaḥ.

53 *Vālmīki Rāmāyaṇa* with the Commentaries of Tilaka, Śivasahāya and Govindarāja 1.2.15 (1.2.14): atredam avadheyam. rāvaṇavadhe jāte 'yodhyārājyaprāptyanantaraṃ nāradaṃ prati praśna iti svayam eva vyākhyātatvād uttarakālikaitacchlokasyaiva vividhaghaṭitasyoktārthasya katakamate kathaṃ saṅgatiḥ. kathaṃ vā sarvajñā satyasarasvatī bhūtam artham āśāsyatvena nirdiśed iti.
54 *Vālmīki Rāmāyaṇa* with the Commentaries of Tilaka, Śivasahāya and Govindarāja 1.2.15 (1.2.14): nāradāt svaguṇaśravaṇānantaraṃ muneḥ svavarṇanecchāṃ jñātvā svacaritrasya ca karuṇārasamayatvena tatpradhānakāvye 'tikaruṇacittasyaivādhikārād ṛṣeḥ karuṇacittatvajijñāsayeva pūrvabhṛgudattaśāpasya punaruktatvakaraṇena dārḍyasampādanāya muner īkṣaṇāya ca bhagavān rāma eva niṣādarūpeṇa paśyato muneḥ puratas tam anādṛtya krauñcaṃ rakṣoviśeṣarūpaṃ jaghāna.
55 Bronner 2010: 156–159.
56 Bronner 2010: 159–169.
57 Bronner 2010: 183–192.
58 Greimas 1970: 188 (cited and translated in Eco 1992: 62). Eco 1984: 201.
59 Hartman 1988: 145.
60 Eco 1992: 60.
61 Hartman 1985: 145–146.
62 Eco 1992: 61.
63 Eco 1992: 62.
64 Doniger 1993: 53–54, Doniger 2009: 212–251.
65 Goldman 2004: 47–86.
66 Eco 1992: 62.
67 Leavitt, forthcoming.
68 Goldman and Sutherland Goldman 1996: 3.
69 Derrida 1976: 158.
70 Irvine 1994: 264.
71 Barthes 1957: 109–159.
72 Bronner 2010: 192.
73 Griffiths 1999: 112–113.
74 Inden, 2000: 13.

4 Rāma in the imperial capital

1 Examples of such an interpretation include Talbot 1995, Chattopadhyaya 1998 and Lorenzen 1999.
2 On asymmetric causal relations, see Lewis 1979.
3 Pollock 1993: 277.
4 Bakker 1986: 61–62.
5 See Cousins 1897: 7ff. and Verma 1973. *Epigraphia Indica* XXV, 7–20.
6 Bharati 1978.
7 Located in Chikmanglur District, site number 91; Padigar 380 cited in Verghese 1995: 52.
8 See for instance Dallapiccola, Fritz, Michell and Rajasekhara 1991 and Fritz, Michell and Rao 1984.
9 *South Indian Inscriptions* IV, no. 252.
10 Fritz, Michell and Rao 1984: 149.
11 Appadurai 1981: 63–64.
12 Fritz, Michell and Rao 1984: 147. See also Inden 1978.
13 Sewell 1962: 228–376 provides full translations of the accounts of Paes and Nuniz.
14 *Caturvargacintāmaṇi* of Hemādri (*vrata khaṇḍa*, vol. 1: 900–920, 970–973) and *Devībhāgavata Purāṇa* 3.26–27.
15 Sanderson 2009: 245–246.

16 The pre-Vijayanagara *Devībhāgavata Purāṇa* does recount the performance of the Mahānavamī by Rāma, but there is no reference in it to a cultic worship of Rāma himself.
17 Appadurai 1981: 89–97.
18 Verghese 1995: 70–71.
19 *Sources of Vijayanagara History*: 77–79.
20 See, for example, Saletore 1940: 193–195.
21 Verghese 1995: 8–9.
22 Lutgendorf 2007: 66–73.
23 Verghese 1995: 78–79.
24 *Vijayanagara Progress in Research*, no. 67.
25 *South Indian Inscriptions* IX, pt. II, no. 595, *South Indian Inscriptions* XVI, no.120.
26 Fritz, Michell, and Rao 1984: 149.
27 Pollock, 2006: 511–524, where Pollock extends Anthony Giddens's global critique of functionalism to a critique of legitimation theory (Giddens 1981).
28 Narayanan 1994a: 65.
29 *Perumāḷ Tirumoḻi* of Kulacēkarāḻvār 10.1–10.
30 Shulman 1987.
31 Shulman, 1979.
32 Shulman, 1991.
33 Shulman 1987: 286.
34 *Irāmāvatāram of Kampaṉ* 1.191–192. The translation is from Shulman 1978: 142.
35 Shulman 1978: 141–146.
36 Hardy 1983: 524.
37 Nayar 1992: 22–25.
38 Ramanujan 1999: 236.
39 *Mahāvīravaibhava* of Vedānta Deśika 47.
40 *Mahāvīravaibhava* of Vedānta Deśika 81.
41 *Mahāvīravaibhava* of Vedānta Deśika 15, 19.
42 *Mahāvīravaibhava* of Vedānta Deśika 36, 72, 76.
43 *Mahāvīravaibhava* of Vedānta Deśika 46.
44 *Mahāvīravaibhava* of Vedānta Deśika 7.
45 *Mahāvīravaibhava* of Vedānta Deśika 14.
46 *Mahāvīravaibhava* of Vedānta Deśika 44.
47 *Mahāvīravaibhava* of Vedānta Deśika 92.
48 *Mahāvīravaibhava* of Vedānta Deśika 77–79.
49 *Vālmīki Rāmāyaṇa* with the Commentaries of Govindarāja, Maheśvaratīrtha and Rāmānuja 6.18.36 (6.12.21): vibhīṣaṇo vā 'vibhīṣaṇas tu dharmātmā' iti vibhīṣaṇasvīkāro dharmavatsvīkāratayā notkarṣāya. rāvaṇasya nṛśaṃsasyeti rāvaṇasvīkāra evotkarṣaḥ syād iti. vibhīṣaṇasvīkāre tatparikarāś catvāra eva rakṣitāḥ syuḥ. rāvaṇasvīkāre tu laṅkāsthāḥ sarve 'pi rakṣitāḥ syur iti mahān lābhaḥ . . . yadi vā rāvaṇaḥ svayaṃ yatsambandhena vibhīṣaṇe 'py atiśaṅkā sa evāstu. svayaṃ sītām apuraskṛtya svayam āgato rāvaṇo vā 'stu. yad vā svayaṃ ayaṃ yadi vibhīṣaṇo na bhavati kiṃtu kāmarūpī rāvaṇa eva vibhīṣaṇabhūmikāṃ parigṛhya yadi āgataḥ tathāpy asyābhayaṃ mayā dattam. tvam api rāvaṇo 'yaṃ na tu vibhīṣaṇa iti vijñāpanāyāpi punar nāgaccheḥ, kiṃtv ānayaivety arthaḥ.
50 *Vālmīki Rāmāyaṇa* with the Commentaries of Govindarāja, Maheśvaratīrtha and Rāmānuja 6.41.66 (6.31.56): maithilīm upādāya samarpya māṃ śaraṇaṃ nabhyeṣi ced idam lokam arākṣasaṃ kartāsmi. śaraṇāgatau tu sarvaṃ kṣamiṣya iti bhāvaḥ. maithilīm upādāyety anena svarṇasteye svarṇapratyarpaṇam antareṇa prāyaścittānadhikāravat sītāpratyarpaṇābhāve śaraṇāgatau tu nādhikāra ity uktam. rāvaṇena śaraṇāgatau kṛtāyāṃ vibhīṣaṇāya kosalarājyaṃ dāsyāmītyabhiprāyaḥ.
51 *Vālmīki Rāmāyaṇa* with the Commentaries of Govindarāja, Maheśvaratīrtha and Rāmānuja 6.59.143 (6.47.132).

52 Wagoner 1996: 853–855.
53 Wagoner 1996: 861–863.
54 Wagoner 2000: 300–315.
55 Wagoner 1996: 870.
56 Flood 2009: 61–87.
57 Eaton 2005: 53. Michell 1995.
58 Asher 1985.
59 Wagoner 2000: 317–319.
60 Flood 2009: 111–112.
61 Wagoner 1999: 242–249.
62 Wagoner 1999: 249–260.
63 Eaton 2005: 96.
64 Wagoner 1999: 247.
65 Eaton 2005: 78–104.
66 Wagoner 2007.
67 Eaton 2000.
68 Verghese 1995: 137.
69 *Epigraphia Carnatica* II, SB. 344.
70 Verghese 1995: 137.
71 Heras 1927: 553–554.
72 Dehejia and Davis 2010.
73 For a comparative study of Appayya Dīkṣita's *Rāmāyanatātparyasaṃgraha* and Vedānta Deśika's *Abhayapradānasāra*, see Bronner 2011.

Conclusion

1 Venkatesan 2007.
2 Indo-Asian News Service 2007.
3 Sharma and Sinha 2007.
4 Rajagopal 2001.

References

Primary sources

Abhayapradānasāra of Vedānta Deśika. Mysore: Sri Venkatesa Sabha, 1968.

Abhayapradānasāra of Periyavāccāṉ Piḷḷai. Tirucci Puttur Agraharam, n.d.

Abhijñānaśākuntala of Kālidāsa. New Delhi: Rashtriya Samskrta Samthana, 2006.

Āṛāyirappaṭi Guruparamparāprabhāva of Piṉpaḻakiya Perumāḷ Cīyar. Tirucci: Puttur Agraharam, 1975.

Bhagavad Gītā with Eleven Commentaries. Mumbai: Gujarati Printing Press, 1935.

Caturvargacintāmaṇi of Hemādri. Varanasi: Kāśī Saṃskṛta Granthamālā, 1985.

Devībhāgavata Purāṇa. New Delhi: Bharatiya Vidya Prakashan, 2001.

Dhvanyāloka of Ānandavardhana with the Commentary of Abhinavagupta. Kashmir Sanskrit Series 135. Varanasi: Chowkamba Sanskrit Office, 1940.

Epigraphia Carnatica. Edited by B. Lewis Rice. Mysore: Archaeological Department, Mysore Archaeological Survey, 1886–.

Epigraphia Indica. Edited by V. Mirashi and L. R. Kulkarni. Calcutta: Archaeological Survey of India., 1888–.

Haṃsasandeśa of Vedānta Deśika. Chennai: Ubhaya Vedanta Granthamala, 1973.

Irāmāvatāram of Kampaṉ. Chennai: Kampan Kalakam, 1976.

Kāvyālaṃkāra of Bhāmaha. Varanasi: Chowkhambha Sanskrit Series Office, 2002.

Kāvyamīmāṃsā of Rājaśekhara. Varodara: Baroda Oriental Intitute, 1934.

Kuvalayānanda of Appayya Dīkṣita. Mumbai: Tukaram Javaji, 1903.

Mahābhārata. Critical Edition. Pune: Bhandarkar Oriental Research Institute, 1933–1966.

Mahāvīravaibhava of Vedānta Deśika in *Vedānta Deśika Stotramālā*. Chennai: Lifco, 1966.

Meghadūta of Kālidāsa. Edited by M. R. Kale. Mumbai: B. D. Mulgaokar, 1947.

Meghadūta of Kālidāsa with the Commentary of Dakṣiṇāvarthanātha. New Delhi: Nag Publishers, 1984.

Muṇḍaka Upaniṣad. Pune: Anandashrama, 1935.

Nāṭya Śāstra with the Commentary of Abhinavagupta. Varodara: Central Library, 1926–1964.

Pādukāsahasra of Vedānta Deśika. Varanasi: Chaukhambha, 1984.

Perumāḷ Tirumoḻi of Kulacēkarāḻvār. Kanchipuram: Kadaikkumidam Granthamala Office, 1966.

Pratimānāṭaka of Bhāsa in *Bhāsanāṭakacakram, Plays Ascribed to Bhāsa*. New Delhi: Motilal Banarsidas, 1962.

Romeo and Juliet of William Shakespeare. New York: Washington Square Press, 1992.
Saṅkalpasūryodaya of Vedānta Deśika. Chennai: Adyar Library, 1948.
Sources of Vijayanagara History. Edited by S. K. Aiyangar. Chennai: University of Madras, 1919.
South Indian Inscriptions. Edited by E. Hultzsch, et al. Chennai: Government Press, 1890–.
Śrīvacanabhūṣaṇa of Piḷḷai Lokācārya with the Commentary of Maṇavāḷamāmuni. Puri: Sriraghunandandanmudralaya, 1926.
Śṛṅgāraprakāśa of Bhoja. Cambridge: Harvard University Press, 1998.
Taittirīya Upaniṣad. Pune: Anandashrama, 1911.
Taniślokam of Periyavāccāṉ Piḷḷai. Tirucci: Puttur Agraharam, n.d.
Tiruvāymoḻi of Nammāḻvār with the Commentary of Vaṭakkutiruvītip Piḷḷai. Chennai: University of Madras Press, 1957–62.
Uttararāmacarita of Bhavabhūti. Varanasi: Chowkamba, 1990.
Vālmīkīyarāmāyaṇa with the Commentaries of Govindarāja, Maheśvaratīrtha and Rāmānuja. Reprint of the Venkatesvara Steam Press Edition. New Delhi: Nag Publishers, 1994.
Vālmīki Rāmāyaṇa with the Commentaries of Tilaka, Śivasahāya, and Govindarāja. New Delhi: Parimal Publications, 1990.
Vijayanagara: Progress of Research. Edited by D. V. Devaraj and C. S. Patil. Mysore: Directorate of Archaeology and Museums, 1983–1984.
Vivekatilaka. Unpublished Mss. R 3409, Government Oriental Manuscripts Library.
Vivekatilaka. Unpublished Mss. 9386, Sarasvati Mahal Library.
Yājñavalkyasmṛti. New Delhi: Nag Publishers, 1985.

Secondary sources

Aiyangar, K. V. Rangaswami. 1942. 'Govindarāja.' In *Annals of the Bhandarkar Oriental Research Institute*: 40–41.
Aiyangar, S. Krishnaswami. 1940–1941. *A History of Tirupati*. Madras: C. Sambaiya Panthulu.
Altekar, G. S. 1987. *Studies on Vālmīki's Rāmāyaṇa*. Pune: Bhandarkar Oriental Research Institute.
Appadurai, Arjun. 1981. *Worship and Conflict Under Colonial Rule: A South Indian Case*. Cambridge: Cambridge University Press.
Asher, Catherine B. 1985. 'Islamic Influence and the Architecture of Vijayanagara.' In *Vijayanagara – City and Empire: New Currents of Research*, edited by Anna Dallipiccola. Stuttgart: Steiner Verlag Wiesbaden.
Bakker, Hans. 1986. *Ayodhyā*. Groningen: Egbert Forsten.
Barthes, Roland. 1957. *Mythologies*. Translated by Annette Lavers. London: Paladin.
Barrett, Douglas E. 1965. *Early Cola Bronzes*. Mumbai: Bhulabhai Memorial Institute.
Bauman, Richard. 1977. *Verbal Art as Performance*. Rowley: Newbury House Publishers.
Behl, Aditya. 2007. 'Presence and Absence in Bhakti: An Afterword.' *International Journal of Hindu Studies* 11.3: 319–324.
Bharati, Agehananda, ed. 1978. *The Smith Āgama Collection: Sanskrit Books and Manuscripts Relating to Pāñcarātra Studies*. Syracuse, NY: Maxwell School of Citizenship and Public Affairs, Syracuse University.
Bhatt, G. H. 1964. 'Rāmāyaṇa Commentaries,' *Journal of the Oriental Institute Baroda* 14: 350–361.

Blackburn, Stuart. 1996. *Inside the Drama House: Rāma Stories and Shadow Puppets in South India*. Berkeley: University of California Press.

Blackburn, Stuart and Flueckiger, Joyce. 1989. Introduction to *Oral Epics in India*, edited by Stuart Blackburn, Peter Claus, Joyce Flueckiger, and Susan Wadley. Berkeley: University of California Press.

Bonazzoli, Giorgio. 1983. 'Composition, Transmission, and Recitation of the *Purāṇas*.' *Purāṇa* 25: 254–280.

Bose, Mandakranta, ed. 2004. *The Rāmāyaṇa Revisited*. Oxford: Oxford University Press.

Brockington, J. L. 1984. *Righteous Rāma: The Evolution of an Epic*. New York: Oxford University Press.

Bronner, Yigal. 2010. *Extreme Poetry: The South Asian Movement of Simultaneous Narration*. New York: Columbia University Press.

——. 2011. 'A Text With a Thesis: The *Rāmāyaṇa* From Appayya Dīkṣita's Receptive End.' In *South Asian Texts in History: Critical Engagements with Sheldon Pollock*, edited by Yigal Bronner, Whitney Cox, and Lawrence McCrea. Ann Arbor: Association for Asian Studies.

——. Forthcoming. 'Birds of a Feather: Vāmana Bhaṭṭa Bāṇa's *Haṃsasandeśa* and its Intertexts.'

Bronner, Yigal, and Shulman, David. 2006. "'A Cloud Turned Goose": Sanskrit in the Vernacular Millennium.' *Indian Economic and Social History Review* 43: 1–30.

Bulcke, Camille. 1962. *Ramkathā: utpatti aur vikās*. Allahabad: Hindi Parishad.

Burghart, Richard. 1978. 'The Founding of the Ramanandi Sect.' *Ethnohistory* 25.2: 121–139.

Carman, John. 1974. *The Theology of Rāmānuja*. New Haven: Yale University Press.

Champakalakshmi, R. 1994. '*Patikam Pāṭuvār*: Ritual Singing as a Means of Communication in Early Medival South India.' *Studies in History*, New Series, 10.2: 199–215.

Chattopadhyaya, Bhrajadulal. 1998. *Representing the Other? Sanskrit Sources and the Muslims*. New Delhi: Manohar.

Clooney, Francis X. 1996. *Seeing Through Texts: Doing Theology Among the Śrīvaiṣṇavas of South India*. Albany, NY: SUNY.

Coats, George W. 1981. 'Parable, Fable, and Anecdote: Storytelling in the Succession Narrative.' *Interpretation* 35: 368–382.

Collins, Steven. 2003. 'What is Literature in Pali?' In *Literary Cultures in History: Reconstructions From South Asia*, edited by Sheldon Pollock. Berkeley: University of California Press.

Cone, Margaret and Gombrich, Richard F. 1977. *The Perfect Generosity of Prince Vessantara: A Buddhist Epic*. Oxford: Clarendon.

Cousins, Henri. 1897. *List of Antiquarian Remains in the Central Provinces and Berār*. Calcutta: Archaeological Survey of India.

Coward, Harold G. and Raja, K. Kunjunni, 1990. *Encyclopedia of Indian Philosophers, Volume V: The Philosophy of the Grammarians*. Edited by Karl Potter. Delhi: Motilal Banarsidas.

Cutler, Norman. 1987. *Songs of Experience: The Poetics of Tamil Devotion*. Indiana University Press.

Dallipiccola, A. L., Fritz, John, Michell, George and Rajasekhara, S. 1991. *The Ramachandra Temple at Vijayanagara*. New Delhi: Manohar Publications and American Institute of Indian Studies.

Dehejia, Vidya and Davis, Richard. 2010. 'Addition, Erasure, and Adaptation: Interventions in the Rock-cut Monuments of Māmallapuram.' *Archives of Asian Art* 60: 1–18.

Derrida, Jacques. 1976. *Of Grammatology*. Translated by Gayatri Spivak. Baltimore: Johns Hopkins University Press.

Doniger, Wendy. 1986. *Dreams, Illusions, and Other Realities*. Chicago: University of Chicago Press.

——. 1993. 'Echoes of the *Mahābhārata*: Why is a Parrot the Narrator of the *Bhāgavata Purāṇa* and the *Devībhāgavata Purāṇa*?' Albany: SUNY.

——. 1998. *Splitting the Difference: Gender and Myth in Ancient Greece and India*. Chicago: University of Chicago Press.

——. 2009. *The Hindus: An Alternative History*. New York: Penguin Books.

Eaton, Richard M. 2000. 'Temple Desecration and Indo-Muslim States.' In *Beyond Turk and Hindu: Rethinking Religious Identities in Islamicate South Asia*, edited by David Gilmartin and Bruce B. Lawrence. Gainesville: University Press of Florida.

——. 2005. *A Social History of the Deccan, 1300–1761: Eight Indian Lives*. Cambridge: Cambridge University Press.

Eco, Umberto. 1992. *Interpretation and Overinterpretation*. Cambridge: Cambridge University Press.

——. 1994. *The Limits of Interpretation*. Bloomington: Indiana University Press.

Fergusen, Charles A. 1994. 'Dialect, Register, and Genre: Working Assumptions About Conventionalization.' In *Sociolinguistic Perspectives on Register*, edited by Douglas Biber and Edward Finegan. New York: Oxford University Press.

Flood, Finbarr B. 2009. *Objects of Translation: Material Culture and Medieval 'Hindu-Muslim' Encounter*. Princeton: Princeton University Press.

Freeman, Rich. 1998. 'Rubies and Coral: The Lapidary Crafting of Language in Kerala.' *Journal of Asian Studies* 57.1: 38–65.

Fritz, John, Michell, George, and Rao, M.S. Nagaraja. 1984. *Where Kings and Gods Meet: The Royal Center at Vijayanagara, India*. Tuscon: University of Arizona Press.

Gennette, Gerard. 1992. *The Architext: An Introduction*. Berkeley: University of California Press.

——. 1997. *Palimpsests: Literature in the Second Degree*. Omaha: University of Nebraska Press.

Gerow, Edwin. 1971. *A Glossary of Indian Figures of Speech*. Paris, Mouton.

——. 1979. 'Plot Structure and the Development of Rasa in the Śakuntalā. Pt. 1.' *Journal of the American Oriental Society* 99.4: 559–572.

——. 1980. 'Plot Structure and the Development of Rasa in the Śakuntalā. Pt. 2.' *Journal of the American Oriental Society* 100.3: 267–282.

Giddens, Anthony. 1981. *A Contemporary Critique of Historical Materialism*. Berkeley: University of California Press.

Goldman, Robert. (trans.) 1984. *The Rāmāyaṇa of Vālmīki: An Epic of Ancient India, Vol. I: Bālakāṇḍa*. Princeton: Princeton University Press.

——. 1992. 'Translating Texts Translating Texts: Issues in the Translation of Popular Texts with Multiple Commentaries.' In *Translation East and West*, edited by Cornelia N. Moore. Honolulu: East–West Center and University of Hawaii.

——. 2005. 'Historicizing the Rāmakathā: Vālmīki's Rāmāyaṇa and its Medieval Commentators.' *India International Quarterly* 31.4: 83–97.

——. 2006. 'How Fast Do Monkeys Fly? How Long Do Demons Sleep? *Rivista Di Studi Sudasiatici*, 1: 7–29.

Goldman, R. P., and Sutherland Goldman, S. J. (trans.) 1996. *The Rāmāyaṇa of Vālmīki: An Epic of Ancient India, Vol. V: Sundarakāṇḍa*. Princeton: Princeton University Press.

Goldman, R. P., Sutherland Goldman, S. J. and van Nooten, B. A. (trans.) 2009. *The Rāmāyaṇa of Vālmīki: An Epic of Ancient India, Volume VI: Yuddhakāṇḍa*. Princeton: Princeton University Press.

Goldman, Sally Sutherland. 2004. 'Gendered Narratives: Gender, Space, and Narrative Structures in Vālmīki's *Bālakāṇḍa*.' In *The Rāmāyaṇa Revisited*, edited by Mandakranta Bose. Oxford: Oxford University Press.

Gopalan, L. V. 1972. *Śrīvaiṣṇava Divya Deśams*. Chennai: Sri Visisistdvaita Pracarini Sabha, 1972.

Greimas, A. J. 1970. *Du sens*. Paris: Seuil.

Griffiths, Paul. 1999. *Religious Reading: The Place of Reading in the Practice of Religion*. Oxford: Oxford University Press.

Groesbeck, Rolf. 1999. 'Cultural Constructions of Improvisation in *Tāyampaka*, A Genre of Temple Instrumental Music in Kerala, India.' *Ethnomusicology* 43.1: 1–30.

Gurumurthy, Prameela. 1994. *Kathākālakṣepa: A Study*. Madras: International Society for the Investigation of Ancient Civilizations.

Hardy, Friedhelm. 1983. *Viraha Bhakti: The Early History of Kṛṣṇa Devotion in South India*. New Delhi: Oxford University Press.

——. 1998. 'South Indian Viṣṇu Temples and the Performing Arts.' *South Asia Research* 18.1: 99–114.

Hartman, Geoffrey. 1988. *Easy Pieces*. New York: Columbia University Press.

Hazra, R. C. 1040. *Studies in the Puranic Records on Hindu Rites and Customs*. Dhaka: University of Dhaka.

Heras, Henry. 1927. *The Aravidu Dynasty of Vijayanagara*. Chennai: B. G. Paul and Co.

Hess, Linda and Schechner, Richard. 1977. 'The Rāmlīlā of Rāmnagar.' *The Drama Review* 21: 51–82.

Hiltebeitel, Alf. 1988. *The Cult of Draupadi, Volume 1. Mythologie: From Gingee to Kurukṣetra*. Chicago: University of Chicago Press.

Hudson, Dennis. 2001. 'The Barley-Corn Pattern of *Bhagavad-Gītā* 12–16,' *Journal of Vaishnava Studies* 9.2: 181–195.

Inden, Ronald. 1978. 'Ritual Authority and Cyclical Time in Hindu Kingship.' In *Kingship and Authority in South Asia*, edited by J. F. Richards. Madison: University of Wisconsin, Department of South Asian Studies.

——. 1985. 'Kings and Omens.' In *Purity and Auspiciousness in Indian Society*, edited by J. B. Carman and Frederique Apffel Marglin. Leiden: E. J. Brill.

——. 2000. *Querying the Medieval: Texts and the History of Practices in South Asia*. Oxford: Oxford University Press.

Indo-Asian News Service. 2007, September 13. 'Advani Calls up PMO to Protest Ram Sethu Affidavit.' *Hindustan Times*.

Irvine, Martin. 1994. *The Making of Textual Culture: 'Grammatica' and Literary Theory, 350–1100*. Cambridge: Cambridge University Press.

Jacobi, Hermann. 1893. *Das Ramayana: Geschichte und Inhalt*. Bonn: F. Cohen.

Jauss, Hans Robert. 1982. *Toward an Aesthetics of Reception*. Minneapolis: University of Minnesota Press.

Johnston, E. H. 1935–1936. *The Buddhacarita; or, Acts of the Buddha*. Calcutta: Baptist Mission Press.

Kirshenblatt-Gimblett, Barbara. 1975. 'A Parable in Context: A Social Interactional Analysis of Storytelling Performance.' In *Folklore: Performance and Communication*, edited by Dan Ben-Amos and Kenneth S. Goldstein. Paris: Mouton.

Knutson, Jesse Ross. 2011. 'The Vernacular Cosmopolitan: Jayadeva's *Gītagovinda*.' In *South Asian Texts in History: Critical Engagements with Sheldon Pollock*, edited by Yigal Bronner, Whitney Cox, and Lawrence McCrea. Ann Arbor: Association for Asian Studies.

Krishnamachariar, M. 1906. *History of the Classical Sanskrit Literature*. Madras: Vaijayanti Press.

Kulke, Herman. 1980. 'Legitimation and Town-Planning in the Feudatory States of Central Orissa.' In *Ritual Space in India: Studies in Architectural Anthropology*, edited by J. Pieper. London: Art and Archaeology Research Papers.

Leavitt, Guy. Forthcoming. *The Poetics and Cosmology of Narrative Time in Sanskrit Literature*. Unpublished dissertation. University of Chicago.

Lefebre, Rosalind. (trans.) 1994. *The Rāmāyaṇa of Vālmīki: An Epic of Ancient India, Volume IV: Kiṣkindhākāṇḍa*. Princeton: Princeton University Press.

Lewis, David. 1979. 'Counterfactual Dependence and Time's Arrow.' *Nous* 13.4: 455–476.

Lorenzen, David. 1999. 'Who Invented Hinduism?' *Comparative Studies in Society and History* 41.4: 630–659.

Ludden, David. 2002. 'Specters of Agrarian Territory in Southern India.' *Indian Economic and Social History Review* 39.2–3: 233–257.

Lutgendorf, Philip. 1991. *The Life of a Text: Performing the Rāmcaritmānas of Tulsidas*. Berkeley, University of California Press.

——. 2007. *Hanumān's Tale: The Messages of a Divine Monkey*. Oxford: Oxford University Press.

Masson, Jeffrey. 1969. 'Who Killed Cock Krauñca? Abhinavagupta's Reflections on the Origins of Aesthetic Experience.' *Journal of the Oriental Institute Baroda* 18: 207–224.

Michell, George. 1995. *Architecture and Art of Southern India: Vijayanagara and the Successor States*. Cambridge, Cambridge University Press.

Monius, Anne. 2000. 'The Many Lives of Daṇḍin: The *Kāvyādarśa* in Sanskrit and Tamil.' *International Journal of Hindu Studies* 4.1: 1–37.

Mumme, Patricia. 1991. 'Rāmāyaṇa Exegesis in Teṉkalai Śrīvaiṣṇavism.' In *Many Rāmāyaṇas: The Diversity of a Narrative Tradition in South India*, edited by Paula Richman. Berkeley: University of California Press.

Nagaswamy, R. 1980. 'Śrī Rāmāyaṇa in Tamilnadu in Art, Thought, and Literature.' In *The Rāmāyaṇa Tradition in Asia*, edited by V. Raghavan. New Delhi: Sahitya Academy.

Narayanan, Vasudha. 1994a. 'The Rāmāyaṇa in the Theology and Experience of the Śrīvaiṣṇava Community.' *Journal of Vaiṣṇava Studies* 2.4: 55–89.

——. 1994b. *The Vernacular Veda: Revelation, Recitation, and Ritual*. Columbia: University of South Carolina Press.

Nayar, Nancy Ann. 1992. *Poetry As Theology: The Śrīvaiṣṇava Stotra in the Age of Rāmānuja*. Weisbaden: Harrassowitz.

Orr, Leslie. 2007. 'Cholas, Pandyas, and "Imperial Temple Culture" in Medieval Tamilnadu.' In *The Temple in South Asia*, edited by Adam Hardy. London: British Academy.

Pollock, Sheldon. (trans.) 1986. *The Rāmāyaṇa of Vālmīki: An Epic of Ancient India, Volume II: Ayodhyākāṇḍa*. Princeton: Princeton University Press.

——. 1991. *The Rāmāyaṇa of Vālmīki: An Epic of Ancient India, Volume III: Araṇyākāṇḍa*. Princeton: Princeton University Press.

——. 1993. 'Rāmāyaṇa and Political Imagination in India.' *Journal of Asian Studies* 52.2: 261–297.

——. 2006. *The Language of the Gods in the World of Men: Sanskrit, Culture, and Power in Premodern India*. Berkeley: University of California Press.

——. 2011 'The Revelation of Tradition: *śruti, smṛti*, and the Sanskrit Discourse of Power.' In *Boundaries, Dynamics and Construction of Traditions in South Asia*, edited by Frederico Squarcini. London: Anthem Press.

Raghavan, V. 1940–1942. 'Uḍāli's Commentary on the Rāmāyaṇa: The Date and Identification of the Author and the Discovery of His Commentary.' *Annals of Oriental Research* 1–8.

——. 1958. 'Methods of Popular Religious Instruction in South India.' *Journal of American Folklore* 71.281: 336–344.

——. 1961. *Some Old Lost Rāma Plays*. Chennai: Annamalai University.

——, ed. 1980. *The Rāmāyaṇa Tradition in Asia*. New Delhi: Sahitya Academy.

Raja, K. K. 1994–1997. 'Malayalam and Maṇipravāḷam.' *Journal of Oriental Research, Madras*: 99–109.

Rajagopal, Arvind. 2001. *Politics after Television: Hindu Nationalism and the Reshaping of the Public in India*. Cambridge: Cambridge University Press.

Raman, Srilata. 2007. *Self-Surrender (Prapatti) to God in Śrīvaiṣṇavism: Tamil Cats and Sanskrit Monkeys*. Abingdon, UK: Routledge.

Ramanujan, A. K. 1989. 'Where Mirrors are Windows: Towards an Anthology of Reflections.' *History of Religions* 28.3: 187–216.

——. 1991. 'Three Hundred Rāmāyaṇas: Five Examples and Three Thoughts of Translation.' In *Many Rāmāyaṇas: The Diversity of a Narrative Tradition in South Asia*, edited by Paula Richman. Berkeley: University of California Press.

Ramanujan, A. K. (with Norman Cutler). 1999. 'From Classicism to *Bhakti*.' In *The Collected Essays of A. K. Ramanujan*, edited by Vinay Dharwadker. Oxford: Oxford University Press.

Rangachari, V. 1914–1915. 'The Successors of Rāmānuja and the Growth of Sectarianism among the Śrívaiṣṇavas.' *Journal of the Bombay Branch of The Royal Asiatic Society* 24: 277–312.

——. 1917. 'The History of Sri Vaishnavism: From the Death of Śrī Vedānta Deśika to the Present Day.' *Quarterly Journal of the Mythic Society* 7.2: 106–118 and 7.3: 197–209.

Richman, Paula. (Ed.) 1991. *Many Rāmāyaṇas: The Diversity of a Narrative Tradition in South Asia*. Berkeley: University of California Press.

——. (Ed.) 2001. *Questioning Ramayanas: A South Asian Tradition*. Berkeley: University of California Press.

Saletore, B. A. 1940. 'Vaiṣṇavism in Vijayanagara.' In *D. R. Bhandarkar Volume*, edited by B. C. Law. Calcutta: Indian Research Institute.

Sanderson, Alexis. 2009. 'The Śaiva Age: The Rise and Dominance of Śaivism During the Early Medieval Period.' In *Genesis and Development of Tantrism*, edited by Shingo Einoo. Tokyo: University of Tokyo, Institute of Oriental Culture.

Sastri, Sayavat, 1963. *Essays on Indology*. New Delhi: Meharchand Lachhmandass.

Schegloff E. A. 1982. 'Discourse as an Interactional Achievement: Some Uses of "Uh Huh" and Other Things That Come Between Sentences.' In *Analyzing Discourse: Text and Talk. Georgetown University Roundtable on Languages and Linguistics*, edited by Deborah Tannen. Washington: Georgetown University Press.

Sewell, Robert. 1962. *A Forgotten Empire: Vijayanagara; A Contribution to the History of India*. New Delhi: Ministry of Information and Broadcasting Publications Division.

Sharma, Tannu and Sinha, Amitabh. 2007. 'UPA "Atonement": Affadavits Withdrawn, Review Promised, 2 ASI Officials Suspended.' *The Indian Express*, 15 September.

Shastri, P. P. S. 1942. 'Rāmāyaṇa Commentaries,' *Annals of the Bhandarkar Oriental Research Institute* 23: 410–417.

Shulman, David. 1978. 'The Cliché as Ritual and Instrument: Iconic Puns in Kampaṉ's *Irāmāvatāram*.' *Numen* 25.2: 135–55.

——. 1979. 'Divine Order and Divine Evil in the Tamil Tale of Rāma.' *Journal of Asian Studies* 38.4: 651–69.

——. 1980. *Tamil Temple Myths: Sacrifice and Divine Marriage in the South Indian Śaiva Tradition*. Princeton: Princeton University Press.

——. 1987. 'The Anthropology of the Avatār in Kampaṉ's *Irāmāvatāram*.' In *Gilgul (Festschrift R. J. Zwi Werblowsky)*, edited by S. Shaked, D. Shulman and G. G. Stroumsa. Leiden: E.J. Brill.

——. 1991. 'Fire and Flood: The Testing of Sītā in Kampaṉ's *Irāmāvatāram*.' In *Many Rāmāyaṇas: The Diversity of a Narrative Tradition in South Asia*, edited by Paula Richman. Berkeley: University of California Press.

——. 2001. 'Bhavabhūti on Cruelty and Compassion.' In *Questioning Ramayanas*, edited by Paula Richman. Berkeley: University of California Press.

Slaje, Walter. 1990. 'A Guide to the Philosophical and Religious Terms in the (*Laghu-*) *Yogavāsiṣṭha*.' *Weiner Zeitschrift für die Kunde Südasiens* 34: 147–179.

——. 1994. *Vom Mokṣopāya-Śāstra zum Yogavāsiṣṭha-Mahārāmāyaṇa:* philologische Untersuchungen zur Entwicklungs- und Überflieferungsgeschichte eines indischen Lehrwerks mit Ausruch auf Heilsrelevanz. Osterreichische Akademie der Wissenschlaften, Philosophisch-historische Klasse Sitzungsberichte, 60. Wien: Verlag der Osterreichischen Akademie der Wissenschaften.

Talbot, Cynthia. 1995. 'Inscribing the Other, Inscribing the Self: Hindu-Muslim Identities in Pre-Colonial India.' *Comparative Studies in Society and History* 37.4: 692–722.

Thiel-Horstmann, Monika. 1991. *Rāmāyaṇa and Rāmāyaṇas*: Wiesbaden: Harassowitz.

van der Veer, Peter. 1988. *Gods on Earth*. London: Athlone Press.

Venkatachari, K. K. A. 1994–1997. 'Observations.' *Journal of Oriental Research, Madras*: 94–97.

Venkatesan, V. 2007. 'Shifting Lines.' *Frontline* 22 September–5 October.

Verghese, Anila. 1995. *Religious Traditions at Vijayanagara: As Revealed Through Its Monuments*. New Delhi: Manohar.

Verma, Omkar Prasad. 1973. *A Survey of Hemadpanti Temples in Maharashtra*. Nagpur: Nagpur University.

Viraraghvacharya, T. 1977. *History of Tirupati: The Thiruvengadam Temple*. Tirupati: Tirumala-Tirupati Devasthanams.

Wagoner, Philip. 1996. "'Sultan Among Hindu Kings": Dress, Titles, and the Islamicization of Hindu Culture at Vijayanagara.' *Journal of Asian Studies* 55.4: 851–880.

——. 1999. 'Fortuitous Convergences and Essential Ambiguities: Transcultural Political Elites in the Medieval Deccan.' *International Journal of Hindu Studies* 3.3: 241–264.

——. 2000. 'Harihara, Bukka, and the Sultan: the Delhi Sultanate in the Political Imagination of Vijayanagara.' In *Beyond Turk and Hindu: Rethinking Religious Identities in Islamicate South Asia*, edited by David Gilmartin and Bruce B. Lawrence. Gainesville: University Press of Florida.

——. 2007. 'Retrieving the Chalukyan Past: the Politics of Architectural Reuse in the Sixteenth-Century Deccan.' *South Asian Studies* 23: 1–29.

Whaling, Frank. 1980. *The Rise of the Religious Significance of Rāma*. New Delhi: Motilal Banarsidass.

Young, Katherine. 1980. *Beloved Places*. Unpublished dissertation, McGill University.

Index